Contemporary American Slang

Contemporary

American

Slang

Second Edition

An Up-to-Date Guide to the Slang of Modern American English

Richard A. Spears, Ph.D.

NTC Publishing Group

Library of Congress Cataloging-in-Publication Data

Spears, Richard A.
    Contemporary American slang / Richard A. Spears.—2nd ed.
        p.   cm.
    Includes index.
    ISBN 0-8442-0297-5
    1. English language—United States—Slang—Dictionaries.
  2. Americanisms—Dictionaries.   I. Title.

    PE2846 .S638   2001
    427'.973—dc21

                                        00-46072

Cover design by Nick Panos
Interior design by Terry Stone

Published by NTC Publishing Group
A division of NTC/Contemporary Publishing Group, Inc.
4255 West Touhy Avenue, Lincolnwood (Chicago), Illinois 60712-1975 U.S.A.

Contents

About This Dictionary

This dictionary is a resource cataloging the meaning and usage of frequently used slang expressions in the U.S.A. It contains expressions that are familiar to many Americans and other expressions that are used primarily within small groups of people. These expressions come from movies, novels, newspaper stories, and everyday conversation. The entries represent the vocabulary found in many places, such as the college campus and urban streets. We hear slang from surfers, weight lifters, and young people in general.

There is no standard test that will decide what is slang and what is not. Expressions that are identified as slang are sometimes little more than entertaining wordplay, and much slang is little more than an entertaining, alternative way of saying something. Slang is rarely the first choice of careful writers or speakers or anyone attempting to use language for formal, persuasive, or business purposes. Nonetheless, expressions that can be called slang make up a major part of American communication in movies, television, radio, newspapers, magazines, and informal spoken conversation.

Young people are responsible for a high proportion of the fad expressions and collegiate wordplay found here. Not surprisingly, there are a large number of clever expressions for drinking alcohol and vomiting from this source. Clever or insulting nicknames for types of people are the major linguistic product of this subgroup. Matters of social taboo have provided many slang expressions as well. Although, strictly speaking, taboo words are not slang, the major taboo words have been included in this dictionary.

Some slang expressions are not standardized in spelling or punctuation. This dictionary usually represents slang expressions in the form in which they were found, except for the following. Entry heads made up of initials that are pronounced as one word—acronyms—are spelled without periods, e.g., "GAPO." Entry heads that are to be pronounced as one or more letter names, e.g., "L.I.Q.," have a period after each letter.

The entries in the following pages come from many sources. Many have been collected by college students and other individuals. Much of the recent material has come directly from television and a lesser amount from contemporary radio and journalism. Standard reference works have been used to verify the meanings and spellings of older material. Most of the examples are concocted and have been edited to exemplify an expression's meaning as concisely as possible. The examples are to be taken as representative of slang usage, not of standard, formal English usage. They are included to illustrate meaning, not to prove the earliest date of print or broadcast dissemination.

Guide to the Use of the Dictionary

1. Entry heads are alphabetized according to an absolute alphabetical order that ignores all punctuation, spaces, and hyphens.
2. Entry heads appear in **boldface type**. When words or expressions that are not entries in this dictionary are cited, they appear in *italics*. Function codes [see No. 8 below] and examples appear in *italics*.
3. An entry head may have one or more alternative forms. The alternatives are printed in **boldface type** and are preceded by "AND." Alternative forms containing commas are separated by semicolons, otherwise by commas.
4. Definitions are in roman type. Alternative or closely related definitions are separated by semicolons.
5. Some definitions contain restrictive comments in square brackets that help to make the definition more clear. These comments limit the context in which the expression can be used.
6. Sometimes the numbered senses of an entry refer only to people or things, but not both. In such cases the numeral is followed by "[with *someone*]" or "[with *something*]."
7. A definition may be followed by comments in parentheses. These comments give additional information about the expression, including cautions, comments on origins, or cross-referencing. Each numbered sense can have its own comments.
8. Every expression is followed by a function code that indicates the grammatical or syntactic function of the expression. These codes are in *italics*. The function codes provide a way of determining the grammatical or syntactic function of a particular expression

as it occurs in its examples. Expressions functioning as nominals (nouns, noun phrases, etc.) are marked *n*. Expressions serving to modify, restrict, or qualify (adjectives, adjective phrases, adverbs, adverb phrases, etc.) are marked *mod*. Expressions that are transitive verbs or transitive verb phrases (a transitive verb, its auxiliaries, object[s], and modifier[s]) are marked *tv*. Expressions that are intransitive verbs or intransitive verb phrases (an intransitive verb, its auxiliaries, and any modifiers) are marked *iv*. Other abbreviations are explained in the following section titled "Terms and Abbreviations."

9. Many expressions have more than one major sense or meaning. These meanings are numbered with boldface numerals.

10. Sometimes a numbered sense will have an alternative form that does not apply to the other senses in the entry. In such cases, "and" plus the alternative forms follow the numeral.

11. Entry heads that contain unfamiliar words or whose spellings are misleading have an indication of pronunciation in IPA symbols. See the symbols and their values in the "Pronunciation Guide."

12. In some entries, comments direct the user to other entries for additional information through the use of the terms "compare to" or "see also." The expressions mentioned are in **this type**.

13. Many of the examples utilize "eye-dialect" spelling to indicate that certain words are contracted or shortened in the slangy speech style of the examples. These words are *gimme* "give me," *gonna* "going to," *kinda* "kind of," *lemme* "let me," *oughtta* "ought to," *outa* "out of," *sorta* "sort of," *wanna* "want to," and *ya* "you."

Pronunciation Guide

Some expressions in the dictionary are followed by a phonetic transcription in International Phonetic Alphabet (IPA) symbols. These expressions include words whose pronunciations are not predictable from their spellings, difficult or unfamiliar words, and words where the stress placement is contrastive or unique. The style of pronunciation reflected here is informal and tends to fit the register in which the expression would normally be used. A [d] is used for the alveolar flap typical in American pronunciations such as ['wɑdɚ] "water" and [ə'nɑɪəledəd] "annihilated."' The transcriptions distinguish between [ɑ] and [ɔ] and between [w] and [ʍ] even though not all Americans do so. In strict IPA fashion, [j] rather than the [y] substitute is used for the initial sound in "yellow." The most prominent syllable in a multisyllabic word is *preceded* by the stress mark, [']. There may be additional prominent or stressed syllables in compounds and phrases, but their weight and placement varies from speaker to speaker and utterance to utterance.

The use of "..." in a transcription indicates that easy-to-pronounce words have been omitted. Parentheses used in a transcription either correspond to parentheses in the preceding entry head or indicate optional elements in the transcription. For instance, in ['ɑrtsi 'kræf(t)si] "artsy-craftsy," the "t" may or may not be pronounced.

The following chart shows the American English values for each of the IPA symbols used in the phonetic transcriptions. To use the chart, first find the large phonetic symbol whose value you want to determine. The two English words to the right of the symbol contain examples of the sound for which the phonetic symbol stands. The letters in boldface type indicate where the sound in question is found in the English word.

[ɑ]	stop top	[ɝ]	bird turtle	[n]	new funny	[tʃ]	cheese pitcher
[æ]	sat track	[f]	feel if	[n̩]	button kitten	[θ]	thin faith
[ɑu]	cow now	[g]	get frog	[ŋ]	bring thing	[u]	food blue
[ɑɪ]	bite my	[h]	hat who	[o]	coat wrote	[ʊ]	put look
[b]	beet bubble	[i]	feet leak	[ɔɪ]	spoil boy	[v]	save van
[d]	dead body	[ɪ]	bit hiss	[ɔ]	caught yawn	[w]	well wind
[ð]	that those	[j]	yellow you	[p]	tip pat	[ʍ]	wheel while
[dʒ]	jail judge	[k]	can keep	[r]	rat berry	[z]	fuzzy zoo
[e]	date sail	[l]	lawn yellow	[s]	sun fast	[ʒ]	pleasure treasure
[ɛ]	get set	[l̩]	bottle puddle	[ʃ]	fish sure	[']	'water ho'tel
[ə]	but nut	[m]	family slam	[t]	top pot		

Terms and Abbreviations

□ (a box) marks the beginning of an example.

Ⲧ marks the beginning of an example that shows the alternative word order of a phrasal verb, i.e., the difference between **call something off** and **call off something**.

AND indicates that an entry head has variant forms that are the same or similar in meaning as the entry head. One or more variant forms are preceded by AND.

acronym is a set of initials pronounced as a single word, as with *UNESCO*.

black describes an expression typically used by or originated by black Americans.

blend is an expression made up of sounds from two other words, like *smoke + fog = smog*.

catchphrase describes an expression meant to catch attention because of its cleverness or aptness.

collegiate describes an expression that is typically heard on college campuses.

combining form is a form of a word used only in combination with another word.

compare to means to consult the entry indicated and examine its form or meaning in relation to the entry head containing the "compare to" instruction.

derogatory describes an expression that insults, mocks, or abuses someone or a class of people.

elaboration is an expression that is built on, or is an expansion of, another expression.

entry head is the first word or phrase, in boldface, of an entry; the word or phrase that the definition explains.

euphemism is a *euphemistic* expression. See the following.

euphemistic describes an expression that is used as a substitute for a less acceptable expression.

exclam. exclamation.

eye-dialect is a class of spelling variants that attempts to capture colloquial pronunciation or indicates that the person who uttered the words or phrases is illiterate.

function code is an indication of the grammatical or syntactic potential of a particular sense of an expression. See No. 8 in the "Guide to the Use of the Dictionary" and *exclam., iv., interj., interrog., mod., n., phr., prep., pro., sent.,* and *tv.* in this section.

iv. intransitive verb. Expressions that are intransitive verbs or intransitive verb phrases (an intransitive verb, its auxiliaries, and modifiers) are marked *iv.*

interj. interjection.

interrog. interrogative.

jocular describes an expression that is intended to be humorous.

military describes expressions that are, or were originally, used in the U.S. military services.

mod. modifier. Expressions serving to modify, restrict, or qualify (adjectives, adjective phrases, adverbs, adverb phrases, etc.) are marked *mod.*

n. nominal. Expressions functioning as nominals (nouns, noun phrases, etc.) are marked *n.*

phr. phrase.

play on refers to wordplay that is based on a particular expression. For instance, "monolithic" is a play on "stoned."

prep. preposition.

pro. pronoun.

see also means to consult the entry indicated for additional information or to find expressions similar in form or meaning to the entry head containing the "see also" instruction.

sent. sentence.

standard English is the widely known and accepted style or register of English taught in schools.

streets describes an expression originating in the streets of urban America.

taboo indicates an expression that is regarded as out of place in public use.

teens describes an expression used typically—but not exclusively—by teenagers.

term of address describes an expression that is used to address someone directly.

tv. transitive verb. Expressions that are transitive verbs or transitive verb phrases (a transitive verb and its auxiliaries, objects, and any modifiers) are marked *tv.*

Numerical Entries

24-7 Go to twenty-four, seven.

404 Go to four-oh-four.

411 Go to four-one-one.

5-O Go to five-oh.

773H Go to seven-seven-three-aitch.

86 Go to eighty-six.

abs ['æbz] *n.* the abdominal muscles. (Bodybuilding. See also **washboard abs**.) □ *I do sit-ups to harden my abs.*

ace 1. *mod.* most competent; the best; top-rated. (Said of persons.) □ *She is an ace reporter with the newspaper.* **2.** *tv.* to pass a test easily, with an A grade. □ *Man, I really aced that test!* **3.** *tv.* to surpass someone or something; to beat someone or something; to ace someone out. □ *The Japanese firm aced the Americans by getting the device onto the shelves first.*

aced ['est] *mod.* outmaneuvered; outscored. □ *Rebecca really got aced in the track meet.* □ *"You are aced, sucker!" shouted Rebecca as she passed Martha in the 100-yard sprint.*

ace out *iv.* to be fortunate or lucky. □ *I really aced out on that test in English.* □ *Freddy aced out at the dentist's office with only one cavity.*

ace someone out *tv.* to maneuver someone out; to win out over someone. Ⓣ *Martha aced out Rebecca to win the first-place trophy.* □ *I plan to ace you out in the first lap.*

action 1. *n.* excitement; activity in general; whatever is happening. □ *This place is dull. I want some action.* □ *How do I find out where the action is in this town?* **2.** *n.* a share of something; a share of the winnings or of the booty. □ *I did my share of the work, and I want my share of the action.* □ *Just what did you do to earn any of the action?*

Adam Henry *n.* an AH = asshole, a jerk. (Treated as a name.) □ *Why don't you get some smarts, Adam Henry?*

adios muchachos [ɑdi'os mu'tʃatʃos] *phr.* the end; good-bye, everyone. (Spanish.) □ *If you step out in front of a car like that again, it's adios muchachos.*

AFAIK *phr.* as far as I know. (Computers and the Internet.) □ *Everything is alright with the server, AFAIK.*

ag AND **aggro** *n.* aggravated. □ *Hey, man. Don't get yourself so aggro!*

aggro Go to ag.

AH *n.* an asshole; a really wretched person. (A euphemistic disguise. Also a term of address. Rude and derogatory.) □ *Look here, you goddamn AH! Who the hell do you think you are?*

A-hole *n.* an asshole; a very stupid or annoying person. (Usually refers to a male. Rude and derogatory.) □ *Tom can be an A-hole before he's had his coffee.*

air-bags *n.* the lungs. □ *Fill those air-bags with good Colorado air!*

air ball *n.* a basketball throw that misses everything, especially the goal. □ *Old Fred has become a master with the air ball. The net will never get worn-out.* □ *Another air ball for Fred Wilson. That's his fourth tonight.*

airbrain Go to airhead.

air guitar *n.* an imaginary guitar, played along with real music or instead of real music. □ *Dave stood near the window while his roommate played air guitar in front of the mirror.*

airhead AND **airbrain** *n.* a stupid person. (Someone with air where there should be brains. Compare to smurfbrain.) □ *What is that loony airhead doing there on the roof?* □ *Some airbrain put mustard in the ketchup squeezer.*

air hose *n.* invisible socks; no socks. □ *How do you like my new air hose? One size fits all.*

alley apple 1. *n.* a lump of horse manure. (See also road apple.) □ *The route of the parade was littered with alley apples after about 20 minutes.* **2.** *n.* a brick or stone found in the rubble of the streets. (Especially a stone that might be thrown.) □ *"Drop it!" the cop called to the kid with an alley apple in his hand.*

all-nighter 1. *n.* something that lasts all night, like a party or study session. □ *After an all-nighter studying, I couldn't keep my eyes open for the test.* □ *Sam invited us to an all-nighter, but we're getting a little old for that kind of thing.* **2.** *n.* a place of business that is open all night. (Usually a café or similar place.) □ *We stopped at an all-nighter for a cup of coffee.* **3.** *n.* a person who stays up all night often or habitually. □ *Fred is an all-nighter. He's not* *worth much in the mornings, though.* □ *I'm no all-nighter. I need my beauty sleep, for sure.*

all over someone **like a cheap suit** *phr.* pawing and clinging; seductive. (A cheap suit might *cling* to its wearer.) □ *She must have liked him. She was all over him like a cheap suit.*

Alpha Charlie *n.* a bawling out; a severe scolding. (From *AC = ass-chewing.*) □ *The cop stopped me and gave me a real Alpha Charlie for speeding.*

ammo ['æmo] **1.** *n.* ammunition. □ *There they were, trapped in a foxhole with no ammo, enemy all over the place. What do you think happened?* **2.** *n.* information or evidence that can be used to support an argument or a charge. □ *I want to get some ammo on the mayor. I think he's a crook.*

ammunition 1. *n.* toilet tissue. □ *Could somebody help me? We're out of ammunition in here!* **2.** *n.* liquor. □ *The cowboy walked in, downed a shot, and called for more ammunition.*

anal applause *n.* the breaking of wind. (Jocular.) □ *Who is responsible for this pungent anal applause?*

animal *n.* a male who acts like a beast in terms of manners, cleanliness, or sexual aggressiveness. (Also a term of address. See also party animal.) □ *Stop picking your nose, animal.*

ankle 1. *n.* an attractive woman. (Typically with *some.*) □ *Now, there's some ankle I've never seen around here before.* **2.** *iv.* to walk [somewhere]. □ *Why should I ankle when I can drive?* **3.** *iv.* to walk away from one's employment; to leave. □ *I didn't fire her. I told her she could ankle if she wanted.*

ankle biter Go to rug rat.

antifreeze *n.* liquor; any legal or illegal alcohol. □ *Here's some antifreeze to stop your teeth from chattering.*

A-number-one Go to A-one.

A-O.K. ['e'o'ke] *mod.* in the best of condition. □ *I really feel A-O.K.*

A-one AND **A-number-one** ['e-'wən AND 'e-'nəmbɚ-'wən] *mod.* of the highest rating. □ *This steak is really A-one!* □ *I would like to get an A-number-one secretary for a change.*

apeshit 1. *mod.* excited; freaked out. (See also go ape(shit) (over someone or something). Usually objectionable.) □ *He was really apeshit* *about that dame.* **2.** *mod.* drunk. (Acting as strangely or comically as an ape.) □ *The guy was really apeshit.*

apple *n.* a baseball. □ *Jim slammed the apple over the plate, but the ump called it a ball.*

armpit *n.* any undesirable place, described as a human armpit. (A nickname for an undesirable town or city.) □ *I won't stay another minute in this armpit!*

(as) fat as a beached whale *phr.* very, very fat. □ *That dame is as fat as a beached whale.*

As if! *exclam.* <an expression said when someone says something that is not true but wishes that it were.> □ *A: I've got a whole lot of good qualities. B: As if!*

ass 1. *n.* the buttocks. (Usually objectionable.) □ *This big monster of a guy threatened to kick me in the ass if I didn't get out of the way.* **2.** *n.* women considered as sexual gratification. (Rude and derogatory.) □ *All he could think about was getting some ass.* **3.** *n.* one's whole body; oneself. (Usually objectionable.) □ *Your ass is really in trouble!* **4.** *n.* a worthless person; a despised person. □ *Who is that stupid ass with the funny hat?*

asshole 1. *n.* the opening at the lower end of the large bowel; the anus. (Usually objectionable.) □ *I was so mad I could have kicked him in the asshole.* **2.** *n.* a worthless and annoying person. (Also a term of address. Rude and derogatory. See also **bouquet of assholes**.) □ *Somebody get this asshole outa here before I bust in his face!*

ass-kisser AND **ass-licker** *n.* a flatterer; an apple polisher; someone who would do absolutely anything to please someone. (Rude and derogatory.) □ *Sally is such an ass-kisser. The teacher must have figured her out by now.*

ass-licker Go to ass-kisser.

ate up with someone or something *mod.* consumed with someone or something; intrigued by someone or something. □ *Bob is really ate up with his new girlfriend.*

atomic wedgie *n.* an instance of pulling someone's underpants up very tightly—from the rear—so that the cloth is pulled between the victim's buttocks; a severe **wedgie**. □ *I'm going to sneak up behind Bob and give him an atomic wedgie.*

attic *n.* the head, thought of as the location of one's intellect. □ *She's just got nothing in the attic. That's what's wrong with her.*

avenue tank *n.* a bus. □ *Watch out for them avenue tanks when you cross the street.*

the **avs** ['ævz] *n.* chance; the law of averages. (Streets.) □ *The avs say that I ought to be dead by now.* □ *It looks like the avs finally caught up with him.*

awesome 1. *exclam.* Great!; Excellent! (Usually **Awesome!** Standard English, but slang when overused.) □ *You own that gorgeous car? Awesome!* **2.** *mod.* impressive. □ *Let me have a look at this awesome new stereo of yours.*

B

backassed *mod.* pertaining to a manner that is backwards, awkward, or roundabout. (Old and widely known. Usually objectionable.) □ *Of all the backassed schemes I've ever seen, this one is tops.*

back-ender Go to **rear-ender**.

bacon *n.* the police; a police officer. (Black. Compare to **pig**.) □ *Keep an eye out for the bacon.*

bad 1. *mod.* powerful; intense. (Black.) □ *Man, that is really bad music!* **2.** *mod.* suitable; excellent. (Black.) □ *I got some new silks that are really bad.*

bad rap 1. *n.* a false criminal charge. □ *Freddy got stuck with a bad rap.* **2.** *n.* a bad reputation. □ *Butter has been getting sort of a bad rap lately.*

bag 1. *tv.* to capture and arrest someone. (Underworld.) □ *They bagged the robber with the loot still on him.* **2.** *n.* an ugly woman. (Rude and derogatory.) □ *Tell the old bag to mind her own business.* **3.** *n.* one's preference; something suited to one's preference. □ *That kind of stuff is just not my bag.* **4.** *tv.* to obtain something. □ *I'll try to bag a couple of tickets for you.* **5.** *n.* a container of drugs. (Drugs. Not necessarily a real bag.) □ *The man flipped a couple of bags out from a little stack he had held under his wrist by a rubber band.* **6.** *iv.* to die. □ *The guy was coughing so hard that I thought he was going to bag right there.* **7.** *tv.* to apply a respirator to someone. (Medical. The respirator has a bag attached to hold air.) □ *Quick, bag him before he boxes.*

bag ass (out of some place**)** AND **barrel ass (out of** some place**); bust ass (out of** some place**); cut ass (out of** some place**); drag ass (out of** some place**); haul ass (out of** some place**); shag ass (out of** some place**)** *tv.* to hurry away from some place;

to get oneself out of a place in a hurry. (Usually objectionable.) □ *I gotta shag ass, Fred. Catch you later.*

bagged 1. AND **in the bag** *mod.* alcohol intoxicated. □ *How can anybody be so bagged on four beers?* **2.** *mod.* arrested. □ *"You are bagged," said the officer, clapping a hand on the suspect's shoulder.*

bag someone *tv.* to put someone on a respirator. (A medical device, part of which is a rubber bag, used to help someone breathe.) □ *Bag this guy quick. He is struggling to get his breath.*

bag some **rays** Go to catch some rays.

bail (out) on someone *iv.* to depart and leave someone behind; to abandon someone. □ *Bob bailed out on me and left me to take all the blame.*

bald-headed hermit AND **bald-headed mouse; one-eyed pants mouse** *n.* the penis. (Usually objectionable.) □ *Somebody said something about the attack of the one-eyed pants mouse, and all the boys howled with laughter.*

bald-headed mouse Go to bald-headed hermit.

ball 1. *n.* a wild time at a party; a good time. □ *Your birthday party was a ball!* **2.** *iv.* to enjoy oneself. □ *The whole crowd was balling and having a fine time.* **3.** *n.* a testicle. (Usually plural. Caution with ball.) □ *He got hit right in the balls.* **4.** *iv.* to depart; to leave. □ *It's late. Let's ball.* □ *We gotta ball. Later.* **5.** *tv. & iv.* to copulate (with someone). (Usually objectionable.) □ *I hear she balled him but good.*

balled up AND **balled-up** *mod.* confused; mixed up. □ *This is really a balled-up mess you've made.*

ball off Go to beat off.

balls 1. *n.* the testicles. (Usually objectionable.) □ *He got hit in the balls in the football game.* **2.** *exclam.* an exclamation of disbelief. (Usually an exclamation: **Balls!** Usually objectionable.) □ *Out of gas! Balls! I just filled it up!* **3.** *n.* courage; bravado. (Usually refers to a male, but occasionally used for females. Usually objectionable.) □ *He doesn't have enough balls to do that!*

ball someone or something **up** *tv.* to mess someone or something up; to put someone or something into a state of confusion. □ *When you interrupted, you balled me up and I lost my place.*

ballsy 1. *mod.* courageous; daring; foolhardy. (Usually said of a male. Usually objectionable.) □ *Who is that ballsy jerk climbing the side of the building?* **2.** *mod.* aggressive; masculine. (Said of a female, especially a masculine female. Usually objectionable.) □ *You act too ballsy, Lillian. You put people off.*

ball up *iv.* to mess up; to make a mess of things. □ *Take your time at this. Go slow and you won't ball up.*

baltic *mod.* cold; very cold. □ *It really looks baltic out there today.*

bamboozle [bæm'buzəl] *tv.* to deceive someone; to confuse someone. □ *The crooks bamboozled the old man out of his life savings.*

bamma *n.* a rural person, such as someone from Alabama; a hick. (Rude and derogatory.) □ *Some bamma in a pickup truck nearly ran me off the road.*

bang 1. *n.* a bit of excitement; a thrill; some amusement. □ *We got a bang out of your letter.* **2.** *n.* the degree of potency of the alcohol in liquor or of a drug. □ *This stuff has quite a bang!* **3.** *n.* an injection of a drug; any dose of a drug. (Drugs.) □ *I need a bang pretty fast.* **4.** *tv. & iv.* to inject a drug. (Drugs.) □ *She banged herself and went on with her work.* **5.** *tv.* to copulate [with] someone. (Usually objectionable.) □ *Did you bang her? Huh? Tell me!* **6.** *n.* an act of copulation. (Usually objectionable.) □ *One bang was never enough for Wallace T. Jones. He was never satisfied.*

bang for the buck *n.* value for the money spent; excitement for the money spent; the cost-to-benefit ratio. □ *I didn't get anywhere near the bang for the buck I expected.*

banging *mod.* good; exciting. □ *We had a banging good time at the concert.*

bang-up *mod.* really excellent. □ *I like to throw a bang-up party once or twice a year.*

bank 1. *n.* money; ready cash. □ *I can't go out with you. No bank.* □ *I'm a little low on bank at the moment.* **2.** *n.* a toilet. (Where one makes a deposit.) □ *I have to got to the bank and make a deposit.*

barf ['barf] **1.** *iv.* to empty one's stomach; to vomit. □ *I think I'm going to barf!* **2.** *n.* vomit. □ *Is that barf on your shoe?* **3.** *iv.* [for a computer] to fail to function. □ *My little computer barfs about once a day. Something is wrong.*

Barney *n.* a nerd; an unattractive male. (From the children's TV dinosaur character.) □ *If you weren't such a Barney, you'd stick up for your own rights.*

barrel ass (out of some place**)** Go to **bag ass (out of** some place**)**.

bashed ['bæʃt] **1.** *mod.* crushed; struck. □ *His poor car was bashed beyond recognition.* **2.** *mod.* alcohol intoxicated. □ *All four of them went out and got bashed.*

bashing *n.* criticizing; defaming. (A combining form that follows the name of the person or thing being criticized.) □ *On T.V. they had a long session of candidate-bashing, and then they read the sports news.*

bazillion [bə'zɪljən] *n.* an indefinite enormous number. □ *Ernie gave me a bazillion good reasons why he shouldn't do it.* □ *Next year's bazillion-dollar budget should make things even worse.*

bazoo ['bɑ'zu OR bə'zu] **1.** *n.* a jeer; a raspberry. □ *They gave Ted the old bazoo when he fumbled the ball.* **2.** *n.* the mouth. □ *You would have to open your big bazoo and tell everything.*

B-ball *n.* basketball; a basketball. (See also **hoops.** Compare to V-ball.) □ *Let's go play some B-ball.*

be about it *iv.* to be ready; to be knowledgeable; to be **cool.** □ *Sam is smart. He's really about it.*

be all over something *iv.* to like something. □ *Jane's really into jazz. I mean she's all over it!*

bean 1. *n.* the head. □ *I got a bump right here on my bean.* **2.** *tv.* to hit someone on the head. □ *Some lady beaned me with her umbrella.*

bean-counter *n.* a statistician; an accountant. □ *When the bean-counters get finished with the numbers, you won't recognize them.* □ *The bean-counters predict a recession sometime in the next decade.*

beans 1. *n.* nothing. □ *You act like you don't know beans about it.* **2.** *n.* nonsense. □ *Come on, talk straight. No more beans!*

bean time *n.* dinnertime. □ *Hey, you guys! It's bean time!* □ *I'm hungry. When's bean time around here?*

be a snap *iv.* to be an easy thing to do. □ *Nothing to it. It's a snap.*

be ass out *iv.* to be broke. (Usually objectionable.) □ *I ain't got a cent. I'm ass out, man.*

beast 1. *n.* an ugly person. □ *Who is that beast with the big hat?* **2.** *n.* a crude, violent, or sexually aggressive male; an **animal**. □ *That beast scares the hell out of me.* **3.** *n.* liquor. □ *Pour me some more of that beast.*

beat 1. *mod.* exhausted; worn-out. □ *The whole family was beat after the game.* **2.** *mod.* down and out; ruined. (From *beat up.*) □ *This thing is beat. I don't want it.* **3.** *mod.* broke. □ *Man, I'm beat. I got no copper, no bread.*

beat box *n.* the person who provides the (verbal) rhythmic beat in a rap song. □ *What makes him sound so good is his beat box.*

beat off AND **ball off; jack off; jag off; jerk off; pull** oneself **off; toss off; wack off; wank off; whack off; whank off; whip off 1.** *iv.* to masturbate. (Usually objectionable.) □ *They say if you beat off too much, you'll get pimples.* **2.** *iv.* to waste time; to waste one's efforts; to do something inefficiently. □ *The whole lot of them were jacking off rather than sticking to business.*

beat one's **meat** Go to beat the dummy.

beat the dummy AND **beat the meat; beat** one's **meat; beat the pup; choke the chicken; whip** one's **wire; whip the dummy; yank** one's **strap** *tv.* to masturbate [of a male]. (Usually objectionable.) □ *Are you going to sit around all day beating the pup?*

beat the meat Go to beat the dummy.

beat the pup Go to beat the dummy.

beat the shit out of someone AND **kick the shit out of** someone; **knock the shit out of** someone *tv.* to beat someone very hard. (Usually objectionable.) □ *Shut up, or I'll beat the shit out of you!*

beautiful *mod.* very satisfying; excellent. □ *Man, this place is beautiful. You got your own sink and toilet right in the room and good strong bars to keep the riffraff out.*

be bum(med) about someone or something *iv.* to be depressed about someone or something. (See also **bummed (out)**.) □ *She's really bum about her grades. They suck.*

beef 1. *iv.* to break wind; to release intestinal gas audibly through the anus. (Usually objectionable.) □ *Why are you all the time beefing? You sick?* **2.** *n.* an act of breaking wind. (Probably short for **beef-hearts**. Usually objectionable.) □ *That was the worse smelling beef I ever smelled!*

beefcake 1. *n.* a display of the male physique. (Compare to **cheese-cake**.) □ *There was some beefcake at the party just to liven things up.* □ *There was one calendar showing beefcake rather than the usual cheesecake.* **2.** *n.* a muscularly handsome male. □ *She's been going out with a real beefcake.*

beef-hearts *n.* audible releases of intestinal gas through the anus. (Rhyming slang for *farts.* Usually objectionable.) □ *What a stink! No more of these beef-hearts!*

beemer ['bimɚ] *n.* a B.M.W. automobile. □ *I had to sell my beemer when the stock market crashed.*

been around (the block) *phr.* sexually experienced. □ *He's just a kid. He hasn't been around the block yet.*

beer 1. *iv.* to drink beer. □ *Fred and Tom sat in there watching the game and beering and belching like two old whales.* □ *Let's just sit here and beer for a while.* **2.** *tv.* to get oneself drunk on beer. □ *I beered myself, but good.* □ *Let's go beer a few.*

beerbong ['birbɔŋ] **1.** *n.* a can of beer prepared for drinking in one gulp. (An opening is made in the bottom of a can of beer. The can, with the opening placed in the mouth, is turned upright, and the tab opener is pulled, releasing all the beer directly into the mouth.) □ *A beerbong is a great way to liven up a party.* **2.** *iv.* to drink beer as described in sense 1. □ *Those guys who were beer-bonging all barfed after it was over.*

begathon *n.* a televised appeal for contributions, especially as con-ducted by U.S. public television stations. □ *It seems like this T.V. station is one long begathon all year long.*

belly fiddle *n.* a guitar. □ *Listen to that guy play that belly fiddle!*

belly-up 1. *mod.* alcohol intoxicated. □ *After four beers, I was belly-up, for sure.* **2.** *mod.* dead. (See also **turn belly-up**.) □ *After the fire, the firm went belly-up.*

bench 1. *tv.* to take someone out of a ball game. □ *If you don't stop fouling, I'll bench you!* **2.** *tv.* to retire someone; to withdraw someone from something. □ *The manager benched the entire sales staff for cheating on their expense reports.*

bench jockey *n.* a player who sits on the bench and calls out advice. □ *The coach told all the bench jockeys to shut up.* □ *Do what you are told, or be a bench jockey for the rest of the season!*

bench warmer *n.* a ballplayer who spends most of the game on the bench waiting to play; a second-rate player. □ *I do what I'm told so I can play every game. I don't want to be a bench warmer.*

benies *n.* benefits. □ *The salary is good, but the benies are almost nonexistent.*

Benjamin AND **Benji** *n.* a one-hundred dollar bill. (Bearing a picture of Benjamin Franklin.) □ *You owe me two Benjamins!*

bent 1. *mod.* alcohol or drug intoxicated. □ *I can get bent on a glass of wine.* **2.** *mod.* dishonest; crooked. □ *I'm afraid that Paul is a little bent. He cheats on his taxes.* **3.** *mod.* angry. □ *Come on, don't get bent. I was only kidding.*

best bud *n.* a best buddy; a best friend. □ *Isn't Bill your best bud? Why are you so mad at him?*

best buy *n.* a sexually loose woman. □ *That chick is a best buy.*

betty 1. *n.* some fake drugs; a bad drug buy. □ *John's supplier slipped him some betty.* **2.** *n.* a good-looking girl or woman. (Usually **Betty.**) □ *Who's your new Betty, Bob?*

bi 1. *n.* the biceps. (Typically **BI.** Usually plural.) □ *I have to work on my BIs and then build up my thighs.* **2.** *mod.* bisexual. □ *Suddenly she suspected that she was getting involved in some sort of strange bi activities.* **3.** *n.* a bisexual person. □ *This information is of interest only to bis and gays.*

bigass 1. *n.* a person with very large buttocks. (Usually objectionable.) □ *Some bigass came in and broke the chair when he sat down.* **2.** *mod.* pertaining to someone who has very large buttocks. (Usually objectionable.) □ *Tell that bigass jerk to get out!* **3.** *mod.* pertaining to a person who is self-important, overbearing, or arrogant; pertaining to anything having to do with arrogance. (Usually objectionable.) □ *Take your bigass ideas and go back where you came from.*

a **biggie** *n.* something or someone important. □ *As problems go, this one's a biggie.*

the **biggie** *n.* copulation. □ *He wanted to do the biggie!*

big gun *n.* an important and powerful person, such as the officers of a company. (Often with *bring in* as in the example.) □ *It went up to the big guns, who said no immediately.* □ *I knew they would bring in the big guns at the last minute.*

big iron *n.* a large, mainframe computer. (Computers. See also iron.) □ *We'll have to run this job on the big iron over at the university.*

big mouth 1. *n.* a person who talks too much or too loudly; someone who tells secrets. (Also a term of address.) □ *Tell that big mouth to shut up.* **2.** *tv.* to spread secrets around. □ *Don't you big mouth this to anyone, but I'm going to have a baby.*

big noise 1. *n.* an important person. □ *If you're such a big noise, why don't you get this line moving?* **2.** *n.* the important current news; the current scandal. □ *What's the big noise around town now?* □ *There's a big noise up on Capitol Hill. Something about budget cuts.*

big stink *n.* a major issue; a scandal; a big argument. □ *There was a big stink made about my absence.*

bike boys *n.* cops; the police. □ *Look out! Here come the bike boys.*

biker *n.* a motorcycle rider. □ *That biker is wearing about a dozen earrings.*

billie AND **bill(y)** *n.* a piece of paper money. (California.) □ *Do you have any billies on you?*

bimbo ['bɪmbo] **1.** *n.* a clownlike person. □ *If that bimbo doesn't keep quiet, I'll bop him.* **2.** *n.* a giddy woman; a sexually loose woman. □ *Now that silly bimbo is a star in the movies.*

bird 1. *n.* a woman. □ *I like the bird you were with last night.* **2.** *n.* a derisive noise made with the lips; a **raspberry**. □ *The third time he fumbled, he was greeted by two thousand mouths making the bird.* □ *You guys making the bird aren't perfect either.* **3.** *n.* an odd person. □ *Some old bird came up to me and tried to sell me a cookbook.* **4.** *n.* an airplane. □ *I like this bird. She's a dream to fly.* **5.** *n.* one-hundred dollars. □ *This thing cost three birds! Bull!*

the **bird** *n.* a rude gesture made with the middle finger. □ *The kid gave me the bird, so I bopped him.*

bird-dog 1. *tv.* to take away another man's girlfriend. □ *Why'd you have to go and bird-dog me, your best buddy?* **2.** *tv.* to supervise someone; to tail someone. □ *I wish you would stop bird-dogging me!*

birdseed 1. *n.* a small amount of money. □ *That's just birdseed compared to what I spend.* □ *Forty billion is birdseed to a government* *with a 600-billion-dollar budget.* **2.** *n.* nonsense. (Based on the B.S. of *birdseed.*) □ *Cut the birdseed. I'm not stupid, you know.*

biscuit ['bɪskət] *n.* the head. □ *She got a nasty little bump on the biscuit.*

bit-bucket *n.* the imaginary place where lost computer data goes. (Computers.) □ *I guess my data went into the bit-bucket.*

bitch 1. *n.* a woman. (Rude in context. Street talk, usually black.) □ *Tell your bitch to be on time the next time we go out!* **2.** *n.* an unpleasant or irritating female. (Rude and derogatory.) □ *How can anyone be expected to deal with a bitch like that?* **3.** *iv.* to complain. (Usually objectionable.) □ *Oh, stop bitching! I'm sick of hearing your noise.* **4.** *n.* a complaint. (Usually objectionable.) □ *I've got a bitch about this new foreman.*

bitch out *iv.* to complain. (Usually objectionable.) □ *You are always bitching out no matter how well off you are.*

bitch session *n.* an informal gathering where people gripe and air their grievances. (Caution with bitch.) □ *The bitch session went on for 40 minutes.* □ *I learned never to open my mouth in those office bitch sessions.*

bitch someone off *tv.* to make someone very angry. (Compare with piss someone off. Usually objectionable.) □ *You know what bitches me off? Soggy French fries, that's what!*

bitch something up *tv.* to mess something up; to ruin or spoil something. (Usually objectionable.) □ *The rain really bitched up our picnic.*

bitch tits *n.* gynecomastia; the development of breast tissue in the male. (From bodybuilding, in reference to breast development caused by steroids. Usually objectionable.) □ *If you don't let up on the gorilla juice, you'll get bitch tits.*

bitchy *mod.* spiteful; moody; rude; complaining. (Caution with bitch.) □ *Who needs a house full of bitchy kids?*

Bite the ice! *exclam.* Go to hell! □ *If that's what you think, you can just bite the ice!* □ *Get a life! Bite the ice!*

blade 1. *n.* a knife. □ *Bring your blade over here and cut this loose.* **2.** *n.* a young man, witty and worldly. □ *One of those blades kept winking at me.* □ *A couple of blades from the international jet set ordered vintage wine for everyone.*

blaze *iv.* to smoke marijuana. □ *Two freshmen are in the restroom blazing.*

blazing *mod.* really good; really good-looking; really hot. □ *We had a blazing time at Jane and Bob's wedding reception.*

bleed like a stuck pig *iv.* to bleed great volumes of blood. □ *I poked a nail into my foot and bled like a stuck pig.*

blimp out *iv.* to overeat. □ *I love to buy a bag of chips and just blimp out.* □ *I only blimp out on weekends.*

blinkers *n.* the eyes. □ *As I opened my blinkers, guess who I saw?* □ *Look at those sexy blinkers!*

blissed (out) AND **blissed-out 1.** *mod.* in a state of emotional bliss. □ *After the second movement, I was totally blissed out.* **2.** *mod.* alcohol or drug intoxicated. □ *She is more than blissed. She is stoned.* □ *My friend is a little blissed out. Can she rest here?*

bliss ninny ['blɪs 'nɪni] *n.* a giddy and disoriented person; a blissed-out person. □ *You silly bliss ninny! Who watches over you, anyway?*

bliss out *iv.* to become euphoric. □ *I blissed out just because it is spring and I am with you.*

blitz ['blɪts] **1.** *n.* a devastating attack. □ *After that blitz from the boss, you must feel sort of shaken.* **2.** *tv.* to attack and defeat someone or something. □ *The team from downstate blitzed our local team for the third year in a row.*

blitzed (out) ['blɪtst . . .] *mod.* alcohol or drug intoxicated. □ *I want to go out and get totally blitzed. I'll show her who's in charge!*

blivit ['blɪvət] *n.* someone or something annoying and unnecessary. □ *Don't be a blivit. Just calm down.*

blixed ['blɪkst] *mod.* mildly drug intoxicated. □ *He was a little blixed when I last saw him.* □ *He has been blixed for hours.*

blooey ['blui] **1.** *mod.* gone; destroyed. □ *Everything is finished, blooey!* □ *All my plans are blooey!* **2.** *mod.* alcohol intoxicated. □ *Reggie is totally blooey. He can't even open his eyes.*

blotto ['blɑdo] *mod.* alcohol intoxicated; dead drunk. □ *Let's get some beer and get blotto.*

blow 1. *tv. & iv.* to leave (someplace) in a hurry. □ *It's late. I gotta blow.* □ *They blew this place before you got here.* **2.** *tv.* to ruin something; to ruin an opportunity. □ *It was my last chance, and I blew it.* **3.** *n.* a setback; an attack. □ *It was a real blow to our* *prestige.* **4.** *tv.* to waste an amount of money; to spend money. □ *Mary blew forty bucks on a second-hand radio.* □ *We blew it all at a fancy restaurant.* **5.** *iv.* to become very angry; to lose one's temper. (See also **blow a fuse.**) □ *Finally I had had enough, and I blew.* **6.** *iv.* to play a musical instrument, not necessarily a wind instrument. □ *He blows, and everybody listens.* **7.** AND **blow-out** *n.* a drinking party. □ *Man, come to my blow-out. It's the best place to go.* **8.** *tv.* to sniff up any powdered drug; to take snuff. (Drugs.) □ *Those guys spend all their time blowing coke.* **9.** *iv.* to smoke marijuana. (Drugs.) □ *He sits there blowing by the hour. How can he afford it?* **10.** *n.* cocaine. (Drugs.) □ *You can get some good blow over at that crack house.* □ *What's blow cost around here?* **11.** *tv.* to perform an act of oral sex on someone, especially males. (Usually objectionable.) □ *Tom was looking for somebody who would blow him for nothing.*

blow a fuse AND **blow** one's **fuse; blow a gasket; blow** one's **cork; blow** one's **lid; blow** one's **top** *tv.* to explode with anger; to lose one's temper. □ *Come on, don't blow a fuse.* □ *Go ahead, blow a gasket! What good will that do?*

blow a gasket Go to **blow a fuse.**

blow a hype *tv.* to overreact; to **spaz out.** □ *I was afraid she would blow a hype about the broken window.*

blow beets *tv.* to empty one's stomach; to vomit. □ *What was in that stew? I feel like I gotta blow beets.*

blow chunks *tv.* to empty one's stomach; to vomit. (Collegiate.) □ *The stuff makes me blow chunks every time I get near it.*

Blow it out your ear! *exclam.* Go away!; I don't believe it! □ *Oh, blow it out your ear, you twit!*

blown away *mod.* overwhelmed; greatly impressed. □ *We were just blown away by your good words.*

blow off 1. *iv.* to goof off; to waste time; to procrastinate. □ *All your best time is gone—blown off.* **2.** *n.* a time-waster; a **goof-off.** (Usually **blow-off.**) □ *Fred is such a blow-off!* □ *Get busy. I don't pay blow-offs around here.* **3.** *n.* the final insult; an event that causes a dispute. (Usually **blow-off.**) □ *The blow-off was a call from some dame named Monica who asked for Snookums.* □ *When the blow-off happened, nobody was expecting anything.*

blow one's **cookies** *tv.* to empty one's stomach; to vomit. □ *Yuck! I think I'm going to blow my cookies.*

blow one's **cool** *tv.* to become angry. (Compare to **keep** one's **cool**.) □ *I almost blew my cool when the dog wet on my pants leg.*

blow one's **cork** Go to blow a fuse.

blow one's **doughnuts** AND **lose** one's **doughnuts** [. . .'donəts] *tv.* to empty one's stomach; to vomit. □ *The stuff was so vile, I thought I would blow my doughnuts.*

blow one's **fuse** Go to blow a fuse.

blow one's **groceries** *tv.* to empty one's stomach; to vomit. □ *She blew her groceries all over the front seat.*

blow one's **lid** Go to blow a fuse.

blow (one's) lunch AND **lose** one's **lunch** *tv.* to empty one's stomach; to vomit. □ *I almost lost my lunch, I ran so hard.*

blow one's **top** Go to blow a fuse.

Blow on it! *exclam.* Cool it!; Take it easy! (As if one were trying to cool something by blowing on it.) □ *It's all right, Tom. Blow on it!* □ *Hey, man. Relax. Blow on it!*

blow-out Go to blow.

blow smoke *tv.* to state something in a way that conceals the truth. □ *She is a master at blowing smoke. She belongs in government.*

blow someone **away** *tv.* to overwhelm someone. □ *The music about blew me away.*

blow someone or something **off 1.** *tv.* to neglect or ignore someone or something. □ *Get it done now. Don't blow it off!* □ *Don't blow me off. Listen! I want it done now!* **2.** *tv.* [with *someone*] to cheat someone; to deceive someone. □ *They blew off a young couple and conned a hundred bucks out of them.* □ *Don't try to blow me off! I know what's what.*

blow someone's **doors off** *tv.* to defeat someone; to surpass someone. (As if someone were going by another vehicle on the highway at such a high speed that the doors would be blown off in passing.) □ *They blew our doors off in sales last year.*

blow Z's [. . . ziz] *tv.* to sleep. (See also **catch** some **Z's**.) □ *I got to blow Z's for a while; then we'll talk.*

boat 1. *n.* a big shoe. □ *Whose boat is that under the coffee table?* **2.** *n.* a big car; a full-size car. □ *How do you stop that boat? Throw out an anchor?*

boat anchor *n.* a useless computer; anything heavy and useless. □ *Why don't you replace that boat anchor with a new model?*

bod ['bɑd] **1.** *n.* a body, especially a nice body. □ *You got a nice bod, Tom.* **2.** *n.* a person. □ *How many bods are coming over tonight?*

boff ['bɑf] **1.** *tv.* to punch someone. □ *Ted boffed Harry playfully.* **2.** *iv.* to empty one's stomach; to vomit. (See also **barf**.) □ *She boffed and boffed, until she was exhausted.* **3.** *tv. & iv.* to copulate with someone. (Usually objectionable.) □ *They were boffing in the faculty lounge and the principal caught them.*

boffo ['bɑfo] **1.** *n.* a box-office hit; a successful play, musical, movie, etc. □ *The last one was a tremendous boffo, but we only broke even.* **2.** *mod.* successful; tremendous. □ *Another boffo success for Wally!*

bogue ['bog] *mod.* bogus; fake. □ *She is so, like, bogue!*

bogus beef AND **bum beef** *n.* a false complaint or charge. (See also **beef**.) □ *The cops took them in on a bogus beef.*

bohunk 1. *n.* a resident of or an immigrant from an Eastern European country, such as Poland, Hungary, etc. (A nickname. Can be perceived as derogatory. Usually objectionable.) □ *The bohunks can really cook up some fine food.* **2.** *n.* an oafish person. (Usually refers to a male. Usually objectionable.) □ *Get outa here, you stupid bohunk!* **3.** *n.* a term of endearment for a close friend or child. (Also a term of address.) □ *Come here, you little bohunk. Let me tuck in your shirt.* □ *Okay, you bohunks, come to dinner now.*

boink *tv. & iv.* to copulate [with] someone. (Usually objectionable.) □ *He said he boinked her twice.*

bokoo AND **boku** ['bo'ku] *mod.* many. (A play on French *beaucoup*.) □ *I've got bokoo things to do today.* □ *There are already boku people invited.*

boku Go to **bokoo**.

bomb 1. *n.* a bad performance or an inherently bad show. □ *They tried as hard as they could, but the thing was a bomb from act one on.* □ *The latest bomb on Broadway, like all bombs, will only go off once. This one finished to a chorus of boos before the final cur-*

tain. **2.** *iv.* to fail. □ *It bombed the minute the first curtain went up.* **3.** AND **bomb out** *iv.* [for a computer program] to fail. □ *You expect a program to bomb a time or two.*

the **bomb** AND **da bomb** *n.* something really great. □ *This tingle is really da bomb.*

bombed (out) *mod.* alcohol or drug intoxicated. □ *They were bombed and looked nearly dead.*

bomb out Go to bomb.

bone 1. *n.* a trombone. (Musicians.) □ *She plays the bone like nobody's business.* **2.** Go to bones; boner.

bonehead 1. *n.* a stupid or stubborn person. □ *You are such a bonehead when it comes to buying cars!* **2.** AND **boneheaded** *mod.* stupid; stubborn. □ *Of all the boneheaded things to do!* □ *Why am I married to the world's greatest, all-time bonehead klutz?* **3.** *mod.* suitable for a stupid person. □ *Are you signed up for that bonehead course?*

boneheaded Go to bonehead.

boner 1. *n.* a silly error; a gaffe. □ *What a boner! You must be embarrassed.* **2.** AND **bone** *n.* an erection. □ *He always gets a boner when he doesn't need it and never when he does.*

bones 1. *n.* dice. □ *Throw them bones and hope for the best.* **2.** *n.* a nickname for a physician. (From *sawbones.* Also the nickname of the doctor on the starship *Enterprise* of *Star Trek* fame. Also a term of address.) □ *This is quite a cut. You'll have to go over to the bones in Adamsville.*

bonk ['bɔŋk] **1.** *tv.* to strike one's head. □ *He bonked his head on the shelf.* **2.** *tv.* to strike someone on the head. □ *He wouldn't move, so I bonked him.* **3.** *tv. & iv.* to copulate [with] someone. (Usually objectionable.) □ *She bonked him all night. At least that's what he said.*

bonkers ['bɔŋkɚz] **1.** AND **crackers** *mod.* insane; crazy. □ *I think I am going bonkers.* **2.** *mod.* slightly intoxicated. □ *I'm just a little bonkers, nothing really serious.*

bonzo ['banzo] *mod.* crazy. □ *You are completely bonzo!*

boob AND **booby** *n.* a woman's breast. (Usually objectionable.) □ *Do you think my boobs will ever grow, Dr. Jones?* □ *That dame's really got boobs!*

boo-bird ['bubə·d] *n.* a person who boos frequently at games or other public events. □ *It was a big day for the boo-birds at Wrigley Field.*

boo-boo ['bubu] *n.* an error. □ *It's only a small boo-boo. Don't stress yourself.*

boob-tube ['bubtub] *n.* a television set. □ *You spend too much time in front of the boob-tube.* □ *What's on the boob-tube tonight?*

booby Go to boob.

boody AND **boodie; bootie; booty 1.** *n.* the buttocks. (Potentially offensive. Usually objectionable.) □ *Get your boodie out on that dance floor and shake it.* **2.** *n.* someone or something disliked. (From sense 1.) □ *Why don't you clean up all this boody? This place is a mess.* **3.** *n.* the female genitals; the vulva. (Usually objectionable.) □ *He wants to get into her boody.* **4.** *n.* women considered as a receptacle for the penis. (Rude and derogatory.) □ *He likes boody better than anything.*

booger Go to boogie.

boogie ['bugi OR 'bʊgi] **1.** *n.* a kind of rock dance. □ *I didn't like the boogie until I learned how to do it right.* **2.** *iv.* to dance rock-style. □ *I don't like to boogie.* **3.** *n.* a party where the boogie is danced. □ *There's a boogie over at Steve's tonight.* **4.** *iv.* to get down to work; to get down to business. □ *All right, it's time to boogie. Cool it!* **5.** AND **booger** *n.* a piece of nasal mucus. (Usually objectionable.) □ *Is that a boogie on your lip, or what?* **6.** *iv.* to leave. □ *Time to boogie. It's late.* **7.** *n.* a tumor. (Medical slang.) □ *Looks like a little boogie down in the lung.* **8.** *iv.* to copulate; to have sex. (Usually objectionable.) □ *Let's go boogie.*

book 1. *iv.* to leave. □ *Let's book. I'm late.* **2.** *tv.* to charge someone with a crime. □ *She looked sort of messy, and they wanted to book her for something, but didn't know what.* **3.** *iv.* to study. □ *I gotta book. Bye.*

boom box *n.* a portable stereo radio. (See also box.) □ *Turn down that damn boom box, or I'll kick it in.*

boom sticks *n.* drumsticks. (Musicians.) □ *He always carries his boom sticks in his back pocket, and he beats on walls, radiators, desks—you name it.* □ *I need new boom sticks. They keep breaking.*

boon *iv.* to leave the road in a car for the boondocks. □ *Tom has a 4-wheel-drive, so we can really boon!*

booster *n.* a shoplifter. □ *Gary was a part-time booster till he got into dope.*

bootie Go to boody.

booty call 1. *n.* sexual arousal. (Usually objectionable.) □ *Sam said he was feeling the booty call and needed to find his woman.* **2.** *n.* calling someone up for sex. (Usually objectionable.) □ *Reg stopped at a phone booth in the bar to make a booty call.*

booze ['buz] **1.** *n.* beverage alcohol. (Slang since the 1500s.) □ *I don't care for booze. It makes me sneeze.* □ *I gotta get some booze in me fast!* **2.** AND **booze up** *iv.* to drink alcohol to excess; to go on a bash. □ *Stop boozing for a minute and listen up, guys.*

booze up Go to booze.

bop ['bɑp] **1.** *tv.* to strike someone or something. □ *I bopped the car on the hood and made a dent.* **2.** *n.* a style of jazz popular in the 1940s. □ *We heard some bop in an old movie.* **3.** *n.* a drug in pill form; a dose of a drug. □ *Give me a bop of that stuff, will ya?*

boss *mod.* excellent; powerful. □ *That is a boss tune.*

bounce 1. *iv.* [for a check] to be returned from the bank because of insufficient funds. □ *My check bounced, and I had to pay a penalty fee.* **2.** *iv.* to leave; to depart. □ *It's late. Let's bounce.* **3.** *tv.* [for a bank] to refuse to honor a check. □ *They bounced another of my checks today.* **4.** *tv.* to throw someone out. □ *Willie bounced me, and I ran to my car and beat it.* **5.** *n.* pep; energy. □ *All these kids have a lot of bounce.*

bounce for something Go to spring for something.

bouquet of assholes *n.* an annoying or disgusting person or thing. (Rude and derogatory.) □ *Don't pay any attention to him. He's just another one of the bouquet of assholes you find around here.*

bow to the porcelain altar *iv.* to empty one's stomach; to vomit. (The porcelain altar is the toilet bowl.) □ *He spent the whole night bowing to the porcelain altar.*

box 1. *n.* a coffin. □ *Put him in a box and put the box in a hole. Then the matter is closed.* **2.** *n.* a portable stereo radio; a (ghetto) box. (See also (ghetto) blaster, boom box.) □ *Does that damn box have to be so loud?* **3.** *n.* the genitals of the male, especially as contained within a garment, such as underwear. (Usually objectionable.) □ *God, did you see the box on him?* **4.** *n.* a piano. □ *She sure can pound the devil out of that box!* **5.** *iv.* to die. □ *The old man looks like he's going to box at any minute.*

boxed in *mod.* in a bind; having few alternatives. □ *I really feel boxed in around here.*

boxed (up) 1. *mod.* alcohol or drug intoxicated. □ *I am way boxed, and I feel sick.* □ *She got boxed up on gin.* **2.** *mod.* in jail. □ *I did it, and I was boxed for a long time for it. Now lay off!* □ *Pat was boxed up for two days till we got bond money.*

bracelets *n.* handcuffs. □ *The cops put the bracelets on Jane and led her away.*

brain bucket *n.* a bike or motorcycle helmet. □ *He refuses to wear a brain bucket when he rides.*

brassed (off) *mod.* angry; disgusted. □ *You look so brassed off with the world. Smile!* □ *I'm not brassed in the least, really.*

bread *n.* money. □ *I need to get some bread to live on.*

break 1. *n.* a chance; an opportunity. □ *I got my first break in show biz when I was only 12.* **2.** *n.* an escape from prison; a prison breakout. □ *I hear there's a break planned for tonight.*

Break a leg! *exclam.* Good luck! (A special theatrical way of wishing a performer good luck. Saying "good luck" is a jinx.) □ *"Break a leg!" shouted the stage manager to the star.*

Break it up! *exclam.* Stop it! (An order to two or more people to stop doing something, such as fighting.) □ *She told the boys to break it up or get sent to the principal's office.*

break one's **balls (to do** something**)** Go to bust (one's**) ass (to do** something).

brew 1. *n.* coffee; occasionally, tea. □ *This is my kind of brew—hot, black, and aromatic.* **2.** *n.* beer; a can, bottle, or glass of beer. □ *Hey, give me a cold brew, will ya?*

brew-ha ['bruhɑ] *n.* beer; a beer. □ *How 'bout another brew-ha, Mike?*

brew-out *n.* a beer blast. □ *Were you at Tom's brew-out? I was too bombed to see who was there.*

brewski AND **brewsky** ['bruski] *n.* beer; a beer. □ *Hey, how 'bout a brewski?*

bring-down 1. *n.* something that depresses someone. □ *Just to see your face was a bring-down.* **2.** *n.* something that brings someone back to reality. □ *The bill for the week's stay was a real bring-down.*

bring someone **on** *tv.* to arouse someone sexually. □ *Look at her! She's doing her best to bring him on! Why are men so stupid?* □ *Are you trying to bring me on or something?*

broad *n.* a woman. (Originally underworld slang. Often jocular. Usually considered rude and derogatory.) □ *When is that broad gonna show up?*

browned (off) *mod.* angry. □ *I am really browned off at you!* □ *The boss is browned—to say the least.*

brownout 1. *iv.* [for the electricity] to fade and dim down. □ *The lights started to brownout, and I thought maybe I didn't pay the bill for the juice.* **2.** *n.* a period of dimming or fading of the electricity. (Something less than a blackout.) □ *There was another brownout today.*

brutal *mod.* excellent; powerful. □ *That last wave was totally brutal.*

B.S. 1. *n.* bullshit; nonsense; deception. (Partly euphemistic. Usually objectionable.) □ *Don't feed me that B.S.! I know the score!* **2.** *tv.* to deceive or attempt to deceive someone with lies or flattery. (Usually objectionable.) □ *Don't try to B.S. me with your sweet talk!*

buck 1. *n.* a dollar. □ *Here's a buck; get me some cigarettes.* **2.** *tv.* to resist something. □ *Don't buck it. Do what you are told.*

bucket 1. *n.* the goal (hoop and net) in basketball. (Sports.) □ *Freddy arced one at the bucket and missed.* **2.** *n.* a hoop or basket in basketball. (Sports.) □ *Four buckets in two minutes. Is that a record, or what?* **3.** *n.* the buttocks. (See also **can**.) □ *Haul your bucket over here and have a seat.* **4.** *n.* an old car. (From **bucket of bolts**.) □ *How much did you pay for that old bucket?*

bucket of bolts *n.* a machine, such as a car or a motorcycle, that is old, run-down, or worn-out. □ *My old bucket of bolts won't start this morning.*

bucko ['bəko] *n.* friend; pal. (Also a term of address.) □ *Hey, bucko, come here a minute.*

bud ['bəd] *n.* a Budweiser™ beer; any beer. (See also **budhead**.) □ *I got buds here. How many you want?*

budget *mod.* [of something] of low quality or cheap. □ *Don't you dare bring back any of that budget pizza!*

budhead ['bədhɛd] *n.* a beer drinker. (Black. See also **bud**.) □ *Here comes Charlie, my favorite budhead. How about a brew, Charlie?*

bug 1. *n.* a flaw in a computer program. □ *As soon as I get the bugs out, I can run my program.* **2.** *n.* a combining form meaning someone who is enthusiastic about something. □ *Mary is a camera bug.* **3.** *n.* an obsession or urge. □ *I had this bug that made me eat all shapes of pasta.* **4.** *tv.* to annoy someone. □ *Stop bugging me, you twit!*

bugly ['bəg li] *mod.* butt + ugly; really ugly. □ *I have never seen such a bugly guy in my life!*

Bug off! *exclam.* Get out!; Go away! □ *Bug off and leave me alone!*

built like a brick shithouse 1. *mod.* pertaining to a very strong and well-built person. (Usually refers to a male. Usually objectionable.) □ *Chuck is built like a brick shithouse. The only fat on him is where his brain ought to be.* **2.** *mod.* pertaining to a beautiful and curvaceous woman. (Refers to the imagined curving and uneven walls of an outhouse built hastily and carelessly of brick. Usually objectionable.) □ *Look at that dame! She's really built like a brick shithouse.*

bull 1. *n.* nonsense; bullshit. □ *Don't give me that bull! I won't buy it.* **2.** *tv. & iv.* to lie to or deceive someone. □ *Stop bulling me!* □ *Is she bulling again?*

bull-dagger Go to bulldiker.

bulldiker AND **bull-dagger; bulldyker** *n.* a lesbian, especially if aggressive or masculine. (Rude and derogatory.) □ *Some old bulldiker strutted in and ordered a beer and a chaser.*

bulldyker Go to bulldiker.

bull-pucky ['bʊlpəki] **1.** *n.* bull dung. □ *Why didn't you watch where you were going? Didn't you expect to find bull-pucky in a barnyard?* □ *How can you tell it's bull-pucky?* **2.** *n.* nonsense; bullshit. □ *That's all just bull-pucky. Don't believe a word of it.*

bullshit 1. *n.* lies; deception; hype; nonsense. (Also an exclamation: **Bullshit!** Widely known and used by both sexes. Usually objectionable.) □ *I've heard enough of your bullshit!* **2.** *tv.* to deceive someone verbally. (Usually objectionable.) □ *Are you trying to bullshit me?* **3.** *iv.* to tell lies; to hype and promote. (Usually objectionable.) □ *Can't you stop bullshitting about how good you are? 4. mod.* false; deceptive. (Usually objectionable.) □ *I'm sick of those bullshit ads on T.V.*

bullshit artist AND **bullshitter** *n.* a person expert at lies, deception, and hype. (See bullshit. Usually objectionable.) □ *What can you expect from a bullshit artist? The truth?*

bullshitter Go to bullshit artist.

bum beef Go to bogus beef.

bummed (out) *mod.* discouraged; depressed. □ *When you're feeling bummed out, think how many problems I have.*

bummer 1. AND **bum trip** *n.* a bad drug experience. (Drugs.) □ *This bummer comes from mixing pills. 2. n.* a disagreeable thing or person. □ *The game was a bummer you wouldn't believe. 3. mod.* disappointing; unpleasant. □ *This bummer car won't start!*

bumming *mod.* down; depressed; suffering from something disagreeable. (Collegiate.) □ *Everybody's bumming. It must be the weather.*

bumping *mod.* [of music] having a good beat. □ *Man, this music is bumping. I can feel the beat.*

bum someone out *tv.* to discourage someone. □ *That darn blowout bummed me out.* ⊤ *The failure of two tires bummed out the race driver.*

bum something (off someone) *tv.* to beg or borrow something (from someone). □ *Can I bum a cigarette off you?*

bum trip Go to bummer.

bunch of fives *n.* the fist, especially when used to strike someone. □ *How would you like a bunch of fives right in the kisser?*

buns *n.* the buttocks. □ *Look at the buns on that guy!*

burb ['bɚb] *n.* a suburb. (Usually plural.) □ *I've lived in the burbs all my life.*

burbed out ['bɚbd . . .] *mod.* looking very middle-class and suburban; decked out like a suburban citizen. □ *She's all burbed out with new clothes and a fancy car.*

burger-flipper *n.* a lowly hamburger cook in a fast-food restaurant. □ *If you drop out of school now, you'll end up being a burger-flipper for the rest of your life.*

burn 1. *n.* a cigarette. □ *Fred just stood there with a burn on his lower lip and his hands in his pockets.* **2.** *tv.* to smoke a cigarette. □ *This nicotine fiend needs to burn one for a fix!* **3.** *tv.* to cheat or rob someone. □ *Tom tried to burn me by selling me a bum watch, but I'm too clever.*

burn someone **down** *tv.* to humiliate someone. □ *Man, don't you ever burn me down like that again!* Ⓣ *You just want to burn down everybody to make yourself seem better.*

bushed ['buʃt] *mod.* exhausted. □ *Another hard day! I'm more bushed than ever.*

bust 1. *n.* a failure. □ *The whole project was a bust from the beginning.* **2.** *n.* a riotous drinking party. □ *There was no beer at the bust. Only wine.* **3.** *n.* a raid by the police. □ *I knew it was a bust the minute they broke in the door.* **4.** *tv.* [for the police] to raid a place and make arrests. □ *We're gonna bust every bookie joint in town.*

busta *n.* a punk; a jerk. (From the nickname *buster*.) □ *Yo, Busta! Tsup?*

bust-ass Go to kick-ass.

bust (one's) ass (to do something**)** AND **break** one's **balls (to do** something**); bust** one's **butt (to do** something**); bust** one's **nuts (to do** something**)** *tv.* to work very hard to do something; to work very hard at something. (Usually objectionable.) □ *You get down there and bust your ass to get the job done right! You hear me?* □ *I've been busting my butt at this job for 30 years, and look where it's got me!*

bust one's **butt (to do** something**)** Go to bust (one's**) ass (to do** something).

bust one's **nuts (to do** something**)** Go to bust (one's**) ass (to do** something).

bust on someone or something *tv.* to attack someone or a group. □ *These three guys busted on Bubba and broke his arm.*

bust (some) suds 1. *tv.* to drink some beer. □ *Let's go out and bust some suds.* **2.** *tv.* to wash dishes. □ *You get into that kitchen and bust some suds to pay for your meal!*

butch *mod.* masculine, when applied to a homosexual person. □ *Her leather jacket is just too, too butch!*

butt ['bət] **1.** *n.* the buttocks. (Caution with **butt**.) □ *The doctor gave him a shot in the butt.* **2.** *n.* a cigarette butt. □ *Whose butts are those in the car ashtray?* **3.** *n.* a cigarette of any kind. □ *You got a butt I can bum?*

butthead *n.* a stupid or obnoxious person of either sex. (Also a term of address. Rude and derogatory.) □ *Don't be such a butthead!*

butthole *n.* the anus; the **asshole**. (Usually objectionable.) □ *Why are you always scratching your butthole?*

butt naked *mod.* totally nude. □ *I was butt naked in the shower and couldn't get the phone.*

button 1. *n.* the termination of a recitation; the punch line of a joke. (The equivalent of a button that is pressed to signal a response.) □ *When I got to the button, I realized that I had told the whole joke wrong.* □ *When I came to the button, I knew I was really going to insult the guy.* **2.** *n.* a police officer's badge or shield. □ *The guy flashed his button, so I let him in.*

buy it *tv.* to die. □ *He lay there coughing for a few minutes, and then he bought it.*

buzz 1. *n.* a call on the telephone. □ *I'll give you a buzz tomorrow.* **2.** *tv.* to call someone on the telephone. □ *I'll buzz Mary and see if she can go.* **3.** *tv.* to signal someone with a buzzer. □ *I'll buzz my secretary.*

buzz-kill *n.* a person or thing that ruins someone's fun; a **bummer**. □ *The news about the suspension was a buzz-kill.*

cackleberry *n.* an egg. (Old.) □ *You want cackleberries for breakfast?*

cake *n.* money. (From **bread**.) □ *I can't scrape together enough cake to do the job.*

cake hole Go to **word hole**.

cakewalk *n.* something very easy. (Compare to **sleepwalk**.) □ *The game was a cakewalk from beginning to end.*

calendar *n.* a month. (Black.) □ *One more calendar, then you get your money.*

call 1. *n.* a decision; a prediction. □ *The ship behaved just as you said it would. Good call.* **2.** *tv.* to challenge someone. (See also **call** someone **out**.) □ *Are you the guy who called me? Who do you think you are?*

Call my service. *sent.* Please call me through my answering service. (Not a friendly or encouraging invitation.) □ *Good to talk to ya, babe. Call my service. Love ya!*

call shotgun *phr.* to call out and claim the seat beside the driver in an automobile. □ *Bob called shotgun so he could sit next to the driver.*

call someone **out** *tv.* to challenge someone to a fight. □ *Carl wanted to call him out but thought better of it.*

campus ['kæmpəs] *tv.* to restrict someone to the grounds of a college campus. (Collegiate.) □ *The dean threatened to campus the entire fraternity for a month.*

can 1. *n.* the head. □ *What do you have in your can, anyway? Lard?* □ *Jerry landed one on Frank's can. Frank crumpled.* **2.** *n.* toilet. □ *Hell, I ain't tired! Where's the can?* □ *I gotta use the can before we leave.* **3.** *n.* jail. □ *I had to spend the night in the can, but it wasn't too bad.* **4.** *tv.* to dismiss someone from employment. □

The jerk canned everybody who played a part in the gag. **5.** *n.* the buttocks. □ *I slipped and fell right on my can.*

candy-ass 1. *n.* a coward; a timid person. □ *Sue is such a candy-ass when it comes to dealing with her children.* **2.** Go to candy-ass(ed).

candy-ass(ed) *mod.* timid; frightened; cowardly. □ *What a candy-assed twit you are!*

cans *n.* earphones. (See also can.) □ *The guy with the cans on his head is the radio operator.*

cap 1. *n.* a capsule of a drug. □ *She spilled the caps on the floor and had to find every single one of them.* **2.** *tv.* to exceed something; to surpass something. □ *I know I can't cap that. That's just super!* **3.** *tv.* to make a capsule. □ *I must have capped 300 placebos today.* **4.** *tv.* to kill someone. □ *One more word and I'll cap you!*

capish [kə'piʃ] *iv.* to understand. (Usually a question.) □ *The matter is settled. No more talk. Capish?*

capper ['kæpɚ] *n.* the climax or clincher of something. □ *The capper of the evening was when the hostess got lathered and couldn't stand up.* □ *When the butler tripped and served Mr. Wilson the entire dessert in his lap, that was the capper to an exciting evening.*

carb ['karb] *n.* carburetor. □ *I learned how to clean and adjust a carb by the time I was in high school.*

carbos ['karboz] *n.* carbohydrates. (Bodybuilding.) □ *You need more protein and less carbos.* □ *Too many carbos will make you fat.*

card 1. *n.* a funny person. □ *Gee, Fred. You're a card. Somebody's gonna have to deal with you.* **2.** *tv.* to check people's I.D. cards for age or other eligibility. □ *They card everybody at the football games, even the parents.*

carry the stick *tv.* to live as a hobo, on the streets. (Streets. From the stick that supports the hobo's bundle.) □ *I even carried the stick for a while in the sixties.*

a **case of the shorts** Go to the shorts.

cash cow *n.* a dependable source of money; a good investment. □ *I put most of my money in a dependable cash cow that pays off once a month.* □ *Mr. Wilson turned out to be the cash cow we needed to start our repertoire company.*

cat 1. *n.* a fellow; a guy; a **dude**. □ *Now, this cat wants to borrow some money from me. What should I do?* **2.** *iv.* to empty one's stomach; to vomit. □ *Looks like somebody catted in the bushes.*

catch some **rays** AND **bag** some **rays** *tv.* to get some sunshine; to tan in the sun. □ *We wanted to catch some rays, but the sun never came out the whole time we were there.* □ *I went to Hawaii to bag some rays.*

catch some **Z's** AND **cop** some **Z's; cut** some **Z's** *tv.* to get some sleep. □ *I gotta catch some Z's before I drop.* □ *Why don't you stop a little bit and try to cop some Z's?*

Catch you later. *sent.* I will talk to you again when I next see you. □ *Can't talk now. Catch you later.*

catholic bagel *n.* a nontraditional bagel made or flavored with cinnamon, blueberries, strawberries, etc. (Jocular.) □ *At breakfast, they had catholic bagels and sweet rolls.*

C.F. Go to **cluster fuck.**

chain(saw) *tv.* to destroy something; to cut something up severely. □ *The senatorial committee tried to chainsaw the nominee, but the full senate voted for confirmation.* □ *We didn't think they'd come in and chain all our plans.*

chamber of commerce *n.* toilet; restroom. □ *Q: Where's Bob? A: Oh, Bob's in the chamber of commerce.*

change the channel *tv.* to switch to some other topic of conversation. □ *Just a minute. I think you changed the channel. Let's go back to the part about you owing me money.* □ *Let's change the channel here before there is a fight.*

chap *tv.* to anger or annoy someone. □ *That whole business really chapped me.*

Charlie Foxtrot Go to **cluster fuck.**

Charlie Noble *n.* a ship's smokestack. (Naval. This is an old naval term, used as slang and in joking.) □ *The captain says I am supposed to take this letter to Charlie Noble.*

chart *n.* a musical score. (Musicians. See also **map.**) □ *Come on, man! Look at the chart! You're making mistakes everywhere.*

chas AND **chez** ['tʃæz AND 'tʃɛz] *n.* matches. (Collegiate. A clipping of *matches*.) □ *Where are my chas?* □ *You got a couple of chez?*

cheaters *n.* sunglasses. (Formerly used for all spectacles. See also shades, sunshades.) □ *Get your cheaters on. The sun's really bright.* □ *Somebody sat on my cheaters!*

check *interj.* okay; yes; yes, it is on the list. □ BILL: *Four quarts of oil.* TOM: *Check.* □ FRED: *Are you ready?* PAUL: *Check.*

check that *tv.* cancel that; ignore that (last remark). □ *Check that. I was wrong.* □ *At four, no, check that, at three this afternoon, a bomb exploded at the riverside.*

cheddar *n.* money. □ *I'm totally out of cheddar. Can you loan me a Benji?*

cheese 1. *n.* vomit. □ *There's cheese on the sidewalk. Look out!* **2.** *iv.* to empty one's stomach; to vomit. □ *She popped into the bushes and cheesed soundlessly.* **3.** *iv.* to smile, as for a photographer who asks you to say "cheese" when a picture is taken. □ *Why are you cheesing? Did something good happen?* **4.** *n.* money. □ *I don't have the cheese to buy a new car.* □ *You have some cheese I can borrow?*

cheesecake 1. *n.* a display of the female form, probably wearing little clothing, often in photographs. (Compare to beefcake.) □ *Women don't like to see all that cheesecake on the walls when they bring their cars in here to be fixed.* □ *Now they're even putting the magazines with cheesecake under the counter.* **2.** *n.* a good-looking woman; good-looking women. □ *Who's the cheesecake in that low-cut job?*

cheesed off *mod.* angry; disgusted. □ *Clare was really cheesed off at the butler.*

cheesehead 1. *n.* a stupid-acting person. □ *Is this cheesehead bothering you?* □ *Why do all the cheeseheads in town ride in my cab in the same day?* **2.** *n.* someone from the state of Wisconsin. (Much cheese is made is Wisconsin. Not usually derogatory.) □ *I moved to Wisconsin and became a cheesehead.*

cheesy *mod.* cheap; tacky. □ *That was a cheesy trick to pull on him.*

cheezer *n.* a very bad smelling release of intestinal gas; a foul-smelling fart. □ *God, who let the cheezer?*

cherry 1. *n.* an inexperienced person; a novice. □ *She's a cherry when it comes to computers.* **2.** *n.* the hymen. (Usually objectionable.) □ *You jerk! All you care about is scoring cherries!*

chewed *mod.* tired; abused. □ *After that argument at the office yesterday, I really felt chewed.*

chew face *tv.* to kiss. (More jocular than crude.) □ *A couple of kids were in a doorway chewin' face.*

chew someone's **ass out** *tv.* to scold someone severely. (Usually objectionable.) □ *The cop was really mad and chewed Bob's ass out.*

chez Go to chas.

chicken *n.* a coward. □ *Come on, let's go. Don't be a chicken.*

chicken out (of something**)** *iv.* to manage to get out of something, usually because of fear or cowardice. □ *Freddy chickened out of the plan at the last minute.*

chicken shit 1. *n.* virtually nothing. (Usually objectionable.) □ *Fifty bucks! That's just chicken shit!* **2.** *mod.* cowardly. (Usually objectionable.) □ *You are such a chicken shit coward! Stand up and fight!* **3.** *n.* worthless. (Usually objectionable.) □ *I don't want this chicken shit pizza! Get me one with pepperoni on it, not dead fish.*

chief ['tʃif] *n.* the person in charge. (Also a term of address.) □ *Okay, chief, where to?*

chill 1. AND **chilly** *n.* a cold can of beer. □ *Hey, toss me a chilly, would ya, buddy?* □ *You ready for another chill?* **2.** *tv.* to kill someone. (Underworld.) □ *I'll chill you with one blast from my cannon, you creep.* **3.** *tv.* to reject someone. □ *The whole gang chilled him, and this really made him come home.*

chill (out) *iv.* to calm down; to be cool; to get cool. □ *All right now, people, chill . . . chill.* □ *Before we can debate this matter, you're all gonna have to chill out.*

chill someone's **action** *tv.* to squelch someone; to prevent someone from accomplishing something. (Black.) □ *Freddie is trying to chill my action, and I'm a little steamed about that.* □ *Just wait! I'll chill his action—just you wait.*

chintzy ['tʃɪntsi] **1.** *mod.* cheap; shoddy. □ *Nobody's gonna buy this chintzy stuff. Throw it out.* □ *What a chintzy car! The door fell off!* **2.** *mod.* stingy; miserly. □ *The chintzy guy left me no tip!* □ *Don't be so chintzy. Give the man a dollar for a cup of coffee.*

chippy 1. AND **chippie** *n.* a part-time prostitute. □ *Some little chippie stopped us to ask for a match. How amateurish.* **2.** *iv.* to play around sexually. □ *So me and my boyfriend was chippying a little in the hall. Why, was you watching?*

chippy around *iv.* to be sexually promiscuous. □ *She has been known to chippy around, but not with just anyone and never for money.* □ *She figures it's her right to chippy around.*

chips *n.* money. □ *She saved some chips over the years and bought herself a little place on the beach.*

chism Go to jism.

chiz ['tʃɪz] *iv.* to relax. (Collegiate.) □ *I gotta get back to my room and chiz awhile.*

choke 1. *iv.* [for a computer] to fail to take in information being fed to it. (Computers.) □ *If you don't have your modem and your software set the same way as the host, your machine will choke.* □ *I did what you told me, but it choked anyway.* **2.** *iv.* to panic before or during a test. (From *choke up.*) □ *She always chokes during a test.*

choker 1. *n.* a cigarette; a cigarette butt. □ *Put that damn choker out in my house!* □ *I can smell a choker the minute somebody lights it.* **2.** *n.* a necktie. □ *Let's go out to eat where I don't have to wear a choker.*

choke the chicken Go to beat the dummy.

chop *n.* a rude remark; a cutting remark. □ *Jerry made some chop about the way I dress.*

chotchke Go to tchotchke.

chow 1. *n.* food. □ *What time is chow served around here?* **2.** *tv. & iv.* to eat (something). (See also **chow down.**) □ *I've been chowing canned tuna and stale bagels to save money.* **3.** Go to ciao.

chow down *iv.* to eat; to take a meal. □ *It's past my time to chow down.*

chow something **down** *tv.* to eat something, probably quickly or without good manners. □ *We can chow this pizza down in about two minutes!* Ⓣ *I found a box of cookies and chowed down the whole thing before anybody knew what I was doing.*

chubby *n.* an erection. (Usually objectionable.) □ *He always gets a chubby when he doesn't need it and never when he does.*

chuck 1. AND **chuck up** *iv.* to empty one's stomach; to vomit. (See also upchuck.) □ *I think I gotta chuck!* **2.** *tv.* to throw something away. □ *Chuck this thing. It's no good.* **3.** *iv.* to eat voraciously. □ *The two guys sat guzzling and chucking till they were full.*

chuck a dummy *tv.* to empty one's stomach; to vomit. □ *Somebody chucked a dummy on the patio.*

the **chuckers** AND the **chucks** *n.* a great hunger; an enormous appetite. □ *Oh, man, I really got the chucks. What time is chow?* □ *The chuckers got my stomach asking if my throat is cut.*

the **chucks** Go to the chuckers.

chuck up Go to chuck.

chunk *iv.* to empty one's stomach; to vomit. (Collegiate.) □ *I think I gotta chunk.* □ *The cat chunked all over the carpet.*

ciao AND **chow** ['tʃɑʊ] Good-bye; Hello. (Italian.) □ *See ya. Ciao.* □ *Chow, baby. Call my service.*

circle-jerk 1. *n.* a gathering of males performing mutual masturbation. (Partly jocular. Usually objectionable.) □ *There were twelve boys involved in a circle-jerk, and the principal caught them.* **2.** *n.* a boring or time-wasting meeting. (From sense 1.) □ *That board meeting was the typical circle-jerk that it always is.*

circle (the drain) *tv. & iv.* to be in the final process of dying; to be in extremis. (Jocular but crude hospital jargon.) □ *Get Mrs. Smith's son on the phone. She's circling the drain.*

clanked *mod.* exhausted; pooped. □ *At the end of the race, the chick was totally clanked.*

clap *n.* a case of gonorrhea. (Very old and still in use.) □ *He thinks he got the clap from her.*

climb *tv.* to scold someone. □ *The boss climbed Harry for being late.*

clincher ['klɪntʃɚ] *n.* the final element; the straw that broke the camel's back. (See also **capper**.) □ *The clincher was when the jerk turned up the volume.*

cling like shit to a shovel AND **stick like shit to a shovel 1.** *iv.* to stick or adhere [to someone or something] tightly. (Usually objectionable.) □ *That oily stuff sticks like shit to a shovel.* **2.** *iv.* to be very dependent on someone; to follow someone around. (Often with an indirect object. Usually objectionable.) □ *She's so dependent. She clings to him like shit to a shovel.*

clinker 1. *n.* a mistake; [in music] a misplayed note. □ *That was a bad clinker in the middle of the soft passage.* □ *Look at the score,* *man! That series of clinkers just isn't there.* **2.** *n.* a worthless person or thing. (From the term for a cinder.) □ *Ralph has turned out to be a real clinker. We'll have to fire him.*

clip 1. *tv.* to cheat someone. □ *That guy in there clipped me for a fiver.* **2.** *n.* a music video; a short film. □ *This next clip is something you'll all recognize.* □ *Stay tuned for more great clips.* **3.** *n.* a fast rate of speed. □ *By traveling at a good clip, we managed to get there before the wedding started.* □ *You were moving at a pretty good clip when you ran into the truck.*

clit AND **clitty** *n.* the clitoris. (Usually objectionable.) □ *Have I got a present for you and your clitty!*

clod *n.* a stupid and oafish person. (Usually refers to a male. Old. Widely known. Usually objectionable.) □ *Don't be such a clod! Put on your tie, and let's go.*

clunk 1. *tv.* to strike someone or something. □ *The branch clunked the roof as it fell.* **2.** *n.* a hit; the sound of a hit. □ *The clunk on the roof was a falling branch.*

clunker 1. *n.* an old car. □ *He drives an old clunker and doesn't have any insurance.* **2.** *n.* someone or something worthless; a **clinker**. □ *We have to get the clunkers off the payroll.*

cluster fuck 1. *n.* an act of group rape. (Also **Charlie Foxtrot** from the initials *C.F.* Usually objectionable.) □ *Look at her! She's just asking for a cluster fuck.* **2.** *n.* any event as riotous as an act of group rape. (Figurative on sense 1. The same allusion as sense 1.) □ *This goddamn day has been one long cluster fuck!*

clutched *mod.* nervous. □ *I get so clutched before a test.*

clutch (up) *iv.* to become very tense and anxious; to freeze with anxiety. □ *I have been known to clutch up before a race.* □ *Cool it, babe! Don't clutch!*

coaster *n.* someone who lives near the ocean. (California.) □ *Tiffany is a coaster now, but she was born, like, somewhere else.*

cob 1. *n.* a sharp poke in the anus. □ *Ouch! That cob hurt!* **2.** *tv.* to give someone a sharp poke in the anus. □ *Tom cobbed Fred when he passed by.*

coin *n.* money. (See also **hard coin**.) □ *I'm sort of short of coin right now. Can it wait?* □ *He made a lot of coin on his last job.*

cojones [ko'honiz] *n.* the testicles. (Spanish. Usually objectionable.) □ *He kicked that old cat right in the cojones and sent it flying.*

cold 1. *mod.* [stopping someone or something] suddenly and totally. □ *That remark stopped her cold.* **2.** *mod.* dead. □ *When I'm cold and buried, I hope people will think of me fondly.*

cold fish *n.* a dull and unresponsive person. □ *I hate to shake hands with a cold fish like that. He didn't even smile.* □ *I hate going out with a cold fish.*

a **cold piece of work** *n.* a person who is difficult to deal with. □ *Buddy, you are a cold piece of work.*

collar 1. *tv.* to arrest someone. □ *The officer tried to collar Carl, but Carl moved away too fast.* **2.** *n.* an arrest. □ *It was a tough collar, with all the screaming and yelling.*

come AND **cum 1.** *iv.* to experience an orgasm. (There is no other single word for this meaning. Usually objectionable.) □ *God, I thought she'd never cum.* **2.** *n.* semen. (Usually objectionable.) □ *Do you think cum is alive?*

come down 1. *iv.* to happen. □ *Hey, man! What's coming down?* □ *When something like this comes down, I have to stop and think things over.* **2.** *n.* a letdown; a disappointment. (Usually **comedown**.) □ *The loss of the race was a real comedown for Willard.* **3.** *iv.* to begin to recover from the effects of alcohol or drug intoxication. □ *She came down slow, which was good.*

come home 1. *iv.* to return to reality. □ *I'm glad you decided to come home.* **2.** AND **come home to haunt** someone *iv.* [for some problem] to cause negative consequences. □ *Eventually every single problem you have avoided dealing with will come home.* □ *All these things come home to haunt you sooner or later.*

come home to haunt someone Go to come home.

Come off it! 1. *exclam.* Stop acting arrogantly! □ *Come off it, Tiff. You're not the Queen of England.* **2.** *exclam.* Give up your incorrect point of view! □ *You are arguing from a foolish position. You're dead wrong. Come off it!*

come on 1. *n.* a lure; bait. (Usually **come-on**.) □ *It's just a come on. Nobody is giving away a decent color T.V. just for listening to a sales pitch.* **2.** *n.* an invitation; a sexual invitation. (Usually **come-on**.) □ *Who could resist a come-on like that?*

come on to someone *iv.* to try to get someone to respond romantically or sexually. □ *She was just starting to come on to me when her parents came home.*

come out of the closet *iv.* to appear publicly as a homosexual. (The phrase has many nonsexual metaphorical meanings.) □ *They say he came out of the closet when he was 8 years old.*

come up for air *iv.* to pause for a break. □ *The kissers—being only human—had to come up for air eventually.* □ *They were taking in money so fast at the box office that there wasn't a minute to come up for air.*

comma-counter *n.* a pedantic person. □ *Comma-counters can be such a pain.*

comp 1. *tv.* to accompany someone [musically]. □ *I have to sing a solo at a wedding and need someone to comp me.* **2.** *tv.* to give something to someone free. (Either as *compensation* for difficulties endured or as a *complimentary* gift.) □ *The movie patron was angry and demanded his money back. The manager comped him with a few free passes, and he was happy.*

con 1. *n.* a convict. □ *Is that guy in the gray pajamas one of the escaped cons?* **2.** *n.* a confidence scheme. □ *They pulled a real con on the old lady.* **3.** *tv.* to swindle or deceive someone. □ *Don't try to con me. I know the score.*

con artist Go to con man.

conehead 1. *n.* a fool; an oaf. □ *Some conehead put sugar in the salt shaker.* **2.** *n.* an intellectual; a **pointy-head**. □ *They build fences around universities to keep the coneheads in.*

conk AND **konk** *n.* the head. □ *Where'd you get that nasty bump on your konk?*

conk out 1. *iv.* [for someone] to collapse. □ *I was so tired I just went home and conked out.* □ *I was afraid I would conk out while I was driving.* **2.** *iv.* [for something] to break down; to quit running. □ *My old car conked out finally.*

con man AND **con artist** *n.* someone who makes a living by swindling people. □ *Gary is a con artist, but at least he's not on the dole.* □ *He looks like a con man, but he's just a sweetie.*

cookie-pusher 1. *n.* a bootlicker; someone who flatters other people for self-serving motives. □ *When you've got a whole office full* *of cookie-pushers, there's always someone to take you to lunch.* □ *Another cookie-pusher came in today to tell me what a great teacher I am.* **2.** *n.* a lazy do-nothing. □ *Is Martin a couch potato or a cookie-pusher? That is the question!*

cool 1. *mod.* unabashed; unruffled; relaxed. □ *She is totally cool and easygoing.* **2.** *mod.* good; excellent. □ *This is a really cool setup!*

cool down *iv.* to calm down. □ *Now, just cool down. Chill, chill. Everything's gonna be real cool.* □ *When things cool down around here, life will be much more livable.*

cooled out *mod.* calm; unabashed. □ *Ted is a really cooled out kind of guy.*

the **cooler** *n.* jail. □ *Do you want to talk, or do you want to spend a little time in the cooler?* □ *Don't keep me in the cooler! I'm innocent!*

Cool it! *exclam.* Calm down! □ *Take it easy! Cool it!* □ *Come on, cool it, man!*

cool off *iv.* to calm down. □ *Now, it's all right. Cool off!*

cool out *iv.* to calm down; to relax. □ *Now, just cool out, man. This will pass.*

cool someone out *tv.* to calm someone; to appease someone. □ *Cool yourselves out, you people. We gotta be sensible.* ⊤ *The manager appeared and tried to cool out everybody, but that was a waste of time.*

cop 1. *tv.* to take or steal something. (Originally underworld.) □ *Somebody copped the statue from the town square.* **2.** *n.* a police officer. □ *The cop wasn't in any mood to put up with any monkey business.*

cop an attitude *tv.* to take a negative or opposite attitude about something. (See also **tude.**) □ *I think you're copping an attitude. Not advised, man. Not advised.*

cop a plea *tv.* to plead guilty to a lesser charge. □ *Walter copped a plea and got off with a week in the slammer.* □ *I wanted to cop a plea, but didn't have the chance.*

cop a squat *tv.* to sit down. □ *Hey, man! Come in and cop a squat.* □ *Cop a squat and crack a tube.*

cop a tube *tv.* to catch a perfect tubular wave. (Surfers.) □ *Mark— as drunk as all get out—said he was gonna go out and cop a tube.*

cop out 1. *iv.* to plead guilty (to a lesser charge). (Underworld. See also cop a plea.) □ *I decided not to cop out and got a lawyer instead.* **2.** *iv.* to give up and quit; to **chicken out** (of something). □ *Why do you want to cop out just when things are going great?* **3.** *n.* a poor excuse to get out of something. (Usually **cop-out** or **copout**.) □ *This is a silly copout.* □ *That's not a good reason. That's just a cop-out.*

copped *mod.* arrested. □ *Jed got himself copped—a speeder.*

copper 1. *n.* a police officer. (Originally underworld. Because the copper "cops" or "takes." See also cop.) □ *See that copper over there? He arrested me once.* □ *The coppers will catch up with you some day.* **2.** *n.* money. (From *copper penny.* See also **rivets**.) □ *How much copper you got on you?*

cop some Z's Go to catch some Z's.

corn *n.* money. □ *I need some corn to pay the rent.*

corpse 1. *n.* an empty liquor or beer bottle. (See also **dead soldier**.) □ *Throw your corpses in the trash can, you jerk!* **2.** *n.* a cigarette butt. □ *The wino picked up the corpse and put it in a little box of them he carried with him.* □ *He is saving corpses to build a real smoke.*

cosmic *mod.* excellent; powerful. □ *Who wants to see a really cosmic movie?*

couch potato *n.* a lazy, do-nothing television watcher. (See also **sofa spud**.) □ *If there was a prize for the best couch potato, my husband would win it.* □ *You are turning into a perfect couch potato.*

Cough it up! *tv.* to give something—typically money—to someone, especially if done unwillingly. □ *You owe me 20 bucks. Cough it up!*

cowboy *n.* a reckless and independent man; a reckless driver. (Also a term of address.) □ *Come on, cowboy, finish your coffee and get moving.* □ *Some cowboy in a new caddy cut in front of me.*

cow chips *n.* dried cow dung. □ *There's a whole field of cow chips out there! Why do you want to buy a bag of the stuff at a nursery?* □ *Break up these cow chips and work them into the soil around the base of the bushes.*

cow flop AND **cow plop** *n.* a mass of cow dung. □ *Mrs. Wilson is out in the pasture gathering cow flops for her garden.*

cow plop Go to cow flop.

coyote-ugly ['kɑɪot 'əgli OR 'kɑɪoti 'əgli] *mod.* extremely ugly. (Said of people. See also **double-bagger**. Supposedly, if one woke up and found one's arm around a **coyote-ugly** person, one would chew off one's arm—in the manner of a coyote escaping from a steel-jaw trap—rather than pull it back away from this person.) □ *Isn't that the most coyote-ugly creep you've ever seen?*

cozy up (to someone) *iv.* to become overly friendly with someone in hope of gaining special favors. □ *Molly cozied up to the prof, hoping for a good grade at least.*

cr@p 1. *n. & iv.* a partially written disguise for **crap** = junk. □ *I asked him what all the cr@p was on the floor.* **2.** *iv.* a partially written disguise for **crap** = dung. □ *The cat cr@pped in the hall last night.*

crab *n.* a louse. (Usually plural.) □ *He's scratching like he's got crabs.*

crack 1. *n.* a joke; a smart-aleck remark. □ *Another crack like that and your nose will be a little flatter than it is.* □ *Who made that crack?* **2.** *n.* a try (that may or may not succeed). □ *Have another crack at it.* □ *One more crack and I'll have it.* **3.** *n.* a unit of something (for a particular price); a use (of something). □ *You would think twice, too, if you remembered that it's seven dollars a crack.* **4.** *n.* the gap between the buttocks. □ *You can take your old summons and stick it up your crack!* □ *You wanna get kicked in the crack?* **5.** *n.* crystalline, smokable cocaine. (Drugs.) □ *This crack seems to have become the drug of choice for punks of all ages.* □ *Crack became popular when it became easy and cheap to process. It's been around for years in medicinal form.* **6.** *iv.* to break down and talk under pressure. (Underworld.) □ *They kept at her till she finally cracked and talked.* □ *We knew you'd finally crack.* **7.** *mod.* [of a person] excellent; top-flight. □ *The dealer's crack salesman was no help at all.* **8.** *tv.* to break into something. (Underworld.) □ *We almost cracked the safe before the alarm went off.*

crack a book *tv.* to open a book to study. (Usually in the negative. See also **book**.) □ *I never cracked a book and still passed the course.* □ *Sally didn't crack a book all semester.*

crack a tube *tv.* to open a can of beer. (See also **tube**.) □ *Why don't you drop over this evening, and we'll crack a few tubes?* □ *Would you crack a tube for me? My hands are full.*

cracked *mod.* crazy. □ *You're cracked if you think I'll agree to that.*

crackers Go to bonkers.

crack open a bottle AND **crack a bottle open; crack the bottle open** *tv.* to open a bottle of liquor. □ *Let's crack open a bottle and celebrate.*

crack someone **up** *tv.* to make someone laugh. □ *She giggled, and that cracked us all up.* ⊤ *The lecturer would talk along sort of boring like, and then all of a sudden he would crack up everybody with a joke.*

cram *iv.* to study hard at the last minute for a test. □ *She spent the night cramming for the test.*

crank 1. *n.* a bothersome person who telephones with a bogus message. □ *A crank called with a bomb threat.* **2.** *mod.* bogus. □ *We had four crank calls threatening to blow up the Eiffel Tower.* **3.** *n.* a crabby person. (Collegiate.) □ *Why are you such a crank? Is something wrong in your life?*

cranking *mod.* exciting; excellent. □ *We had a massively cranking time at your party.*

crap ['kræp] **1.** *n.* junk; worthless matter. □ *Why don't you just throw this crap away?* □ *Get your crap off my bed!* **2.** *n.* dung. (Crude. Caution with topic.) □ *There's dog crap on the lawn.* **3.** *n.* nonsense; lies. □ *I've had enough of your crap. Now talk straight, or out you go.* □ *Cut the crap!* **4.** *iv.* to defecate. (Crude. Caution with topic.) □ *Your dog crapped on my lawn!*

crap-house Go to shit-house.

crap-list Go to shit-list.

crap out *iv.* to evade something; to **chicken out (of** something). □ *Now, don't crap out on me at the last minute.* □ *Fred crapped out, so there are only three of us.*

crapped (out) *mod.* dead; finished. (Not prenominal. From dice, not from the other senses of **crap**.) □ *After a serious encounter with a rattlesnake, my two dogs were crapped by dawn.*

crapper 1. *n.* a toilet; an outhouse. □ *Man, I gotta go! Where's the crapper around here?* **2.** *n.* someone who tells lies or exaggerates; a bullshit artist. □ *She's such a crapper. You can't believe a word she says.*

crappy 1. *mod.* messed up with dung; dungy. □ *Clean off your crappy shoes before you go in there!* **2.** *mod.* lousy. □ *This has been a real crappy day for me.*

crash 1. *tv. & iv.* to attend a party or other event uninvited. □ *Some clown tried to crash the rally, but my dad called the cops.* **2.** *iv.* to spend the night. □ *I crashed at a friend's place in the city.* **3.** *iv.* to sleep. □ *I crashed till noon.* □ *If I don't crash pretty soon, I'm going to die!* **4.** *n.* a place to sleep. □ *I think I know of a crash for tonight.* □ *Molly's on the phone, looking for a crash.* **5.** *iv.* [for a computer] to stop working. □ *This thing crashes every time I hit a certain key.* □ *My machine hasn't crashed since I got it.* **6.** *n.* a total failure of a computer. □ *Most of my data was lost in the crash.* **7.** *iv.* [for any electronic device] to fail. □ *My stereo crashed, so I've been watching T.V.* **8.** *iv.* [for a securities market] to lose a significant portion of its value in a short time. □ *The market crashed and scared the stuffing out of everybody.* **9.** *n.* a collapse of a securities market. □ *After the crash, a lot of people swore off the market for good.* **10.** *iv.* to pass out from drinking alcohol to excess. □ *About midnight I crashed, and I woke up here.* □ *Let's get Wilbur home before he crashes for good.*

crash and burn 1. *iv.* [for a young man] to fail brilliantly in a romance. (Collegiate. See also **go down in flames**.) □ *It stands to reason that if Ken hadn't shot me down, I wouldn't have crashed and burned.* **2.** *iv.* to fail spectacularly. □ *I have to be prepared. I don't want to crash and burn if I don't have to.*

crasher *n.* a person who attends a party uninvited. (See also **crash**.) □ *The crashers ruined the party, and my dad called the cops.*

crater *n.* an acne scar. □ *Ted has a nasty crater on his cheek.* □ *Walter was always sort of embarrassed about his craters.*

crater-face AND **pizza-face** *n.* a person with acne or many acne scars. (Intended as jocular. Rude and derogatory.) □ *I gotta get some kind of medicine for these pimples. I'm getting to be a regular crater-face.*

cream 1. *tv.* to beat someone; to outscore someone. □ *The other team creamed us, but we had better team spirit.* **2.** *n.* semen. (Usually objectionable.) □ *His father found some cream in the john and went into a purple rage.* **3.** *tv.* to copulate [with] someone, usually a female. (Usually objectionable.) □ *He acted like he wanted to cream her.*

cream puff 1. *n.* a weakling; a wimpy person. □ *Don't be a cream puff all your life! Join a health club!* **2.** *n.* a used car that is in very good condition. □ *This one is a real cream puff. Only driven to church by a little old lady.* □ *This cream puff is loaded, air and everything.*

creased *mod.* exhausted. □ *What a day. I am totally creased.*

crib 1. *n.* a location where thieves gather to plot; a dwelling for thieves, prostitutes, etc. (Underworld.) □ *The police busted a crib over on Fourth Street.* □ *They use a basement over there for a crib.* **2.** *n.* a dwelling. (Black.) □ *Where's your crib, man?* □ *My good threads are back at my crib.*

crisco ['krɪsko] *n.* a fat person. (Cruel. Also a rude term of address. The brand name of a baking shortening.) □ *Some crisco came in and ordered 10 large fries.*

croak 1. *iv.* to die; to expire; to succumb. □ *I was afraid I'd croak.* **2.** *tv.* to kill someone. □ *The car croaked the cat just like that.*

crock (of shit) 1. *n.* a mass of lies and deception worth no more than dung. (Usually objectionable.) □ *That's nothing but a crock of shit! I don't believe a word of it.* **2.** *n.* a person who tells lies. (Rude and derogatory.) □ *He's just a crock of shit. He never tells the truth.* **3.** *n.* a braggart. (Rude and derogatory.) □ *He's such a crock. He makes everything he has done sound ten times better than it really is.*

cromagnon [kro'mægnən] *n.* an ugly male. (Collegiate.) □ *Who is that cromagnon you were with last night?* □ *That was no cromagnon. That was your blind date for next weekend.*

crotch-cobra *n.* the penis. (Usually objectionable.) □ *He held his hands over his crotch-cobra and ran for the bedroom.*

crotch rot *n.* a severe fungal itch, perhaps with a rash, in the crotch; any skin disease of the crotch or vaginal area. (Usually objectionable.) □ *Man, do I have a case of crotch rot.*

crowd 1. *tv.* to pressure or threaten someone or something. □ *Don't crowd me!* □ *Carl began to crowd Reggie—which was the wrong thing to do.* **2.** *tv.* to gang up on someone or something. (Black.) □ *They moved in from all sides, carrying clubs, and began to crowd us.*

crud ['krəd] **1.** *n.* nastiness; junk; worthless matter. □ *This is just crud. Get rid of it.* **2.** *n.* a repellent person. (Also a term of address.) □ *Don't be such a crud!* □ *That crud kept trying to paw me!*

crud(d)y AND **cruddie** ['krədi] *mod.* nasty; awful. □ *What is this cruddy stuff on my plate?* □ *It's just chocolate mousse, and it's not cruddie.*

cruise 1. *iv.* to travel at top speed. □ *This old caddy can really cruise.* **2.** *iv.* to drive around looking for friends or social activity. □ *We went out cruising, but didn't see anybody.* **3.** *iv.* to move on; to leave. □ *Listen, I gotta cruise.* □ *Time to cruise. Got a test tomorrow.*

crunchers *n.* the feet. □ *My crunchers are sore from all this walking.* □ *New shoes can be hard on your crunchers.*

crunchie *n.* a soldier; a marching infantry soldier. (Military. See also crunchers.) □ *A couple of crunchies were complaining about the Army.*

crunchy *mod.* [of someone] loving nature, plants, and animals. (The type of person who lives on granola.) □ *He's such a crunchy guy, always saving whales and trees.*

cry hughie ['kraɪ 'hjui] *iv.* to empty one's stomach; to vomit. □ *He is in the john crying hughie.*

cry ruth ['kraɪ 'ruθ] *tv.* to empty one's stomach; to vomit. (See also ruth.) □ *Someone is in the bushes crying ruth.*

crystals *n.* the testicles. (From *crystal balls.*) □ *He got hit right in the crystals. It was real embarrassing, as well as painful.*

cube ['kjub] **1.** *n.* a very square person. □ *This nerd was the most unbelievable cube you have ever seen.* □ *Not just an L7, a real cube.* **2.** *n.* a die, one of a pair of dice. (Usually in the plural.) □ *She shook the cubes, saying, "Baby needs shoes!"*

cuff *tv.* to put a charge on one's bill. □ *Would you cuff this for me, please?* □ *Sorry, I can't cuff any more charges.*

cull *n.* a socially unacceptable person. □ *Who's the cull driving the Edsel?* □ *This place is filled with aging culls. Let's split.*

cum ['kəm] **1.** Go to come. **2.** AND **cume** ['kjum] *n.* a cumulative average, such as a grade-point average. □ *My cume is not high enough to get into law school.*

cum(e) Go to cum.

cunt 1. *n.* the female genitals; the vulva. (One of the English four-letter words. Usually objectionable.) □ *He thought he could see her cunt through her swimming suit.* **2.** *n.* women considered as nothing more than a receptacle for the penis; a wretched and despised woman. (Rude and derogatory.) □ *Jed announced that he really needed some cunt, bad.* **3.** *n.* a wretched and disgusting male. (Rude and derogatory.) □ *Don't act like such a cunt, you twit!*

cupcake *n.* an attractive woman. (Also a term of address.) □ *Hey, cupcake, what ya doing?* □ *Who is that cupcake driving the beemer?*

curly *n.* a bald person, almost always a male. (Also a jocular term of address.) □ *Well, Curly, looks like you got your dome sunburned!*

cushy ['kʊʃi] *mod.* soft; easy. (From *cushion*.) □ *That's a cushy kind of life to lead.*

cuss someone out *tv.* to rebuke someone; to scold someone severely. □ *Don't cuss me out! I can't take it.* T *You can't cuss out people you don't know!*

cut 1. *mod.* alcohol intoxicated. □ *He got cut on beer, which is unusual for him.* **2.** *tv.* to dilute something. □ *She always cuts her eggnog with cola. Yuck!* **3.** *n.* a share of the loot or the profits. (Originally underworld.) □ *You'll get your cut when everybody else does.* **4.** *n.* a single song or section of music on a record or compact disc. □ *This next cut is one everybody likes.* **5.** *tv.* to eliminate something; to stop (doing something). □ *Okay, chum, cut the clowning.* **6.** *mod.* muscular; with well-defined muscles, especially in reference to the abdominal muscles. □ *He works out and he's really cut!* **7.** *mod.* circumcised. (Not usually prenominal.) □ *I'm not cut and neither is my brother.*

cut a fart AND **cut one; let a fart; let one** *tv.* to release intestinal gas through the anus. (Usually objectionable.) □ *Fred cut a fart right in the middle of English class, and nobody moved a muscle.*

cut and run *iv.* to stop what one is doing and flee. □ *At the first warning, we cut and run.*

cut ass (out of some place) Go to **bag ass (out of** some place).

cut no ice (with someone) *tv.* to have no influence on someone; to fail to convince someone. □ *So you're the mayor's daughter. It still cuts no ice.*

cut one Go to cut a fart.

cut one's **wolf loose** *tv.* to go on a drinking bout; to get drunk. □ *I'm gonna go out and cut my wolf loose tonight.*

cut out *iv.* to leave; to run away. □ *It's late. I think I'll cut out.*

cut-rate *mod.* cheap; low-priced. □ *Where are your cut-rate sweaters?*

cuts *n.* sharply defined musculature, especially in the abdominal area. □ *Look at the cuts on that guy! What great abs!*

cut someone **in (on** something) *tv.* to permit someone to share something. □ *You promised you would cut me in on this caper.*

cut some **Z's** Go to catch some Z's.

Cut the crap! *exclam.* Stop the nonsense! □ *Cut the crap. Talk straight or get out.*

cut up (about someone or something) *mod.* emotionally upset about someone or something. □ *She was all cut up about her divorce.*

da bomb Go to *the* **bomb**.

damage *n.* the cost; the amount of the bill (for something). □ *Okay, waiter. What's the damage?* □ *As soon as I pay the damage, we can go home.*

dap ['dæp] *mod.* well-dressed. (From *dapper*.) □ *Who is that dap-looking dude?*

dark Monday AND **dark Sunday; dark night** *n.* an evening when a theater is closed and no performances are held. □ *I couldn't get tickets for the 16th. That's dark Monday.* □ *Monday night is always dark night.*

dark night Go to **dark Monday**.

dark Sunday Go to **dark Monday**.

dead 1. *mod.* quiet and uneventful. □ *Things were sure dead around this town this summer.* **2.** *mod.* very tired. □ *I went home from the office, dead as usual.* **3.** *mod.* dull; lifeless; flat. □ *This meal is sort of dead because I am out of onions.*

dead man Go to **dead soldier**.

dead marine Go to **dead soldier**.

dead one Go to **dead soldier**.

dead president *n.* a piece of U.S. paper money. (Refers to the pictures of presidents on the bills.) □ *This silly magazine costs three dead presidents!*

dead soldier AND **dead man; dead marine; dead one 1.** *n.* an empty liquor or beer bottle. □ *Toss your dead soldiers in the garbage, please.* **2.** *n.* a cigarette butt. (Less common than sense 1.) □ *The bum found a dead soldier on the ground and picked it up.*

deck 1. *tv.* to knock someone to the ground. □ *I was so mad I almost decked him.* **2.** *n.* a pack of cigarettes. □ *Can you toss me a deck of fags, please?* □ *Why don't you stop in there and buy a deck?*

deduck ['didək] **1.** *n.* a tax deduction. (From *deduct.*) □ *Interest is no longer a deduck.* □ *I need a few more deducks this year.* **2.** AND **duck** *n.* a deduction from one's paycheck. □ *More of my pay goes to deducks than I get myself.*

deejay Go to disk jockey.

deep pockets 1. *n.* a good source of money. □ *We need to find some deep pockets to finance this venture.* **2.** *n.* a rich person. □ *The lawyer went after the doctor who was the deep pockets of the organization.* □ *I want to find the deep pockets who arranged all this.*

def ['dɛf] *mod.* better; cool. (Black. From *definitive.*) □ *What a def set of threads!*

definately *mod.* definitely. (A misspelling that is so widely used in Internet news groups as to be considered part of the Internet jargon.) □ *I am definately going to look at your home page!*

defrosted *mod.* "even" with someone who has insulted, embarrassed, or angered one. (Black. See also chill.) □ *He yelled at her till he was defrosted, and then things settled down.* □ *Bob was finally defrosted when he insulted Alice.*

delish [də'lɪʃ] *mod.* delicious. □ *Oh, this cake is just delish!*

delts ['dɛlts] *n.* the deltoid muscles. (Bodybuilding.) □ *How do you get delts like that?*

desk jockey *n.* someone who works at a desk in an office. (Patterned on *disk jockey.*) □ *The desk jockeys at our place don't get paid very well.*

dialog *tv.* to attempt to deceive someone; to attempt to seduce someone. □ *Ron was dialoging some dame when her brother came in and told him to leave.*

diarrhea of the mouth *n.* an imaginary medical condition that is supposed to account for someone talking too much. (Jocular.) □ *She's really afflicted with diarrhea of the mouth.*

dicey ['dɑɪsi] *mod.* touchy; chancy; touch and go. □ *Things are just a little dicey right now.* □ *I'm working on a dicey deal with the city right now.*

dick 1. *n.* a detective; a police officer. (Underworld. From *detective.*) □ *Some dicks were around looking for you.* **2.** *n.* the penis. (Usually objectionable.) □ *She told some dirty joke about a dick,* *but everybody just sat there and looked straight ahead.* **3.** *n.* a stupid person, usually a male. (Rude and derogatory.) □ *What stupid dick put this thing here in the way?* **4.** *n.* nothing. (Usually objectionable.) □ *The whole idea isn't worth dick.* **5.** *tv. & iv.* to copulate [with] a woman. (Usually objectionable.) □ *If you think I'm going out with a guy who only wants to get me dicked, you're crazy.* **6.** *tv.* to cheat or deceive someone. (Usually objectionable.) □ *That salesman dicked me for ten extra bucks.*

dick around *iv.* to waste time; to goof off. (Usually objectionable.) □ *Stop dicking around and get to work!*

diddly-shit AND **doodly-shit 1.** *n.* anything at all. (Usually in the negative. Usually objectionable.) □ *I don't give a diddly-shit what you do!* **2.** *mod.* virtually worthless; useless. (Usually objectionable.) □ *I'm gonna take this diddly-shit watch back to the store and get my money back.*

diddly-squat AND **(doodly-)squat** ['dɪdliskwɑt AND 'dudliskwɑt] *n.* nothing. (Folksy. Originally black or southern.) □ *This contract isn't worth diddly-squat.*

dig 1. *tv. & iv.* to understand something. □ *I just don't dig what you are saying.* □ *Sorry. I just don't dig.* **2.** *tv.* to appreciate something; to like something. □ *He really digs classical music.*

digs *n.* a dwelling; a dwelling and its furnishings. □ *Nice digs. You like it here?*

Dig up! *exclam.* Listen up!; Pay attention! (Black.) □ *Dig up, man! This is important.*

dike AND **dyke** *n.* a lesbian; a bulldiker. (Usually intended and perceived as derogatory. Also a term of address. Usually objectionable.) □ *I guess she was a dike. She looked mean enough.*

dikey AND **dykey** *mod.* in the manner of a lesbian; pertaining to lesbians. (Usually objectionable.) □ *She walks kinda dikey, doesn't she?*

dinero [dɪ'nɛro] *n.* money. (Spanish.) □ *I don't have as much dinero as I need, but other than that, I'm doing okay.* □ *You got some dinero I can borrow?*

ding *tv.* to shoot, dent, or knock something. □ *A rock dinged my left fender.*

ding-dong 1. *n.* the penis. (Usually objectionable.) □ *He held his hands over his ding-dong and ran for the bedroom.* **2.** *n.* a stupid person of either sex. □ *You silly ding-dong! Try again.* **3.** *mod.* damned. (A euphemism.) □ *Get your ding-dong junk outa my way!*

dingleberry 1. *n.* a blob of fecal matter clinging to the hairs around the anus. (Usually objectionable.) □ *Is there no permanent cure for the heartbreak of dingleberries?* **2.** *n.* a stupid-acting person of either sex. (Usually objectionable.) □ *You are such a dumb dingleberry! Wise up!*

dingle(-dangle) *n.* the penis. (Usually objectionable.) □ *Come on, Billy. Shake your dingle and put it away.*

dingus 1. *n.* a thing or gadget. □ *I have a little dingus that helps me clean venetian blinds.* **2.** AND **dingy** *n.* the penis; the male "thing." (Usually objectionable.) □ *Jimmy, shake your dingus and put it away!*

dingy 1. ['dɪŋi] *mod.* loony; giddy. □ *That friend of yours sure does act dingy sometimes.* **2.** Go to **dingus**.

dink 1. *n.* A person of East Asian [including Japanese] nationality or decent; originally a person of Chinese nationality or descent. (Rude and derogatory.) □ *This place is full of dinks!* **2.** *n.* the penis, especially a small one. (Usually objectionable.) □ *God, Fred, you really got a dink. Is it full-grown yet?* **3.** AND **DINK** *n.* Double Income, No Kids; a (young) married couple with two incomes and no children. (Acronym.) □ *The whole neighborhood is populated by dinks. Not a single child on the block.* **4.** Go to **DNK**.

dip(head) Go to **dipshit**.

dipshit 1. AND **dip(head); dipstick** *n.* an oaf; a jerk. (Rude and derogatory.) □ *Is there a convention of dipsticks or something here today?* □ *Look, dipshit, I'm in a hurry.* **2.** *mod.* pertaining to someone or something obnoxious, stupid, or offensive. (Usually objectionable.) □ *Here's another one of his dipshit ideas.*

dipstick Go to **dipshit**.

dirt 1. *n.* low, worthless people. □ *I am not dirt. I'm just temporarily financially embarrassed.* **2.** *n.* scandal; incriminating secrets. □ *What's the dirt on Molly?* □ *I don't want to know about anybody's dirt!*

the **(dirty) dozens** *n.* a game of trading insulting remarks about relatives. (Black. See also **play the dozens.**) □ *Man, what's with you? Always the dirty dozens. You just gotta start something all the time.* □ *Freddy is out giving the dozens to Marty.*

dish the dirt *tv.* to spread gossip; to gossip. □ *Let's sit down, have a drink, and dish the dirt.*

disk jockey AND **deejay; disc jockey; D.J.** *n.* a radio announcer who introduces music from phonograph records or compact discs. (Compare to **desk jockey.**) □ *The disk jockey couldn't pronounce the name of the singing group.*

ditch 1. *tv.* to dispose of someone or something; to abandon someone or something. □ *The crooks ditched the car and continued on foot.* □ *The pilot ditched the plane in the lake and waded ashore.* **2.** *tv. & iv.* to skip or evade someone or something. □ *Todd ditched class today.*

ditsy AND **ditzy** ['dɪtsi] *mod.* pretentious; haughty; snobbish. □ *Who is that ditsy old girl who just came in?* □ *This table is too ditzy with all this fancy silver stuff.*

ditz ['dɪts] *n.* a giddy, absentminded person. □ *You silly ditz!* □ *I'm getting to be such a ditz!*

ditzy Go to ditsy.

divot ['dɪvət] *n.* a toupee; a partial toupee. (See also **rug.**) □ *I think that Sam is wearing a little divot.* □ *His divot slipped, but no one laughed.*

D.J. Go to disk jockey.

DNK ['dɪŋk] *phr.* did not keep (a medical) appointment. (Medical.) □ *Why did you write DNK next to the patient's name?*

do 1. *n.* a party; a social event. □ *We had a smashing time at your little do.* □ *I'm having a do for a friend this weekend. Would you like to come?* **2.** *tv. & iv.* to use a drug or drugs in general. □ *Is Tracy doing dust again?* **3.** AND **doo** *n.* a hairdo. □ *Nice do. Is it new?* □ *I can't go out in this rain and get my doo wet!* **4.** *iv.* to serve (a purpose) well. (Usually with *will* or *won't*.) □ *That won't do at all!* **5.** Go to doo-doo. **6.** *tv.* to copulate [with] someone. (Usually objectionable.) □ *He did Martha, then he did Sue, then he did Gloria.*

do a fade *tv.* to leave; to sneak away. □ *Carl did a fade when he saw the cop car.*

do a job on someone or something *tv.* to ruin someone or something; to harm someone or something in some way. □ *The cops did a job on Walter, but he still wouldn't talk.*

do **a mean** something *tv.* to do something well habitually. □ *John plays the piano quite well. Fred says that John plays a mean piano.* □ *Tom says that his father plays a mean game of golf.*

do a number on someone *tv.* to cheat or betray someone; to do something bad to someone. □ *They really did a number on me in that store.*

do a number on something **1.** *tv.* to urinate or defecate on something. □ *Billy did a number on the bathroom floor.* **2.** *tv.* to damage or ruin something; to destroy something. □ *That huge truck really did a number on my car.*

do a slow burn *tv.* to be quietly angry. □ *I did a slow burn while I was getting my money back.*

do a snow job on someone *tv.* to deceive or confuse someone. □ *Don't try to do a snow job on me. I know all the tricks.*

doc(s)-in-a-box *n.* a walk-in emergency health care center, as found in shopping centers. □ *When I was injured, I went immediately to the docs-in-a-box in the mall.*

dog 1. *n.* a foot. (Usually plural.) □ *I gotta get home and soak my dogs.* **2.** *n.* an ugly woman. □ *I'm no dog, but I could wish for some changes.* **3.** *n.* something undesirable or worthless; merchandise that no one wants to buy. □ *Put the dogs out on the sale table so people will see them.* **4.** *n.* dog dung. □ *There's some fresh dog on the lawn!* **5.** *tv.* to follow someone. □ *The cop dogged Lefty for a week.* **6.** *tv.* to stay with one and haunt one. □ *Will this memory dog me all the days of my life?* **7.** *tv.* to eat something; to eat something as a dog eats. □ *Here, dog a couple of crackers and cheese. That should keep you from starving.* **8.** *tv.* to criticize someone or something. □ *My mom always dogs me because I don't clean my room.*

dog meat *n.* a dead person. (Typically in a threat.) □ *Make one move, and you're dog meat.*

dome *n.* the head, especially if bald. □ *I need a new hat for my shiny dome.*

dome-doctor *n.* a psychologist or psychiatrist. □ *They sent Reggie to a dome-doctor, but it didn't help.*

done over *mod.* beaten; outscored. □ *The other team was done over, and they knew it.*

Don't make a federal case out of it! *sent.* Don't make such a fuss!; This isn't as important as you are making it. □ *So, I dropped a whole dozen eggs! I'll clean it up. Don't make a federal case out of it!*

doodly-shit Go to diddly-shit.

(doodly-)squat Go to diddly-squat.

doo-doo AND **do 1.** *n.* dung; fecal material. □ *There's dog doo-doo on your shoe.* **2.** *iv.* to defecate. □ *Mommy, the cat's doo-dooing in the kitchen!*

doofer AND **dufer** ['dufɚ] *n.* a (found or borrowed) cigarette saved for smoking at another time. (It will "do for" later.) □ *Sam always has a doofer stuck behind his ear.*

doofus AND **duffis** ['dufəs] *n.* a jerk; a nerd. □ *Hank, you are acting like a doofus. Stop standing on your head.*

dook ['duk] **1.** *mod.* really bad. □ *This day was really dook!* **2.** *iv.* to defecate. □ *Mom, I gotta dook.*

dope 1. *n.* a stupid person. □ *I'm not such a dope.* □ *That dope has done it again!* **2.** *n.* drugs in general; marijuana. □ *Lay off the dope, will ya?* **3.** *n.* news; gossip. □ *I got some dope on the tavern fire if you want to hear it.* **4.** *mod.* excellent. □ *That jacket is really dope!*

dope something **out** *tv.* to figure out something from the dope or information available. □ *I think I can dope this thing out from the evidence available.* Ⓣ *We can dope out the truth from her testimony if we have to.*

dorf ['dorf] *n.* a stupid person; a weird person. □ *You are a prize-winning dorf.*

dork 1. *n.* the penis. (Usually objectionable.) □ *He held his hands over his dork and ran for the bedroom.* **2.** *n.* a stupid and worthless person. (Usually objectionable.) □ *You silly dork! Don't do that!*

dorky ['dorki] *mod.* strange; weird; undesirable; typical of a dork (sense 2). □ *That is a real dorky idea. Just forget it.* □ *Let me out of this dorky place!*

double-bagger 1. *n.* a hit good for two bases in baseball. □ *Wilbur hit a nice double-bagger in the top of the fourth.* □ *The hit was good for a double-bagger.* **2.** *n.* a very ugly person. (With a face so ugly that it takes two paper bags to conceal it. See also coyote-ugly.) □ *Fred is what I would call a double-bagger. What a mug!*

double buffalo Go to double nickels.

double-deuces *n.* the number 22. □ *The National Weather Service says it's going down to the double-deuces tonight.* □ *He hit the old double-deuces today. That's right, 22 years old!*

double nickels AND **double buffalo** *n.* the number 55; the 55-mile-per-hour speed limit. (Originally citizens band radio. The buffalo was once on one side of the nickel.) □ *You'd better travel right on those double nickels in through here. The cops are out.* □ *The double buffalo is enforced on this road.*

douche bag *n.* a repellent person; a disliked person. (Crude.) □ *Oh, shut up, you old douche bag!*

dough ['do] *n.* money. (See also bread.) □ *I got a lot of dough for that ring I found.* □ *I need some dough to buy groceries.*

down 1. *tv.* to eat or drink something down quickly. □ *He downed a can of soda and burped like a thunderclap.* **2.** *mod.* behind in a score. □ *We're three points down with two minutes to play.* **3.** *mod.* finished; completed; behind one. □ *Well, I've got the test down. Now what?* □ *One down and three to go.*

downbeat *mod.* cool; easygoing. □ *He is sort of a downbeat character—no stress.* □ *I had sort of a downbeat day. Not your typical Monday.*

downer AND **down(ie) 1.** *n.* a barbiturate or a tranquilizer. □ *Too much booze with those downers, and you're dead.* **2.** *n.* a bad drug experience; a **down trip.** □ *That stuff you gave me was a real downer.* □ *Dust is a downie for most people.* **3.** *n.* a depressing event; a bad situation; a **down trip.** □ *These cloudy days are always downers.* □ *My birthday party was a downie.*

down(ie) Go to downer.

down trip 1. *n.* a bad and depressing drug experience. (Compare to **downer**.) □ *Todd is still suffering from that down trip he had.* □ *For some of them, one down trip is enough.* **2.** *n.* any bad experience. (Compare to **downer**.) □ *Today was a classic down trip.*

D.Q. *n.* Dairy Queen™, a protected trade name for a franchise fast-food store specializing in frozen desserts. (Teens and collegiate.) □ *The D.Q. is closed for the winter.*

drafty *n.* a draft beer; beer. □ *How about a cold drafty?* □ *You about ready for another drafty, Tom?*

drag 1. *n.* something dull and boring. □ *What a drag. Let's go someplace interesting.* **2.** *n.* an annoying person; a burdensome person. (Compare to **s(c)hlep**.) □ *Clare was a drag whether she wanted to be or not.* **3.** *n.* a puff of a cigarette. □ *One more drag and he coughed for a while and stubbed out the fag.* **4.** *tv.* to pull or puff on a cigarette. □ *She dragged a couple and sat in the funk for a while.* □ *When she dragged a fag, you could see her relax and get straight.* **5.** Go to **in drag**.

drag ass around *iv.* to go around looking very sad and depressed. □ *Why do you drag ass around all the time, Tom?*

drag ass (out of some place**)** Go to **bag ass** (out of some place).

dragged out *mod.* exhausted; worn-out. □ *I feel so dragged out. I think I need some vitamins.* □ *After the game, the whole team was dragged out.*

drain the bilge *iv.* to empty one's stomach; to vomit. □ *Fred left quickly to drain the bilge.*

dreck ['drɛk] *n.* dirt; garbage; feces. (From German via Yiddish.) □ *What is all this dreck in the corner?*

the **drink** *n.* the water of the ocean, lake, pond, etc. □ *Stay away from the edge of the boat unless you want to fall in the drink.*

drinkies ['drɪŋkiz] *n.* drinks; liquor. □ *Okay, kids, it's drinkies all around.*

Drink up! *exclam.* Finish your drink!; Finish that drink, and we'll have another! □ *Okay, drink up! It's closing time.* □ *Drink up, and let's get going.*

drinkypoo ['drɪŋkipu] *n.* a little drink of liquor. □ *Just a little drinkypoo, my dear.*

droid ['drɔɪd] *n.* a robotlike person; a **nerd**. (From *android*.) □ *The droids are taking over this campus.*

droob AND **drube** ['drub] *n.* a dullard; an oaf. □ *Who's the droob standing by the punch bowl?* □ *That drube is my brother!*

drop 1. *tv.* to knock someone down. □ *Jim dropped Willard with a punch to the shoulder.* □ *The swinging board hit him and dropped him.* **2.** *tv.* to take a drug, specifically L.S.D. □ *Ted dropped some stuff and went on a trip.* □ *Now he doesn't drop even once a month.*

drop one's **cookies** *tv.* to empty one's stomach; to vomit. (See also **toss** one's **cookies**.) □ *If you feel like you're going to drop your cookies, don't do it on the carpet.*

drop someone **some knowledge** *tv.* to give someone some information. □ *Come on, what's the 411? Drop some knowledge on me.*

drop the ball *tv.* to fail at something; to allow something to fail. □ *I didn't want to be the one who dropped the ball, but I knew that someone would flub up.* □ *Sam dropped the ball, and we lost the contract.*

drube Go to droob.

ducats AND **duc-ducs** ['dəkəts AND 'dəkdəks] *n.* money. (See also **gold**.) □ *Who's got enough ducats to pay for the tickets?*

duc-ducs Go to ducats.

duck 1. *n.* a male urinal bedpan. (Hospitals.) □ *Somebody in room 212 needs a duck.* **2.** *tv.* to avoid someone or something. □ *Clare is ducking her responsibility.* **3.** Go to deduck. **4.** *n.* a ticket. (Probably akin to **ducats**.) □ *Did you buy the ducks early, or do we have to stand in line?*

duck-butt 1. *n.* a very large pair of buttocks. □ *What an enormous duck-butt!* **2.** *n.* a person with very large buttocks. (Rude and derogatory.) □ *That chair will hold anybody but a real duck-butt.*

ducks Go to duck (sense 4).

duck-squeezer *n.* someone with strong concerns about the environment and conservation, especially rescuing oil-covered ducks. (See also **eagle freak**.) □ *Some duck-squeezers were complaining about what the new dam might do.*

dude ['dud] *n.* a male friend; a guy. (Also a term of address.) □ *Who's the dude with the big car?* □ *Hey, dude, what's happening?*

dude up *iv.* to dress up. □ *Let's dude up and go out.*

dufer Go to doofer.

duffer ['dəfɚ] **1.** *n.* a foolish oaf; a bumbler. □ *Todd's just a duffer—he's not really serious at it.* **2.** *n.* an unskilled golfer. □ *Those duffers up ahead are holding up the game.*

duffis Go to doofus.

duke 1. *iv.* to empty one's stomach; to vomit. (Collegiate. Rhymes with puke.) □ *She's in the john, duking like a goat.* **2.** *n.* a fist. (Always plural.) □ *Okay, brother, put your dukes up.* □ *The guy's got dukes like hams.* **3.** *n.* one's knee. (Always plural.) □ *He went down on his dukes and prayed for all sorts of good stuff.*

duke someone **out** *tv.* to knock someone out with the fist. (See also duke.) □ *Wilbur tried to duke the guy out first.* ⊤ *Bob duked out the mugger with a jab to the cheek.*

dumb-ass AND **stupid-ass 1.** *mod.* stupid; dumb. □ *That was a real dumb-ass thing to do.* **2.** *n.* a stupid person. (Rude and derogatory.) □ *Don't be such a dumb-ass! You know what I mean!*

dumbshit 1. *n.* a very stupid person. (Rude and derogatory.) □ *He's a dumbshit. He can't do any better than that.* **2.** *mod.* stupid; dumb. (Usually objectionable.) □ *That was really a dumbshit thing to do.*

dumbski ['dəmski] **1.** *n.* a stupid person. □ *He's not the dumbski he seems to be.* **2.** *mod.* stupid; dumb. □ *What a dumbski jerk!* □ *It is not a dumbski idea!*

dummy 1. *n.* an empty liquor or beer bottle. □ *Toss your dummies over here, and I'll put them in the bin.* **2.** *n.* a cigarette butt. □ *The tramp collected dummies until he had enough for a smoke.* **3.** *n.* a stupid person. (Rude and derogatory.) □ *Don't be such a dummy!* **4.** *n.* the penis. (Usually objectionable.) □ *He held his hands over his dummy and ran for the bedroom.*

dump *n.* an act of defecation. □ *We stopped while John took a dump.*

Dump it! *tv.* throw it away. □ *We don't need it. Get rid of it! Dump it! It's just junk.*

dump on someone **1.** *iv.* to scold someone severely. □ *Please, don't dump on me. I've had a hard day.* **2.** *iv.* to place a large burden of guilt or grief on someone; to give someone all of one's troubles. □ *She had had a bad day, so she dumped on me for about an hour.*

dupe 1. *n.* a potential victim of a confidence trick. □ *I don't want to be a dupe for anybody.* **2.** *tv.* to trick someone; to swindle someone. □ *You tried to dupe me!* □ *I did not try to dupe you. It was an honest mistake.* **3.** *n.* a duplicate; a copy. □ *Make a dupe of this before you send it off.* □ *I've got a dupe in the files.*

dust 1. *iv.* to leave; to depart. □ *Well, it's late. I gotta dust.* **2.** *tv.* to defeat someone; to win out over someone. □ *We dusted the other team, 87 to 54.*

dust someone **off** *tv.* to give someone a severe pounding or beating. □ *Reggie threatened to dust Carl off.* T *Bob dusted off Larry, and then he started for Tom.*

dust-up *n.* a fight. □ *There was a dust-up at the party that ruined the evening for everyone.*

dweeb ['dwib] **1.** *n.* an earnest student. (Collegiate.) □ *The dweebs get all the A's, so why work?* **2.** *n.* a strange or eccentric person; a nerd. □ *Here comes a dweeb. Ask him for some money.*

dyke Go to dike.

dykey Go to dikey.

dynamite ['daɪnəmaɪt] **1.** *n.* anything potentially powerful: a drug, news, a person. □ *This chick is really dynamite!* **2.** *mod.* excellent; powerful. □ *These tacos are dynamite, too.*

E

eagle freak *n.* someone with strong concerns about the environment and conservation, especially the preservation of the eagle. (Jocular and slightly derogatory.) □ *The eagle freaks oppose building the dam.*

ear candy *n.* soft and pleasant popular music; music that is sweet to the ear. □ *I find that kind of trivial ear candy more annoying than loud rock.*

earful ['irfʊl] **1.** *n.* a tremendous amount of gossip. □ *I got a big earful about Sally.* **2.** *n.* a scolding. □ *Her mother gave her an earful when she finally got home.*

ear hustling *n.* eavesdropping. □ *Your ear hustling will get you in trouble, especially when people are talking about you.*

earp AND **urp** ['ɚp] **1.** *iv.* to empty one's stomach; to vomit. □ *Somebody earped here!* □ *I wish people could urp silently.* **2.** *n.* vomit. □ *There's earp on your shoe.* □ *Throw something over the urp in the flower bed.*

easy make *n.* someone who can be copulated with without much trouble. □ *She's got a reputation as an easy make.*

easy mark *n.* a likely victim. □ *Merton looks like an easy mark, but he's really quite careful.*

eat 1. *tv.* [for something] to bother or worry someone. □ *What's eating you, Bill?* **2.** *tv.* to absorb the cost or expense of something. □ *We'll eat the costs on this one. It's the least we can do.* **3.** *tv.* to perform oral sex on someone. (Usually objectionable.) □ *She said she wanted to eat me!*

eco freak AND **eco nut** ['iko frik AND 'iko nət] *n.* someone with strong concerns about the environment and conservation. (From ecology.) □ *It's we eco nuts who think about the future of our planet!*

eco nut Go to eco freak.

eddress *n.* an electronic address. □ *Please tell me your eddress so I can send you some e-mail.*

effing AND **F-ing** *mod.* fucking. (Usually objectionable.) □ *What an effing stupid idea!* □ *Of all the F-ing stupid things to do!*

effing around AND **F-ing around** *iv.* fucking around; messing around. (See also **fuck around with** someone. Usually objectionable.) □ *They were F-ing around with the switch and turned it on accidentally.*

eggbeater 1. *n.* an outboard boat motor. □ *My eggbeater has been acting up, so I didn't go out on the lake today.* □ *By the time you get about 20 eggbeaters on the lake at once, it's really pretty noisy.* **2.** *n.* a helicopter. (See also **rotorhead**.) □ *The eggbeater landed on the hospital roof.*

the **eighty-eight** *n.* a piano. (Pianos have 88 keys.) □ *Sam can really beat the eighty-eight.*

eighty-six AND **86** *tv.* to dispose of someone or something; to nix someone or something. □ *Please take this out and 86 it.* □ *He wants $400? 86 that! We can't afford it.*

el cheapo [ɛl 'tʃipo] **1.** *n.* the cheap one; the cheapest one. (Mock Spanish.) □ *Give me a good one. I don't want one of those el cheapos.* □ *I can only afford el cheapo.* **2.** *mod.* cheap. □ *The el cheapo brand won't last.*

em ['ɛm] *n.* an empty liquor bottle. □ *Put your ems in the garbage, not on the floor.*

ends 1. *n.* money. (Streets.) □ *You got enough ends to get you through the week?* **2.** *n.* shoes. □ *You even got holes in your ends.*

enforcer *n.* a bully; a thug or bodyguard. □ *Walter is too tender-hearted to be a good enforcer.*

Enough, already! *exclam.* That is enough! Stop! □ *Please stop! Enough, already!*

ESAD! *tv.* Eat shit and die!; take what's coming to you. (Usually objectionable.) □ *All right, you bastard, ESAD!*

evil *mod.* excellent. (See also **wicked**.) □ *This wine is really evil!*

Excellent! *exclam.* Fine! (Like **awesome**, this expression is a standard word used frequently in slang contexts.) □ *A new stereo? Excellent!* □ *Excellent! Way rad!*

Excuse me for breathing! Go to (Well,) pardon me for living!

Excuse me for living! Go to (Well,) pardon me for living!

eyeball *tv.* to look hard at someone or something. □ *I eyeballed the contract and saw the figures.* □ *The two eyeballed each other and walked on.*

eye-in-the-sky *n.* an overhead surveillance camera, usually in a dome; a traffic police helicopter. □ *The cops used an eye-in-the-sky to get the evidence and make the arrest.*

eyepopper *n.* someone or something visually astonishing. □ *The picture of the proposed building was a real eyepopper.*

fab ['fæb] *mod.* fabulous. □ *Man, what a fab stereo!* □ *Your pad is not what I'd call fab. Just okay.*

face *tv.* to reject a member of the opposite sex. (Collegiate. Usually passive.) □ *I've been faced again, and I hate it!* □ *Sally was faced by Todd, and she won't speak to him or anybody else.*

face card *n.* an important person; a self-important person. (As with the royal characters in playing cards.) □ *Who's the face card getting out of that big black car?* □ *Reggie is the face card in the local mob.*

faced *mod.* alcohol intoxicated. (From **shit-faced**.) □ *Who is that guy on the corner who looks so faced?*

face man *n.* a good-looking young man with no personality. (Collegiate.) □ *Harry is just a face man and as dull as dishwater.* □ *Norm is the perfect face man—all looks and no brains.*

face-off ['fesɔf] *n.* a confrontation. (From hockey.) □ *The face-off continued for a few moments till both of them realized that there was no point in fighting.*

face time 1. *n.* time spent face-to-face with someone. (As opposed to over the telephone or by e-mail, etc.) □ *I need to have more face time with my children.* **2.** *n.* time spent with one's face showing on television, as with an actor or news reader. □ *Marge is always trying to rewrite various scenes so she gets more face time.*

fack ['fæk] *iv.* to state the facts; to tell (someone) the truth. (Black.) □ *That dude is not facking with me.* □ *Now is the time to start facking. Where were you?*

fade 1. *iv.* to leave. □ *I think that the time has come for me to fade. See ya.* **2.** *iv.* [for someone] to lose power or influence. □ *Ralph is fading, and someone else will have to take over.*

fag-bashing Go to **fag-busting**.

fag-busting AND **fag-bashing** *n.* doing violence to homosexuals. (Usually objectionable.) □ *What's this strange need you have for fag-bashing? What's your problem?*

faggot AND **fag** *n.* a male homosexual. (Rude and derogatory.) □ *Bob got fired for calling Bill a faggot.*

fairy *n.* a male homosexual. (Rude and derogatory.) □ *Bob got fired for calling Bill a fairy.*

fake off *iv.* to waste time; to **goof off.** □ *Hey, you guys, quit faking off!*

falsies *n.* artificial breasts; stuffing for making the breasts appear larger and more shapely. □ *I don't care if she is wearing falsies. She's got a beautiful smile.*

family jewels *n.* the testicles. (Jocular and euphemistic. They are necessary to produce a family.) □ *Hey, careful of the family jewels!*

fanny-bumper *n.* an event that draws so many people that they bump into one another. □ *The fire on 34th Street turned into a real fanny-bumper.*

far-out 1. *mod.* cool; great; extraordinary. □ *You want to hear some far-out heavy metal?* **2.** *mod.* very hard to understand; arcane; highly theoretical. □ *I can't follow your far-out line of reasoning.*

fart 1. *iv.* to release intestinal gas through the anus. (Usually objectionable.) □ *Okay, who farted?* **2.** *n.* the sound or odor of the release of intestinal gas. (Usually objectionable.) □ *Who made that smelly fart?* **3.** *n.* a stupid, despicable, and annoying person. (Usually objectionable.) □ *The guy's nothing but a fart. Just forget him.*

fart around *iv.* to waste time; to do something ineffectually or inefficiently. (Usually objectionable.) □ *Stop farting around and get to work!*

fart off *iv.* to waste time; to **goof off.** (Usually objectionable.) □ *Why are you farting off when there's work to be done?*

fast buck Go to **quick buck.**

fat *mod.* well supplied; having an overabundance of something. (See also **phat** (sense 1).) □ *We're fat with paper, but there's not a printer ribbon in sight.*

fat-ass(ed) *mod.* having large buttocks. □ *Get your fat-ass self outa my car!*

fat lip Go to lip.

fat skrill *n.* lots of money (See also skrill.) ☐ *The car cost some real fat skrill.*

feeb ['fib] *n.* an oaf; a stupid person. (From *feebleminded*.) ☐ *Don't be a feeb. Wake up!*

feeby AND **feebee** ['fibi] *n.* the F.B.I., the Federal Bureau of Investigation. ☐ *The locals were going to call in the feebies, but the prosecutor said to wait.* ☐ *The feeby is in on this already.*

fender-bender ['fɛndɚbɛndɚ] **1.** *n.* a minor accident. (Compare to rear-ender.) ☐ *There are a couple of fender-benders on the expressway this morning, so be careful.* ☐ *A minor fender-bender blocked traffic for a while.* **2.** *n.* a reckless driver who may cause minor accidents. ☐ *I can't get insurance on my 17-year-old, who is a hopeless fender-bender.* ☐ *Don't give up on young fender-benders.*

fettie *n.* money. (Possibly from *confettie*.) ☐ *I need some fettie to pay the rent.*

a **few ticks** *n.* a few minutes; a few seconds. ☐ *Just wait. I'll be there in a few ticks.*

fiddle-fart Go to monkey-fart.

F-ing Go to effing.

F-ing around Go to effing around.

fink ['fɪŋk] **1.** *n.* a guard hired to protect strikebreakers. ☐ *Management called in the finks.* ☐ *We would've settled if the finks hadn't showed up.* **2.** *n.* a strikebreaker. ☐ *The finks moved in with clubs.* **3.** *n.* an informer. (See also rat fink.) ☐ *Molly has turned into a fink. She told everything to the cops.* **4.** *n.* any strange or undesirable person. ☐ *You are being such a fink. Stop it!*

fink on *someone iv.* to inform on someone; to betray someone. ☐ *If you fink on me, I'll get even with you.*

fish-kiss 1. *tv. & iv.* to kiss (someone) with puckered-up lips. (Collegiate.) ☐ *He can fish-kiss like an expert, which is like being an expert at nothing.* ☐ *He fish-kissed me, then ran back to his car.* **2.** *n.* a kiss made with puckered-up lips. (Collegiate.) ☐ *The actor planted a big fish-kiss right on her lips and frightened her.*

fitshaced *mod.* drunk. ☐ *He goes out and gets really fitshaced almost every night.*

fitted *mod.* well-dressed; properly outfitted. □ *Sam got himself all fitted and looks like a real playa!*

five-finger discount *n.* the acquisition of something by shoplifting. □ *Reggie used his five-finger discount to get the kind of gift Molly wanted.* □ *I got this candy with my five-finger discount.*

five-oh AND **5-O** *n.* the police. (From an old television program, *Hawaii 5-O.*) □ *Somebody called the 5-O! Let's go.*

fix 1. AND **fix-up** *n.* a dose of a drug, especially for an addict who is in need of drugs. (Drugs. It fixes or eases the suffering of withdrawal.) □ *It was clear that the prisoner needed a fix, but there was nothing the cops would do for him.* □ *Carl arranged to get a fix-up into the con.* **2.** *n.* a bribe. □ *The agent paid a fix to the cops.*

fla(c)k ['flæk] **1.** *n.* complaints; criticism; negative feedback. □ *We're getting a lot of flack for that news broadcast.* **2.** *n.* publicity; hype. □ *Who is going to believe this flack about being first-rate?* □ *It's all flak and no substance.* **3.** *n.* a public relations agent or officer. □ *There were flacks all over the place telling lies and making false promises.*

flack (out) *iv.* to collapse in exhaustion; to go to sleep. □ *I just have to go home now and flack out.* □ *Betsy flacks out at nine every night.*

flag ['flæg] **1.** *tv.* to fail a course. □ *I'm afraid I flagged algebra.* **2.** *n.* the grade of F. □ *I got three flags and an A.* **3.** *tv.* to arrest someone. □ *The cop flagged Molly for soliciting.*

flake 1. *n.* a person who acts silly or giddy. □ *Sally is such a flake!* **2.** Go to flake (out).

flake down *iv.* to go to bed; to go to sleep. □ *After I flake down for about three days, I'll tell you about my trip.*

flake (out) 1. *iv.* to pass out from exhaustion; to fall asleep. □ *I just flaked out. I had had it.* □ *After jogging, I usually flake for a while.* **2.** *iv.* to behave like a **flake** (sense 1); to be unreliable. □ *Bob flaked out on us and failed to show up at the last minute.*

flaky ['fleki] *mod.* unreliable. □ *She's too flaky to hold the job.*

flash 1. *n.* something suddenly remembered; something suddenly thought of. □ *I had a flash and quickly wrote it down.* □ *After we talked awhile, a flash hit me. Why don't we sell the house?* **2.** *n.* a very short period of time; an instant. □ *I'll be there in a flash.* □ *It was just a flash between the time I said I'd be there and when I showed up.* **3.** *tv.* to display something briefly. □ *You'd better not flash a wad like that around here. You won't have it long.* □ *The cop flashed her badge and made the pinch.*

flashback *n.* a memory of the past; a portrayal of the past in a story. (Almost standard English.) □ *Suddenly, Fred had a wonderful flashback to his childhood.*

flash on something *iv.* to remember something suddenly and vividly. □ *I was trying to flash on it, but I couldn't bring it to mind.*

flash the hash *tv.* to empty one's stomach; to vomit. □ *Dave left quickly to go out and flash the hash, I think.*

flat-ass *mod.* absolutely; totally. (From a general slang term *flat-out.*) □ *She opened it up as flat-ass fast as it would go.*

flat-chested *mod.* with little or no female breast development. □ *I wish I wasn't so flat-chested!*

flat on one's **ass** AND **on** one's **ass 1.** *mod.* fallen on one's buttocks. □ *She tripped over the chair and was flat on her ass in no time.* **2.** *mod.* totally broke and without any funds. □ *I'm on my ass and I need a few bucks to tide me over.*

flexed out of shape *mod.* very angry. □ *The boss was completely flexed out of shape.*

flick *n.* a movie. □ *That was a pretty good flick, right?*

fling up *iv.* to empty one's stomach; to vomit. □ *I was afraid I was going to fling up.*

fling-wing *n.* a helicopter. (See also **eggbeater**.) □ *The fling-wing from the radio station is hovering over the traffic jam.* □ *There must be a dozen fling-wings up there making all that noise.*

flip *iv.* to go crazy. □ *Wow, I've got so much to do, I may just flip.*

flip one's **lid** Go to flip one's **wig**.

flip one's **wig** AND **flip** one's **lid** *tv.* to go crazy; to lose control. □ *I flipped my lid when I got the news.*

flip (out) *iv.* to lose control of oneself. □ *Wow, I almost flipped out when I heard about it.* □ *He got so mad that he flipped.*

flipping burgers *tv.* what school dropouts end up doing. (An occupation that offers practically no opportunities for advancement.)

□ *Do you want to spend the rest of your life flipping burgers! Do your damn homework!*

flip side 1. *n.* the "other" side of a phonograph record. □ *On the flip side, we have another version of "Love Me Tender" sung by Sally Mills.* □ *Give a listen to the flip side sometime.* **2.** *n.* the "other" side of something, such as an argument. □ *I want to hear the flip side of this before I make a judgment.* □ *On the flip side, he is no bargain either.* **3.** *n.* the return trip of a long journey. (Citizens band radio.) □ *See ya. Catch you on the flip side, maybe.*

flip the script 1. *tv.* to lie; to change one's story. □ *The guy flips the script depending on who's listening.* **2.** *tv.* to turn the tables on someone. □ *Now he's the one who's in trouble! That's really flipping the script!*

flub something **up** *tv.* to do something incorrectly; to mess up a procedure. □ *Now don't flub this up.* ⊤ *I never flub up anything.*

flub (up) 1. AND **flub-up** *n.* an error; a blunder. □ *I tried not to make a flub, but I did.* □ *Who is responsible for this flub-up?* **2.** *iv.* to make a confused mess of something. □ *You are flubbing up again, aren't you?* □ *I do my best to keep from flubbing.*

fluff-stuff ['fləfstəf] *n.* snow. □ *All this fluff-stuff looks pretty, but it's no fun to shovel it.*

fly *mod.* knowledgeable; alert and in the know. □ *This dude is fly. There's no question about it.* □ *We don't need any more fly birds around here.*

flying-fuck 1. *n.* an imaginary act of copulation where the male leaps or dives onto and into the female. (Usually objectionable.) □ *The movie showed some jerk allegedly performing a flying-fuck, just for laughs.* **2.** AND **French-fried-fuck** *n.* something totally worthless. (Usually objectionable.) □ *This thing isn't worth a flying-fuck!* □ *I wouldn't give you a French-fried-fuck for all the crummy cars like that in the world.*

foam *n.* beer. □ *How about some more foam?*

fomp ['famp] *iv.* to play around sexually. (Collegiate.) □ *Jerry wanted to fomp, and I wanted to get him out of my sight.*

fooey Go to phooey.

foot it *tv.* to go somewhere on foot; to walk or run. (Compare to **ankle, shank it.**) □ *I have to foot it over to the drugstore for some medicine.*

Fork you! *exclam.* Fuck you! (A partial disguise. Rude and derogatory.) □ *Fork you, you stupid twit!*

fosho *mod.* For sure. □ *I'll be there on time fosho.*

fossil 1. *n.* an old-fashioned person. □ *Some old fossil called the police about the noise.* **2.** *n.* a parent. (See also **rent(al)s.**) □ *My fossils would never agree to anything like that.*

four-oh-four AND **404** *phr.* the answer to your question is unknown; the location you seek is unknown. (From the Internet message: *Error - 404* that is received when the Internet cannot find the address you are seeking.) □ *Q: Where's the kitchen? A: 404. You'll have to find it yourself.*

four-one-one AND **411** *n.* information; the details about something or someone. (In the U.S., the telephone number of directory assistance or "information" is 411.) □ *What's the 411 on the new guy in the front office?*

four-topper *n.* a restaurant table that will seat four people. (Restaurant jargon.) □ *Please seat these two couples at the four-topper in the corner.*

fox *n.* an attractive person, typically a young woman. □ *Man, who was that fox I saw you with?*

fox trap *n.* an automobile customized and fixed up in a way that will attract women. □ *I put every cent I earned into my fox trap, but I still repelled women.* □ *To you it's a fox trap; to me it's a sin-bin.*

foxy ['fɑksi] **1.** *mod.* sexy, especially having to do with a woman. □ *Man, isn't she foxy!* **2.** *mod.* smelly with perspiration odor. □ *Somebody in this taxi is a little foxy.* □ *Subway cars can sure get foxy in the summer.*

foxy lady *n.* a sexually attractive young woman. □ *You are really a foxy lady, Molly.* □ *A couple of foxy ladies stopped us on the street.*

fragged ['frægd] *mod.* destroyed; ruined. □ *My clothes are fragged, and I need a haircut.*

frantic *mod.* great; wild. □ *We had a frantic time at Chez Freddy.* □ *His party was really frantic.*

freaked (out) AND **freaked-out 1.** *mod.* shocked; disoriented. □ *I was too freaked out to reply.* □ *Man, was I freaked.* **2.** *mod.* tired out; exhausted. □ *I'm too freaked out to go on without some rest.* □ *The chick is really freaked. Let her rest.*

freaker ['frikɚ] **1.** *n.* an incident that causes someone to freak out. (Collegiate.) □ *Wasn't that weird? A real freaker.* □ *Did you see that near miss? What a freaker!* **2.** *n.* a freaked-out person. (Collegiate.) □ *Some poor freaker sat in the corner and rocked.*

freaking *mod.* damned; unsuitable or unacceptable. □ *Get your freaking socks off my bed.* □ *What is this freaking mess on my plate?*

freak (out) 1. *iv.* to panic; to lose control. □ *I was so frightened, I thought I would freak.* **2.** ['frikaʊt] *n.* a wild party of any type; any exciting happening. (Usually **freak-out** or **freakout.**) □ *There is a big freak-out at Freddy's joint tonight.* **3.** ['frikaʊt] *n.* a freaked-out person. (Usually **freak-out** or **freakout.**) □ *Some poor freak-out sat in the corner and rocked.* □ *Who's the freakout in the corner?*

freak someone **out** *tv.* to shock or disorient someone. □ *The whole business freaked me out.* ⊤ *I didn't mean to freak out everybody with the bad news.*

freebie AND **freebee; freeby** ['fribi] *n.* something given away free. □ *They gave me a freebie with my purchase.* □ *I expect a freebee when I spend a lot of money like that.*

the **freeze** *n.* the act of ignoring someone. □ *Everybody seems to be giving me the freeze.* □ *I got the freeze from Julie. What did I do wrong?*

freeze *tv.* to ignore someone; to give someone the cold shoulder. □ *They froze him because he didn't act like a civilized human being.*

French 1. *n.* an act of oral sex. (Usually objectionable.) □ *How much is a French at a cathouse like that?* **2.** *mod.* referring to oral sex. (Usually objectionable.) □ *He tried some French stuff on her, and she nearly killed him.* **3.** *tv.* to perform oral sex on someone. (Usually objectionable.) □ *He wanted her to French him.* **4.** *tv. & iv.* to kiss someone using the tongue; to French kiss. □ *I wouldn't French kiss her on a bet!*

French-fried-fuck Go to flying-fuck.

French kiss 1. *n.* kissing using the tongue; open-mouth kissing. □ *What's French about a French kiss?* **2.** *tv.* to kiss someone, using the tongue. (Usually **French-kiss**.) □ *Kids like to try to French-kiss each other at an early age. It's part of growing up.* □ *He tried to French-kiss me, but I stopped him.*

fricking *mod.* lousy; damn. (A euphemism for **fucking**.) □ *What a fricking mess you've made of this!*

frig 1. *tv. & iv.* to copulate [with] someone. (Usually objectionable.) □ *Bob and Mary were in the back room frigging.* **2.** *tv.* to ruin something. □ *Stop frigging my stereo!*

frigging *mod.* damn; damnable. (A euphemism for **fucking**. Usually objectionable.) □ *I'm tired of this frigging job! I quit!*

friz ['frɪz] *n.* a Frisbee™. □ *If I could find my friz, we could go out and whirl a few.*

from (the) git-go *mod.* from the very start. (See also **git-go, jump (street)**.) □ *This kind of thing has been a problem from the git-go.*

fronts *n.* clothing; a sports jacket. (Black.) □ *You got some good-looking fronts there.*

froody ['frudi] *mod.* grand; wonderful. □ *The curtains parted to the most froody, funky set I've ever seen.*

frost *tv.* to make someone angry. □ *That really frosts me.*

frosted (over) *mod.* angry; annoyed. □ *The clerk was really frosted over when I asked for a better one.* □ *Why was he so frosted?*

frosty 1. AND **frosty one** *n.* a beer; a cold beer. □ *Hey, toss me a frosty, will ya?* **2.** *mod.* **cool**; really **cool** and mellow. □ *That music is really frosty.* □ *We had a frosty time, didn't we?*

frosty one Go to **frosty**.

froth *n.* a beer. □ *Would you like some froth?*

froyo *n.* frozen yogurt. □ *Let's stop at the store and get some froyo.*

fruit AND **fruiter** *n.* a male homosexual. (Rude and derogatory.) □ *I walked in and the place was full of fruits!* □ *Harvey was the kind of fruiter that made you sit up and take notice.*

fruitcake 1. *n.* a silly-acting person. (Also a term of address.) □ *You can be such a silly fruitcake sometimes.* □ *Some fruitcake put salt in the sugar bowl.* **2.** *n.* a male homosexual. (Rude and derogatory. An elaboration of **fruit**.) □ *We went into this bar, but it was filled with fruitcakes, so we left.*

fruiter Go to fruit.

fruity 1. *mod.* silly-acting. □ *He's a fruity guy. Always silly and weird.* **2.** *mod.* in the style or manner of a male homosexual. (Usually objectionable.) □ *The entertainers were sort of fruity, but other than that, the show was okay.*

fuck 1. *tv. & iv.* to copulate [with] someone. (Taboo. Usually objectionable.) □ *They want to fuck all night.* □ *She fucked him all night.* **2.** *n.* an act of copulation. (Taboo. Usually objectionable.) □ *I need a fuck.* **3.** *n.* a person with whom one can copulate. (Taboo. Usually objectionable.) □ *Man, he's a good fuck if I ever saw one.* **4.** *n.* semen. (Taboo. Usually objectionable.) □ *Clean up that fuck before somebody sees it!* **5.** *exclam.* an exclamation of anger or exasperation. (Usually **(Oh,) fuck!** Taboo. Usually objectionable.) □ *Fuck! The hell you do!* □ *Oh, fuck! I'm outa beer.*

fuck around with someone AND **fuck** someone **around** *tv. & iv.* to harass or intimidate someone; to give someone a hard time. (Taboo. Usually objectionable.) □ *Don't fuck around with me all the time! Give me a break.* □ *You fuck me around too much. I'm quitting!*

fuck around with something *iv.* to fiddle or toy with something. (Taboo. Usually objectionable.) □ *Please, don't fuck around with my stuff.*

fuck-brained 1. *mod.* stupid; mindless. (Taboo. Usually objectionable.) □ *What a stupid, fuck-brained idea!* □ *I don't know why I'm stuck in this fuck-brained job.* **2.** *mod.* obsessed with sex. (Taboo. Usually objectionable.) □ *All he thinks about is dames. He is totally fuck-brained.*

fucked out 1. *mod.* exhausted from copulation. (Taboo. Usually objectionable.) □ *They went at it until they were both fucked out.* **2.** *mod.* totally exhausted from doing anything. (As exhausted as if one had been copulating excessively. Taboo. Usually objectionable.) □ *Some fucked-out dude was lying on the floor, and another was collapsed on the chair.*

fucked up *mod.* messed up; confused; ruined. (Taboo. Usually objectionable.) □ *Man, are you fucked up! You need a vacation.* □ *This whole project is so fucked up, it'll take months to straighten out.*

fuckhead *n.* a stupid and obnoxious person. (Taboo. Usually objectionable.) □ *Don't be such a fuckhead! Go back there and stand up for yourself!*

fucking *mod.* damnable; lousy; cursed. (Taboo. Usually objectionable.) □ *Get that fucking idiot out of here!* □ *Somebody had better clean up this fucking mess.*

Fuck it (all)! 1. *exclam.* <an expression of anger and despair>; Damn! (Taboo. Usually objectionable.) □ *Oh, fuck it all! I don't care what you do!* □ *Fuck it all! I broke my toe!* **2.** *tv.* To hell with it!; Forget it! (Taboo. Usually objectionable.) □ *Your idea is stupid. Fuck it! Try something else.*

fuck someone **around** Go to fuck around with someone.

fuck someone or something **up** *tv.* to damage or ruin someone or something. (Taboo. Usually objectionable.) □ *Please don't fuck my stereo up.* ⊡ *You fuck up everything you get your hands on!*

fuck someone **over** *tv.* to give someone a very hard time; to abuse someone physically or mentally. (Taboo. Usually objectionable.) □ *The big guys fucked him over for a while and then let him go.*

fuck someone's **mind (up)** *tv.* to confuse or disorient someone; [for a drug] to affect or destroy someone's mind. (Taboo. Usually objectionable.) □ *She's really fucked your mind up. I'd stay away from her if I were you.* □ *I don't know what this stuff is, but it really fucked my mind.*

fuck up 1. *iv.* to mess up; to fail. (Taboo. Usually objectionable.) □ *Don't fuck up this time or you're fired.* **2.** *n.* a mess; a hopeless hodgepodge. (Usually hyphenated. Taboo. Usually objectionable.) □ *When you went home yesterday, you left behind a first-class fuck-up. Now you can clean it up.* □ *Who's responsible for this fuck-up?* **3.** *n.* someone who does everything wrong; someone who messes everything up. (Usually hyphenated. Taboo. Usually objectionable.) □ *Poor Wille is such a fuck-up. What a mess he has made.*

fuck with someone *iv.* to cause trouble for someone; to threaten someone. (Taboo. Usually objectionable.) □ *Don't fuck with me if you know what's good for you!*

fuck with something *iv.* to meddle with something. (Taboo. Usually objectionable.) □ *Stop fucking with the radio!*

Fuck you! *tv.* Go to hell! (Taboo. Usually objectionable.) □ *Fuck you, you shit!* □ *Fuck you, if that's what you think.*

fugly ['fəgli] *mod.* fat and ugly. (Collegiate.) □ *Man, is that dog of yours ever fugly! What or who did it eat?*

full of it Go to full of shit.

full of shit AND **full of it** *mod.* full of lies; stupid. (Usually objectionable.) □ *You're full of shit, you liar!*

funk ['fəŋk] **1.** *n.* a bad odor; a stench. □ *Open the windows and clear out this funk.* **2.** *n.* a depressed state. □ *As soon as I get out of my winter funk, I'll be more helpful.*

funky AND **phunky 1.** *mod.* strange; far-out. □ *I like your funky hat.* **2.** *mod.* basic and simple; earthy. □ *Everything she does is so funky.* **3.** *mod.* smelly; obnoxious. □ *Get your funky old socks outa here.* □ *This place is really funky. Open some windows.*

funky-drunk *mod.* alcohol intoxicated; stinking drunk. □ *The guy is funky-drunk, and I think he's going to be sick.*

fur *n.* the police. (See also fuzz.) □ *No fur ain't never gonna get me!*

futz Go to phutz.

the **fuzz** AND the **fuzz man; fuzzy (tail)** *n.* the police; a jail keeper; a detective. □ *The fuzz is onto you.* □ *See if you can distract the fuzz man while I lift his keys.*

fuzz AND **fuzzle** *iv.* to get drunk. □ *They were just sitting there fuzzling away the day.*

the **fuzz man** Go to the fuzz.

fuzz station *n.* a police station. (See also the fuzz.) □ *He had to spend about an hour at the fuzz station, but nothing happened to him.* □ *Drop by the fuzz station and pick up a copy of the driving rules.*

fuzzy (tail) Go to the fuzz.

F-word *n.* the word fuck. (A euphemism that can be used to refer to the word alone without reference to the various meanings of the word.) □ *They said the F-word seven times in the movie we saw last night.*

G

G. Go to **grand**.

gaffle *tv.* to steal something. □ *Somebody gaffled my bike!*

gang-bang AND **gang-shag 1.** *n.* an act of serial copulation, with one female and a group of males. □ *It was nothing but a gang-bang, and a drunken one at that.* □ *Old Sally used to like a good gang-shag every now and then.* **2.** *n.* group rape of a woman. □ *There was another gang-bang in the park last week.* **3.** *iv.* to perform an act of serial copulation, as in senses 1 or 2. □ *A bunch of guys gang-banged Sally, for a fee, of course.*

gangbanger *n.* a member of a street gang. □ *The gangbangers threatened the old lady too often, and finally she pulled out a can of mace and gave them a little lesson in good manners.*

gang-shag Go to **gang-bang**.

gank *tv.* to steal something. □ *Who ganked my bike!*

GAPO AND **gapo** ['gæpo] *n.* giant armpit odor; a bad underarm odor. □ *Who's got the gapo in here?* □ *That cab driver really has the GAPO.*

garbage something **down** *tv.* to gobble something up; to bolt something down. □ *Don't garbage your food down!* T *That guy will garbage down almost anything.*

gaucho ['gɑutʃo] *tv. & iv.* to expose the buttocks (at someone), usually through a car window; to **moon**. □ *Wally gauchoed the cops as they went by.* □ *Victor would gaucho at the drop of a hat—so to speak.*

gazoo [gə'zu] *n.* the buttocks; the anus. □ *He fell down flat, smack on his gazoo.* □ *Look at the monstrous gazoo on that guy.*

gear 1. *mod.* excellent. □ *This jazz is really gear!* **2.** *n.* "*"; an asterisk. □ *Why is there a gear after this word?* □ *The gear stands for anything you want it to stand for.*

gee ['dʒi] **1.** *exclam.* Wow! (An abbreviation of *Jesus!*, although not always recognized as such. Usually **Gee!**) □ *Gee! What a mess!* □ *Golly gee, do I have to?* **2.** *mod.* gross; disgusting. (From the initial letter of **gross**.) □ *This is just too gee!*

geek AND **geke 1.** *n.* a disgusting and repellent person. (Rude and derogatory.) □ *The convention was a seething morass of pushy sales geeks and glad-handers.* □ *Who's the geek who just came in?* **2.** *n.* an earnest student; a hardworking student. (Usually objectionable.) □ *Martin is a geek, but he will go places with his brains.* **3.** *n.* a person, soldier or civilian, of an East Asian country, especially in wartime. (Rude and derogatory.) □ *Wally is tired of geeks and the way they talk.*

geke Go to **geek**.

george 1. *tv. & iv.* to copulate [with] a woman. (Usually objectionable.) □ *He was in the back room georging some dame.* **2.** *iv.* to defecate. (Usually objectionable.) □ *Man, I gotta george!*

Get a life! *exclam.* Change your life radically! (Compare to **Get real!**) □ *You are such a twit! Get a life!* □ *Get a life, you clown!*

Get cracking! *command* Get moving!; Get started!; Hurry up! □ *Hurry up! Get cracking!*

get down 1. *iv.* to lay one's money on the table. (Gambling.) □ *Okay, everybody get down.* **2.** *iv.* to concentrate; to do something well. □ *Come on, Sam, pay attention. Get down and learn this stuff.* **3.** *iv.* to copulate. (Black.) □ *All Steve wants to do is get down all the time.*

get face *tv.* to gain respect; to increase one's status. (The opposite of *lose face*.) □ *He's doing his best in life to get face.*

get into something *iv.* to become deeply involved with something. □ *I got into computers when I was in junior high school.* □ *When did you get into foreign films?*

get it 1. *tv.* to understand a joke; to understand a point of information. □ *Don't you get it?* □ *Sorry. I don't get it.* **2.** *tv.* to get punished. □ *I just know I'm going to get it when I get home.*

get it on 1. *tv.* to begin something. □ *Time to go back to work. Let's get it on!* □ *Get it on, you guys! Time to start your engines.* **2.** *tv.* to begin dancing. □ *Let's go out there and get it on!* **3.** *tv.* [for people] to copulate. (Usually objectionable.) □ *Come on, baby, let's get it on.* □ *I don't want to get it on with you or any other creep.*

4. *tv.* to undertake to enjoy oneself. □ *I can really get it on with that slow jazz.* **5.** *tv.* to get an erection; to become sexually aroused. (Usually objectionable.) □ *He's too tired to get it on.*

get it up 1. *tv.* to get an erection of the penis. (Usually objectionable.) □ *He's so drunk all the time, he can hardly get it up.* **2.** *tv.* to get excited about something. □ *I just couldn't get it up about going off to college.*

get lip *tv.* to get some kissing; to neck. (Teens.) □ *Jim's been out getting lip again. Look at the lipstick.*

get naked *iv.* to enjoy oneself thoroughly; to relax and enjoy oneself. □ *Let's all go out and get naked tonight.*

get off 1. *iv.* to reach an understanding with someone. (Not slang.) □ *We just weren't getting off well at all, so we broke up.* **2.** Go to **get off (on** something**)**.

Get off my ass! AND **Get off my tail!; Get off my back!** *exclam.* Leave me alone! (Usually objectionable.) □ *Stop pestering me! Get off my ass!* □ *If you don't get off my back, I'm gonna slug you!*

Get off my back! Go to **Get off my ass!**

Get off my bumper! 1. *exclam.* Stop following my car so closely! □ *Don't follow me so close! Get off my bumper!* **2.** *exclam.* Stop monitoring me!; **Get off my ass!** □ *Look, man. I can take care of myself. Get off my bumper!*

Get off my tail! Go to **Get off my ass!**

get off (on something**) 1.** *iv.* to get pleasure from something. □ *I don't get off on music anymore.* □ *I listen, but I just don't get off.* **2.** *iv.* to take a drug and experience the effects. □ *Carl likes to get off, but he's got his business to run.* □ *Molly likes getting off on grass better than anything else.*

get off the dime *iv.* [for something or someone] to start moving. (To get off the dime that one stopped on in *stop on a dime* or turned on in *turn on a dime*.) □ *I wish this organization could get off the dime.*

get one's **nuts off** Go to **get** one's **rocks off**.

get one's **rocks off** AND **get** one's **nuts off** *tv.* [for a male] to copulate or ejaculate. (Usually objectionable.) □ *He went into town to get his nuts off.*

get one's **rocks off (on** something) *tv.* to enjoy something. (See also get one's rocks off.) ☐ *I really get my rocks off on heavy metal.*

get one's **shit together 1.** *tv.* to get oneself organized. (Usually objectionable.) ☐ *I gotta get my shit together and study for the test tomorrow.* **2.** *tv.* to assemble one's belongings. (Usually objectionable.) ☐ *Hurry up and get your shit together so we can get going.*

get one's **ticket punched** *tv.* to die; to be killed. (Literally, to be canceled.) ☐ *Poor Chuck got his ticket punched while he was waiting for a bus.*

get on one's **horse** *iv.* to prepare to leave. ☐ *It's late. I have to get on my horse.*

Get out of here! *exclam.* You are just kidding me!; You are making that up! ☐ *Get out of here! That can't be so!*

Get out of my face! *exclam.* Stop arguing with me!; Stand back! Don't confront me with your arguments and challenges! ☐ *Beat it! Get out of my face!* ☐ *Get outa my face if you know what's good for you.*

Get real! *exclam.* Start acting realistically! (Compare to **Get a life!**) ☐ *Hey, chum! You are way off base! Get real!*

get someone's **motor running 1.** *tv.* to get someone excited. ☐ *I've got some news that'll really get your motor running.* **2.** *tv.* to get someone sexually aroused. ☐ *She knows how to get his motor running.*

get some **yokes on** *tv.* to build up one's muscles. (Bodybuilding.) ☐ *If I keep working at this, I know I can get some yokes on.*

get to first (base) (with someone) *iv.* to achieve a basic or initial level of intimacy with someone, such as getting some attention or even getting kissed. ☐ *I'm too shy. I just know I can't get to first base with her.*

get to someone **1.** *iv.* [for someone or something] to annoy someone after a period of exposure to the annoyance. ☐ *Her remark got to me after I thought about it.* **2.** *iv.* [for someone or something] to please or entice someone. ☐ *Lovely flowers and things like that get to me.*

get with it 1. *iv.* to modernize one's attitudes and behavior. ☐ *You really have to get with it, Ernie.* **2.** *iv.* to hurry up and get busy;

to be more industrious with something. □ *Let's get with it. There's a lot of work to be done.*

Get your ass in gear! *exclam.* Get going!; Start working or performing well. (Usually objectionable.) □ *You have to get moving and get to work. Get your ass in gear!*

Get your nose out of my business! AND **Keep your nose out of my business!** *exclam.* Mind your own business and leave me alone. □ *Get your nose out of my business! This is not your affair.*

ghetto bird *n.* someone who hangs around the [black] neighborhood. □ *Sam is just a ghetto bird who has lots of skills but no job.*

(ghetto) blaster AND **(ghetto) box** ['gɛdo blæstɚ AND 'gɛdo bɑks] *n.* a portable stereo radio. (Often carried on the shoulder, especially by blacks.) □ *Hey, turn down that ghetto blaster in here!* □ *You can't bring that box on this bus!*

(ghetto) box Go to (ghetto) blaster.

ghost turd *n.* a wad of lint as found under beds, etc. (Jocular. Something insubstantial left behind by a ghost. Usually objectionable.) □ *Good grief! Look at the ghost turds under this bed!*

giffed ['gɪft] *mod.* alcohol intoxicated. (From T.G.I.F. = Thank God it's Friday. Said of people who celebrate the end of the workweek by drinking liquor.) □ *He left the tavern pretty giffed.*

gig 1. *n.* a onetime job; an engagement. (Musicians.) □ *I had a gig out on the west side, but I couldn't get there.* □ *The gig was canceled because of the snow.* **2.** *iv.* to play or perform. (Musicians.) □ *I didn't gig at all last week. I'm getting hungry for a job.* **3.** *n.* any job of an assignment nature; a onetime job such as when a newspaper reporter is assigned to write a particular story. □ *I didn't want that election gig, but I got it anyway.* □ *Wally is tired of getting the crime gigs.*

gimp *n.* a crippled person; a person with a limp. (Rude and derogatory.) □ *They fixed all the buses so the gimps can get on and off.*

girked *mod.* intoxicated with heroin. □ *He shot himself up and was girked in no time.*

gism Go to jism.

git-go ['gɪtgo] *n.* the very beginning. (Black. See also from (the) git-go.) □ *Clear back at the git-go, I told you this wouldn't work.*

give a fuck (about someone or something**)** Go to give a shit (about someone or something).

give a shit (about someone or something**)** AND **give a fuck (about** someone or something**)** *tv.* to care about someone or something. (Usually objectionable.) □ *If you think I give a shit about you or anyone else, you're full of shit.*

Give it a rest! *exclam.* Shut up! (The *it* is a mouth. Compare to Give me a rest!) □ *Give it a rest! You talk too much.*

Give it up! *exclam.* Quit now!; Stop, you will continue to fail! □ *Oh, give it up! You can't do it right.*

Give me a break! Go to Give me a rest!

Give me a rest! AND **Give me a break!** *exclam.* Lay off!; That is enough! (Compare to Give it a rest!) □ *Haven't I told you everything you need to know? Give me a rest!*

Give me five! Go to Give me some skin!

Give me (some) skin! AND **Slip me five!; Give me five!** *exclam.* Shake [or slap] my hand! (A request for some form of hand touching in greeting. See also give someone five, high five.) □ *Hey, man! Give me some skin!* □ *Give me skin, my man! Slip me five!*

give someone **five** AND **slip** someone **five 1.** *tv.* to give someone a helping hand. □ *Hey, give me five over here for a minute, will ya?* **2.** *tv.* to slap hands in greeting. (See also high five.) □ *Jerry gave John five as they passed in the corridor.*

give someone **the gate** *tv.* to get rid of someone. □ *The guy was a pest, so I gave him the gate.*

give someone **the go-by** *tv.* to bypass someone; to ignore someone. (See also go-by.) □ *Gert gave us all the go-by when she got rich.*

gizzum Go to jism.

glad-hand *tv.* to greet someone effusively. □ *The senator was glad-handing everyone in sight.*

glad-hander *n.* someone—such as a politician—who displays effusive friendship. □ *The glad-handers were out in full force at the Independence Day parade.*

glad rags *n.* fancy clothes; best clothing. (Old.) □ *You look pretty good in your glad rags.*

glitch ['glɪtʃ] *n.* a defect; a bug. □ *There is a glitch in the computer program somewhere.* □ *I'm afraid there's a glitch in our plans.*

glitz ['glɪts] *n.* flashiness and glamour. □ *The place was nothing but eager sales geeks and phony glitz.* □ *The glitz was blinding, and the substance was invisible.*

glitzy ['glɪtsi] *mod.* fashionable; glamorous. □ *It was a real glitzy place to hold a meeting.* □ *Some glitzy blonde sang a couple of songs, and then the band played again.*

glock *n.* a gun; a revolver. □ *Sam was carrying a glock and threatened to end the argument his own way.*

go 1. *n.* a try (at something). □ *Let me have a go at it this time.* □ *I'd like to have another go at it, if I could.* **2.** *n.* a drink of liquor; a dose of a drug. □ *She had one go and then sat back for a while.* □ *Another go and she was essentially stoned.*

go ape(shit) (over someone or something**)** *iv.* to get very excited about someone or something. (Usually objectionable.) □ *She really went apeshit over the ice cream.*

goat *n.* a fast and powerful car; a Pontiac GTO. □ *Hey, man, where'd you get that goat?* □ *His goat conked out on him.*

gob ['gɑb] **1.** *n.* a blob or mass of something. □ *I'd like a big gob of mashed potatoes, please.* □ *Take that horrid gob of gum out of your mouth!* **2.** *n.* a large amount of something. (Usually in the plural.) □ *I've just got gobs of it if you need some.* □ *Money? I need gobs and gobs.*

go bananas *iv.* to go mildly crazy. □ *Sorry, I just went bananas for a minute.*

go belly-up Go to turn belly-up.

go bitchcakes *iv.* to go wild or crazy. (Usually objectionable.) □ *All this talk just makes me go bitchcakes.*

go blooey AND **go flooey** [go 'blui AND go 'flui] *iv.* to fall apart; to go out of order. □ *Suddenly, all my plans went blooey.* □ *I just hope everything doesn't go flooey at the last minute.*

(Go) blow it out your ear! *tv.* Go away and stop bothering me with your nonsense. □ *What a stupid thing to say. Go blow it out your ear!*

go-by ['gobaɪ] *n.* an instance of ignoring or passing by (someone). (See also **give** someone **the go-by.**) □ *I got the go-by from her every time I saw her.*

Go chase yourself! AND **Go climb a tree!; Go fly a kite!; Go jump in the lake!; Go soak your head!** *exclam.* Beat it!; Go away! □ *Oh, go chase yourself! Get out of my face!* □ *Go soak your head! You're a pain in the neck.*

Go climb a tree! Go to Go chase yourself!

go down 1. *iv.* to happen. □ *Hey, man! What's going down?* □ *Something strange is going down around here.* **2.** *iv.* to be accepted. (See also **swallow.**) □ *The proposal didn't go down very well with the manager.* **3.** *iv.* to be arrested. (Underworld.) □ *Lefty didn't want to go down for a job he didn't do.* □ *Wally said that somebody had to go down for it, and he didn't care who.*

go down in flames *iv.* to fail spectacularly. □ *The whole team went down in flames.* □ *I'd hate for all your planning to go down in flames.*

go down the chute Go to go down the tube(s).

go down the tube(s) AND **go down the chute** *iv.* to fail totally; to be ruined. □ *The whole project is likely to go down the tubes.* □ *All my plans just went down the chute.*

gofer Go to gopher.

go flooey Go to go blooey.

Go fly a kite! Go to Go chase yourself!

Go for it! *exclam.* Do it!; Try it! □ *Go for it! Give it a try!* □ *It looked like something I wanted to do, so I decided to go for it.*

Go fuck yourself! *exclam.* Go to hell!; Get out of here! (Taboo. Usually objectionable.) □ *Go fuck yourself, you creep!*

go home in a box *iv.* to be shipped home dead. □ *Hey, I'm too young to go home in a box.*

Go jump in the lake! Go to Go chase yourself!

gold *n.* money. (See also **ducats.**) □ *Do you have enough gold to pay the bill?*

golden *mod.* excellent; really cool. □ *Look at the guy she is with. He is golden.*

gomer ['gomɚ] **1.** *n.* a stupid oaf; a social reject. (From the television character Gomer Pyle.) □ *That old gomer happens to be my Uncle Ben.* **2.** AND **goomer** ['gumɚ] *n.* a person unwelcome in a hospital. (Supposedly an acronym for "Get out of my emergency room.) □ *I don't want that worthless goomer back in the emergency room!*

gone 1. AND **gone under** *mod.* unconscious. □ *He's gone. Prop his feet up and call an ambulance.* □ *He's gone under. You can begin the procedure now.* **2.** AND **gone under** *mod.* alcohol or drug intoxicated. □ *Those chicks are gone—too much to drink.* □ *Ted is really gone under.* **3.** *mod.* cool. □ *She is one real gone chick.*

gone under Go to gone.

gonzo ['gɑnzo] **1.** *n.* a silly or foolish person. □ *Some gonzo is on the phone asking for the president of the universe.* □ *Tell the gonzo I'm out.* **2.** *mod.* crazy; wild and uncontrollable. □ *The guy is totally gonzo!*

goo ['gu] *n.* some sticky substance; gunk. □ *There is some sort of goo on my plate. Is that meant to be my dinner?*

goob ['gub] *n.* a pimple. (Short for **guber**.) □ *I have the world's greatest goob right on the end of my nose.*

goober Go to guber.

goober-grease ['gubɚgris] *n.* peanut butter. □ *Pass me some of that goober-grease, will ya?*

good trip 1. *n.* a good session with L.S.D. or some other drug. □ *Paul said he had a good trip, but he looks like the devil.* **2.** *n.* any good time. □ *Compared to the last class, this one is a good trip.*

goof ['guf] **1.** *n.* a foolish oaf; a goofy person. □ *Sometimes I'm such a goof. I really messed up.* **2.** AND **goof up** *iv.* to make a blunder. □ *This time, you really goofed.* **3.** *n.* a blunder; an error. □ *This goof is yours, not mine.*

goof around Go to goof off.

goofball AND **goofer** *n.* a stupid person; a fool. □ *Chuck acts like a goofer, but he's really with it.*

goofed (up) 1. *mod.* messed up; out of order. □ *All my papers are goofed up.* □ *Everything on my desk is goofed. Who's been here?* **2.** *mod.* confused; distraught. □ *I'm sort of goofed up today. I think I'm coming down with something.* □ *I was up too late last* *night, and now I'm all goofed up.* **3.** *mod.* high on drugs. □ *Bob's a little goofed up after partying too much.* □ *He comes to class goofed up every day.*

goofer Go to goofball.

goof off 1. AND **goof around** *iv.* to waste time. □ *Quit goofing off.* □ *Get busy. Stop goofing around.* **2.** *n.* a time-waster; a jerk. (Usually **goof-off**.) □ *I'm no scholar, but I am no goof-off either.*

goof on someone *iv.* to play a prank on someone; to involve someone in a deception. □ *Hey, don't goof on me. I'm your buddy!* □ *The kid goofed on Chuck, and he thought it was a pretty good joke.*

goof something **up** AND **goof up (on)** something *tv.* to mess something up. □ *Now don't goof it up this time.* □ *I hope I don't goof up the report again.*

goof up Go to goof.

goof up (on) something Go to goof something up.

goofus ['gufəs] **1.** *n.* a gadget. □ *Where is that little goofus I use to pry open these cans?* **2.** AND **goopus** *n.* a foolish oaf. (Also a term of address.) □ *You're just acting like a goofus. Be serious!* □ *Hey, goopus! Come here!*

goofy ['gufi] *mod.* silly. □ *Stop acting so goofy! What will the neighbors say?* □ *You are really a goofy chick.*

goombah ['gumbɑ] *n.* a buddy; a trusted friend. (Also a term of address. Ultimately from Italian.) □ *Hey, goombah! How goes it?*

goomer Go to gomer.

goophead ['guphɛd] *n.* an inflamed pimple. (Patterned on *blackhead*.) □ *You ought to see the goophead on your nose!*

goopus Go to goofus.

goose egg 1. *n.* a score of zero. □ *We got a goose egg in the second inning.* □ *It was double goose eggs for the final score.* **2.** *n.* a bump on the head. □ *You've got quite a goose egg there.* □ *I walked into a door and got a big goose egg on my forehead.* **3.** *n.* a failure; a zero. (Similar to sense 1.) □ *The outcome was a real goose egg. A total mess.* □ *The result of three weeks' planning is one big goose egg.*

goozlum ['guzləm] *n.* any gummy, sticky substance: syrup, gravy, soup. □ *Do you want some of this wonderful goozlum on your ice cream?* □ *Just keep putting that goozlum on my mashed potatoes.*

gopher AND **gofer** ['gofɚ] **1.** *n.* someone who goes for things and brings them back. (From *go for.*) □ *You got a gopher who can go get some coffee?* **2.** *n.* a dupe; a pawn; an underling. □ *The guy's just a gopher. He has no say in anything.*

go postal *iv.* to become wild; to go berserk. □ *He made me so mad I thought I would go postal.*

gorilla juice *n.* steroids. (Bodybuilding. Steroids build muscle tissue rapidly.) □ *Andy really wanted to get hold of some gorilla juice, but his parents said no.* □ *Do all those muscle-bound creatures take gorilla juice?*

gork ['gork] **1.** *n.* a fool; a dupe. □ *He acts like such a gork sometimes.* **2.** AND **GORK** *phr.* an alleged hospital chart notation of the diagnosis "God only really knows." □ *I see old Mr. Kelly is in again with a hundred complaints. His chart says GORK.* □ *He's down with gork again.* **3.** *tv.* to give a patient sedation. □ *He'll quiet down after we gork him.*

gorked (out) ['gorkt . . .] *mod.* heavily sedated; knocked out. □ *Once the patient was gorked, he was more cooperative.* □ *The guy in 226 is totally gorked out now.*

Go soak your head! Go to Go chase yourself!

gotcha ['gatʃə] **1.** *phr.* I got you!; I've caught you! (Usually **Gotcha!**) □ *I gotcha, and you can't get away.* □ *Ha, ha! Gotcha! Come here, you little dickens.* **2.** *n.* an arrest. (Underworld.) □ *It was a fair gotcha. Reggie was nabbed, and he went along quietly.* **3.** *phr.* I understand you. □ *Gotcha! Thanks for telling me.*

go tits up *iv.* to die; to go to ruin; to fall apart. (A play on *go belly up,* which has the same meaning. Refers to an animal, like a goldfish, that turns belly up when it dies.) □ *Her firm went tits up after the stock market crash.*

gourd ['gord] *n.* the head. □ *I raised up and got a nasty blow on the gourd.*

go West *iv.* to die. □ *When I go West, I want flowers, hired mourners, and an enormous performance of Mozart's* Requiem.

go zonkers *iv.* to go slightly crazy. □ *What a day! I almost went zonkers.*

grabbers *n.* the hands. □ *Wash your grubby little grabbers before coming to the table.*

grade-grubber 1. *n.* an earnest, hardworking student. (In the way a pig roots or grubs around for food.) □ *If there are too many grade-grubbers in a class, it will really throw off the grading scale.* **2.** *n.* a student who flatters the teacher in hopes of a higher grade. □ *Toward the end of a semester, my office is filled with grade-grubbers.*

grand AND **G.** *n.* one thousand dollars. □ *That car probably cost about 20 grand.* □ *Four G.s for that thing?*

grape(s) *n.* champagne; wine. □ *No more of the grapes for me. It tickles my nose.*

grapes of wrath *n.* wine. (A play on the title of a John Steinbeck novel.) □ *Fred had taken a little too much of the grapes of wrath.*

grave-dancer *n.* someone who profits from someone else's misfortune. (From the phrase *dance on someone's grave.*) □ *I don't want to seem like a grave-dancer, but his defeat places me in line for a promotion.* □ *The guy's a grave-dancer. Anything to get ahead.*

gravel-pounder *n.* an infantry soldier. (Military.) □ *Do you really want to join the Army and be a gravel-pounder?*

gravity check *n.* a fall, as from a surfboard, bike, etc. □ *She rounded the turn and had a sudden gravity check, resulting in a scraped elbow.*

gravy *n.* extra or easy money; easy profit. □ *Virtually every cent that came in was pure gravy—no expenses and no materials costs at all.* □ *After I pay expenses, the rest is pure gravy.*

gravy train *n.* a job that brings in a steady supply of easy money or gravy. □ *This kind of job is a real gravy train.*

grease *n.* protection money; bribery money. □ *Walter was in charge of making sure that enough grease was spread around city hall.* □ *See that the commissioner of the park district gets a little grease to help us get the contract.*

greaser ['grizɚ OR 'grisɚ] *n.* a rough and aggressive male, usually with long, greased-down hair. □ *Donna has been going out with a real greaser.*

green AND **green folding; green stuff** *n.* money; paper money. □ *How much green you got on you?*

green folding Go to green.

greenie ['grini] *n.* a bottle of Heineken™ (brand) beer. (It comes in a green bottle.) □ *Tom ordered a greenie and had it put on his tab.*

green stuff Go to green.

greldge ['grɛldʒ] **1.** *n.* something nasty or yu(c)ky. □ *What is this greldge on my shoe?* **2.** *exclam.* Nuts!; Darn! (Usually **Greldge!**) □ *Oh, greldge! I'm late!*

gripe one's **ass** AND **gripe** one's **butt** *tv.* to annoy someone; to bother or irritate someone. (Usually objectionable.) □ *You really gripe my ass when you act like that!* □ *That kind of thing really gripes my butt.*

gripe one's **butt** Go to gripe one's ass.

grit *n.* courage; nerve. □ *It takes a lot of grit to do something like that.*

gritch ['grɪtʃ] **1.** *iv.* to complain. (A blend of *gripe* and bitch.) □ *Stop gritching all the time.* □ *Are you still gritching about that?* **2.** *n.* a complainer; a griper. □ *You are getting to be such a gritch.*

groaty Go to grody.

grod(dess) ['grad(əs)] *n.* an especially sloppy man or woman. (Patterned on *god* and *goddess*.) □ *Hello, grods and groddesses, what's new?*

grody AND **groaty** ['grodi] *mod.* disgusting. (From *grotesque.* See also **grotty**.) □ *What a grody view of the street from this window.* □ *These shoes are getting sort of groaty. I guess I'll throw them out.*

gronk ['grɔŋk] *n.* a nasty substance, such as dirt that collects between the toes. □ *I don't want to hear any more at all about your gronk.*

gronk (out) *iv.* to conk out; to crash, as with a car or a computer. □ *My car gronked out on the way to work this morning.* □ *This computer program gronks every time I start to run it.*

groove *n.* something pleasant or cool. □ *This day has been a real groove.* □ *Man, what a groove!*

grooved ['gruvd] *mod.* pleased. □ *I am so grooved. I'll just kick back and meditate.*

groove on someone or something *iv.* to show interest in someone or something; to relate to someone or something. □ *Fred was beginning to groove on new-age music when he met Phil.*

grooving *mod.* enjoying life; being cool. □ *Look at those guys grooving in front of the television set.*

groovy 1. *mod.* cool; pleasant. □ *Man, this music is groovy.* □ *What a groovy day!* **2.** *mod.* out of date; passé. (California.) □ *Your clothes are so groovy. They barf me out.*

gross ['gros] *mod.* crude; vulgar; disgusting. □ *This food is gross!*

gross-out 1. *n.* something disgusting. □ *This whole day has been a total gross-out.* □ *That horror movie was a real gross-out.* **2.** *mod.* disgusting; gross. □ *What a gross-out day this has been!*

gross someone **out** *tv.* to disgust someone. □ *Those horrible pictures just gross me out.* ⊤ *Jim's story totally grossed out Sally and the rest of the kids.*

grotty ['grɑdi] *mod.* highly undesirable. (Originally British. From grotesque. See also **grody**.) □ *What is this grotty stuff they serve here?*

grub ['grəb] **1.** *n.* food. □ *Hey, this grub's pretty good.* **2.** AND **grub up** *iv.* to eat [a meal]. □ *When do we grub?* □ *Let's grub and get going.* **3.** *tv.* to eat something; to eat a meal. □ *Are you going to grub that whole pizza?* **4.** *n.* an earnest student. (Collegiate. See also **grade-grubber**.) □ *Martin is not exactly a grub. He gets good grades without trying.* □ *The test was so hard, even the grubs did poorly.* **5.** *n.* a sloppy person. (From grub worm.) □ *Sorry I look like a grub. I've been doing some plumbing.* **6.** Go to **grubbies**.

grub(ber)s Go to **grubbies**.

grubbies AND **grub(ber)s** ['grəbiz AND 'grəb(ɚ)z] *n.* worn-out clothing; clothing one wears for the occasional dirty job. □ *I have to go home, put some grubbies on, and paint the house.*

grubby ['grəbi] *mod.* unclean; untidy; unshaven. □ *I feel grubby, and I want a shower.*

grub on something *iv.* to eat something. □ *What are you grubbing on? It looks horrible.*

grubs Go to **grubbies**.

grub up Go to **grub**.

grunch Go to **grunge**.

grunge AND **grunch** ['grəndʒ AND 'grəntʃ] **1.** *n.* any nasty substance; dirt; gunk. □ *There's some gritty grunge on the kitchen floor.* □ *What's that grunch on your tie?* **2.** *n.* an ugly or nasty person; a repellent person. □ *Alice thinks that Carl is a grunge.* □ *Some grunch came by and dropped off this strange package for you.*

grungy ['grəndʒi] *mod.* dirty and smelly; yu(c)ky. □ *Get your grungy feet off the table!* □ *What is this grungy stuff on the closet floor?*

gubbish *n.* nonsense; useless information. (Computers. A combination of *garbage* and *rubbish*.) □ *I can't make any sense out of this gubbish.*

guber AND **goober** ['gubɚ] *n.* a facial pimple. (See also goob.) □ *Wow, look at that giant guber on my nose.* □ *How does anybody get rid of goobers?*

guck ['gək] *n.* a thick, sticky substance; yu(c)k. □ *What is this guck on the bottom of my shoe?* □ *The doctor painted some nasty guck on my throat and told me not to swallow for a while.*

gucky ['gəki] *mod.* thick and sticky; yu(c)ky. □ *This is a gucky day. Look at the sky.* □ *There is a lot of gucky oil and grease on the garage floor.*

gump ['gəmp] *n.* a fool; an oaf. □ *Don't act like such a gump!*

gun 1. *n.* a hired gunman; a bodyguard, an assassin, or a member of a gang of criminals. (Underworld and Western.) □ *Willie and his guns came by to remind Gary of what he owed Mr. Big.* **2.** *n.* a leader; the key member of a group. □ *Who's the gun around here?* **3.** *tv.* to race an engine; to rev up an engine. □ *See how loud it is when I gun it?* **4.** Go to guns.

gunk ['gəŋk] *n.* any nasty, messy stuff. □ *Get this gunk up off the floor before it dries.*

gunner *n.* an earnest student. (Collegiate.) □ *The gunners in my algebra class always get the A's.*

guns *n.* the biceps. □ *Look at the guns on that guy!* □ *He lifts weights to build up his guns.*

gusto ['gəsto] **1.** *n.* beer. (Black.) □ *How about another tube of gusto?* **2.** *iv.* to drink beer. (Black.) □ *Don't you ever do anything but gusto?*

gut ['gət] **1.** *n.* the belly; the intestines. □ *What a gut that guy has.* □ *Tom poked Bill right in the gut.* **2.** *mod.* basic; fundamental. □ *This is a gut issue, and we have to deal with it now.* **3.** *mod.* easy.

(Said of a course in school.) □ *That's a gut course. Nothing to it.* **4.** *n.* an easy course in school. □ *That course is a gut.*

guts ['gəts] **1.** *n.* courage; bravado. □ *It takes guts to do something like that.* **2.** *n.* the belly; the intestines. □ *Ted poked Frank right in the guts.* **3.** *n.* the inner workings of anything. □ *There's something wrong in the guts of this clock.* **4.** *n.* the essence of something. □ *Let's discuss the real guts of this issue.*

gweeb ['gwib] *n.* a studious student. (Collegiate. A variant of dweeb.) □ *I'm in a physics class full of gweebs.*

hack 1. *n.* a taxi. □ *I drove a hack for a few months; then I quit.* **2.** *n.* a cough. □ *That's a nasty hack you've got there.* **3.** *n.* a professional writer who writes mediocre material to order. □ *This novel shows that even a hack can get something published these days.* □ *That hack can't even write her name!* **4.** *n.* a reporter. □ *Newspaper hacks have to know a little of everything.* **5.** *tv.* to write clumsy or inefficient computer programs. □ *I can hack a program for you, but it won't be what you want.* **6.** *tv.* to break into a computer electronically to steal data or corrupt it or for the challenge of breaking in. □ *I'm gonna hack the bank's computer because they bounced a check of mine.* **7.** *tv.* to annoy someone. □ *This really hacks me!* **8.** *n.* anyone who does poor or undesirable work. □ *Oh, he's just a hack. What can you expect?*

hacked ['hækt] **1.** *mod.* worn-out; ready to quit. □ *We were all hacked at the end of the climb.* **2.** AND **hacked off** *mod.* angry; annoyed. □ *Wally was really hacked off about the accident.* □ *Oh, Wally is always hacked about something.*

hacker 1. *n.* a taxi driver. □ *You wonder how some of these hackers keep their licenses.* **2.** *n.* a sloppy or inefficient computer programmer. □ *This program was written by a real hacker. It's a mess, but it works.* **3.** *n.* a generally unsuccessful person. □ *Poor Pete is just a hacker. He'll never go anyplace.* **4.** *n.* someone who breaks into a computer electronically. □ *Some hacker broke into our computer!*

had Go to taken.

hairy *mod.* hazardous; difficult. □ *That was a hairy experience!*

hairy-ass(ed) *mod.* strong and virile. (Usually objectionable.) □ *He's a big, hairy-assed kinda guy.*

half-ass(ed) *mod.* clumsy; awkward and ineffectual. (Usually objectionable.) □ *She only made a half-ass try at passing the test.*

halvsies ['hævziz] *mod.* with each person paying half. □ *Let's make it halvsies, and I pay for the parking, too.*

hamburger *n.* a stupid and worthless person—meat. □ *The guy is just hamburger. You can't teach him anything.*

hammer *n.* the accelerator of a vehicle. □ *She pressed down the hammer, and off they went.*

hang a huey ['hæŋ ə 'jui AND 'hæŋ ə 'hjui] *tv.* to make a U-turn. (The first pronunciation of *Huey*, with no *hj*, is probably the original version.) □ *Hang a huey at the next corner.*

hang a left *tv.* to turn left. □ *Hey, here! Hang a left here!*

hang a louie ['hæŋ ə 'lui] *tv.* to turn left. □ *Go another block and hang a louie.*

hang a ralph ['hæŋ ə 'rælf] *tv.* to turn right. □ *He skied down the easy slope and hung a ralph near a fir tree.*

hang a right *tv.* to turn right. □ *Hang a right about here.*

hang five AND **hang ten** *tv.* to stand toward the front of a surfboard or diving board and hang the toes of one or both feet over the edge. (Teens and collegiate.) □ *The coach told her to hang ten and not to look down.* □ *Get out there and hang five. You can swim. Nothing can go wrong.*

hang it up *tv.* to quit something. □ *I finally had enough and decided to hang it up.* □ *Oh, hang it up! It's hopeless.*

hang loose AND **stay loose** *iv.* to relax and stay cool. □ *Just hang loose, man. Everything'll be all right.* □ *Stay loose, chum. See ya later.*

hang ten Go to hang five.

hang tough (on something**)** *iv.* to stick to one's position (on something). □ *I decided I'd hang tough on it. I tend to give in too easy.*

hang up 1. *n.* a problem or concern; an obsession. (Usually **hang-up.**) □ *She's got some serious hang-ups about cats.* □ *I don't have any hang ups at all. Well, almost none.* **2.** *iv.* to say no; to cancel out of something. □ *If you don't want to do it, just hang up. I'll understand.*

hard coin *n.* lots of money. (See also coin.) □ *A car like that takes hard coin.*

hard-off *n.* a dull and sexless male. (The opposite of hard-on.) □ *Wally is a silly hard-off. He seems asleep half the time.*

hard-on *n.* an erection of the penis. (Usually objectionable.) □ *He must have had his last hard-on years ago.*

hard up 1. *mod.* alcohol intoxicated. □ *After a couple of six-packs, Wally found himself a little hard up.* **2.** *mod.* in need of drugs or alcohol. □ *The old hobo was hard up for a drink.* **3.** *mod.* desperate for companionship. □ *Freddie said he was hard up and needed a date.*

hardware 1. *n.* a weapon; a gun. (Underworld and Western.) □ *I think I see your hardware showing.* **2.** *n.* computer parts, as opposed to computer programs. □ *The software is okay, so it must be the hardware that's off.*

harsh *mod.* bad; rude. □ *She's a harsh lady and doesn't care how you feel.* □ *Man, this hamburger is harsh. What did you put in it?*

harsh toke 1. *n.* an irritating puff of a marijuana cigarette. (Drugs.) □ *Wow, that was a harsh toke. Yuck!* **2.** *n.* anything or anyone unpleasant. (From sense 1.) □ *Sally can sure be a harsh toke when she wants.*

hate someone's **guts** *tv.* to hate someone very much. □ *You're horrible. I hate your guts!*

haul ass (out of some place**)** Go to bag ass (out of some place).

have a buzz on *tv.* to be tipsy or alcohol intoxicated. (*Have got* can replace *have.*) □ *Both of them had a buzz on by the end of the celebration.*

have a hard-on for someone *tv.* to wish to do someone physical damage; to seek revenge on someone. (The aggressor and victim are usually males. Usually objectionable.) □ *Albert had a hard-on for Walter. He was going to kill him if the chance came up.*

have a shit-fit *tv.* to have a fit; to throw a temper tantrum. (Usually objectionable.) □ *If I'm not home on time, my father'll have a shit-fit.*

have a spaz [. . . spæz] *tv.* to get angry or hysterical. (Teens and collegiate.) □ *If my dad hears about this, he'll have a spaz.*

have a wild hair up one's **ass 1.** *tv.* to act in a hyperactive and energetic manner. (Usually objectionable.) □ *She has a wild hair up her ass about something. I don't know what.* □ *I'm sorry I was so rude. I guess I had a wild hair up my ass or something.* **2.** *tv.* to be obsessed with some strange or offbeat idea. (Usually objectionable.) □ *You're acting like you've got a wild hair up your ass. Calm down.*

have good vibes *tv.* to have good feelings (about someone or something). (*Have got* can replace *have*.) □ *I know everything will go all right. I have good vibes.*

have hot pants (for someone**)** AND **have the hots (for** someone**)** *tv.* to be sexually aroused over someone in particular; to lust after someone. (Also with *got* as in the second example.) □ *She really has hot pants for him.* □ *She's really got the hots for him.*

have it all together *tv.* to be mentally and physically organized; to be of sound mind. (*Have got* can replace *have*.) □ *Try me again later when I have it all together.*

have one's **nose wide open** *tv.* to be in love. □ *Sam's not dense. He's got his nose wide open. It's that Sally.*

have shit for brains *tv.* to be exceedingly stupid. (Usually objectionable.) □ *You have shit for brains if you think you can get away with it.*

have someone **by the short hairs** *tv.* to have someone in an awkward position; to have dominated someone. (This refers to the shorter pubic hairs. Sometime euphemized to *neck hairs*.) □ *They've got me by the short hairs. There's nothing I can do.*

have the hots (for someone**)** Go to have hot pants (for someone).

a **head 1.** *n.* a headache. □ *Man, do I have a head. You got any aspirin?* **2.** *n.* a hangover. □ *How do you get rid of a head so you can go to work?*

head 1. *n.* a member of the drug culture; a hippie or a person who drops out of mainstream society because of drug use. (From the 1960s and 1970s.) □ *You still see a few heads around, even today.* **2.** *n.* a smart person; an intellectual person. □ *I'm no head, but I am sure you made a mistake in your addition.*

the **head** *n.* a toilet; a restroom. (Originally nautical.) □ *Where's the head around here?* □ *Ralph is in the head. He'll be back in a minute.*

headache 1. *n.* an annoying person or thing. □ *Here comes that Kelly Johnson. He's a real headache.* **2.** *n.* liquor. □ *Pour me some more of that headache, will you?*

headfucker *n.* a person, situation, or a drug that confuses someone or disorients someone mentally. (Taboo. Usually objectionable.) □ *This day was a real headfucker!* □ *Why did you have to lay this headfucker on me?*

heave ['hiv] *iv.* to empty one's stomach; to vomit. □ *He heaved and heaved and sounded like he was dying.*

heavy 1. *n.* a villain. (Especially in movies, etc.) □ *He is well known for playing heavies in the movies.* □ *Do I always have to be the heavy?* **2.** *mod.* important; profound; serious. □ *I have some heavy things to talk over with you, Sam.* **3.** *mod.* really fine. □ *Man, this is some heavy chocolate cake!*

heavy artillery *n.* powerful or persuasive persons or things. □ *Finally, the mayor brought out the heavy artillery and quieted things down.* □ *The heavy artillery seemed to know how to handle matters.*

heavy bread AND **heavy money** *n.* a great deal of money. □ *Man, that car cost some heavy bread.* □ *It takes heavy money to run a household like this.*

heavy into someone or something *mod.* much concerned with someone or something; obsessed with someone or something. (Black.) □ *Freddie was heavy into auto racing and always went to the races.* □ *Sam is heavy into Mary.*

heavy money Go to heavy bread.

heavy scene *n.* a serious state of affairs; an emotionally charged situation. □ *Man, that meeting was really a heavy scene.*

helium head ['hiliəm 'hɛd] *n.* a fool; an **airhead.** □ *Well, what's that helium head done now?*

hellhole *n.* a very hot place; a troublesome place. □ *The auditorium was a regular hellhole and somebody even fainted.*

Hello? *exclam.* Did you hear me?; Are you aware that I am talking to you? □ *A: I don't want any of that. B: Here, have some. A: Hello? No, I don't want any!*

hep ['hɛp] *mod.* aware; informed. (See also **hip.**) □ *The chick is simply not hep.*

Here's the deal. *tv.* This is the plan, scheme, or proposition. □ *Okay, here's the deal. You pass the ball to Bob, and I'll run in the opposite direction.*

herped up *mod.* infected with herpes. □ *Stay away from him unless you want to get herped up.*

herpie AND **herp** *n.* someone who is infected with herpes. □ *How would you like to find out you've been going out with a herp?* □ *If you want to end up a herpie for the rest of your life, go ahead.*

hick(e)y ['hɪki] **1.** *n.* a love bite; a mark on the skin caused by biting or sucking. (See also **monkey bite**.) □ *She wore a high collar to cover up a hickey.* **2.** *n.* a pimple, especially if infected. □ *Wouldn't you know I'd get a hickey like this right when I have to have my picture taken!*

hides *n.* drums. (See also **skins**.) □ *Andy can really bang those hides.*

high 1. *mod.* alcohol or drug intoxicated. □ *Wally is a little high for so early in the evening.* **2.** *n.* a state of euphoria caused by drugs or alcohol. □ *His life is nothing but one high after another.*

high five 1. *n.* a greeting where the palm of the hand is raised and slapped against another person's palm similarly raised. (Compare to **low five**.) □ *They exchanged a high five and went on with the show.* **2.** *tv. & iv.* to greet someone as described in sense 1. □ *They high fived and went off together.*

hip 1. *mod.* informed; aware. (See also **hep**.) □ *The guy is just not hip. He's a nerd.* **2.** *tv.* to tell someone; to inform someone. □ *Hey, man, hip me to what's going on!*

hip-shooter *n.* someone who talks without thinking; someone who speaks very frankly. (Like a person who shoots a gun "from the hip.") □ *The press secretary is a hyper and a hip-shooter. She won't last long.*

hipster ['hɪpstɚ] *n.* a youth of the 1950s, characterized by an interest in jazz and **cool** things. □ *Were the hipsters the ones with the big shoulder pads?*

history *n.* someone or something that is part of the past and now dead or gone. □ *Don't make a move! If this gun goes off, you're history.*

hit 1. *n.* a success; something that meets with approval. □ *The fudge with nuts in it was a great hit at the sale.* **2.** *n.* a drink of liquor; a dose of a drug. (See also **bop**.) □ *He had a hit of sauce and went out to finish his work.*

hit me on the hip *tv.* call me on my pager. (Pagers are usually worn attached to one's belt or carried in a pants pocket.) □ *When you need me, just hit me on the hip.*

hit the books AND **pound the books** *tv.* to study hard. □ *I spent the weekend pounding the books.* □ *I gotta go home and hit the books.*

hit the bricks AND **hit the pavement 1.** *tv.* to start walking; to go into the streets. □ *I have a long way to go. I'd better hit the bricks.* □ *Go on! Hit the pavement! Get going!* **2.** *tv.* to go out on strike. □ *The workers hit the pavement on Friday and haven't been back on the job since.* □ *Agree to our demands, or we hit the bricks.*

hit the fan *tv.* to become publicly known; to become a scandal. (From the phrase *when the shit hit the fan.*) □ *I wasn't even in the country when it hit the fan.* □ *It hit the fan, and within ten minutes the press had spread it all over the world.*

hit the pavement Go to hit the bricks.

hit the sack *tv.* to go to sleep; to go to bed. □ *It's late. I'm going to hit the sack.*

H.J.'s Go to Hojo's.

ho(e) *n.* a prostitute; a whore. □ *Get them hoes outa here!*

hog 1. AND **hog cadillac** *n.* a large car; a souped-up car. (See also road hog.) □ *How do you like my new hog?* □ *That hog cadillac needs new shocks.* **2.** *n.* a police officer; a **pig.** □ *The hogs are on to you.*

hog cadillac Go to hog.

Hojo's AND **H.J.'s** ['hodʒoz] *n.* a Howard Johnson's restaurant or hotel. (Collegiate.) □ *Let's hit Hojo's for some grub.*

hole up *iv.* to hide (somewhere). □ *I just want to hole up until the whole matter is settled.*

Hollywood 1. *mod.* having phony glitter. □ *Who is this Hollywood dame who just came in?* **2.** *n.* a gaudily dressed person in sunglasses. (Also a term of address.) □ *Hey, Hollywood! What's cooking?* □ *Ask Hollywood over there to take off his shades and make himself known.*

homeslice *n.* a best friend. □ *Willie's my homeslice, my best bud.*

homo 1. *n.* a homosexual. (Usually a male. Rude and derogatory.) □ *Bob got fired for calling Bill a homo.* **2.** *mod.* homosexual. (Usually objectionable.) □ *Have you ever been to a homo bar?*

honcho ['hɑntʃo] **1.** *n.* the headman; the boss. (Usable for either sex.) □ *The marketing honcho couldn't say when the product would be on the shelves.* □ *The top honcho at the water department was no help at all.* **2.** *tv.* to manage or boss something. □ *Who's supposed to honcho this affair?*

honey ['həni] *n.* beer. □ *You want another can of honey?*

honk 1. *n.* a drinking spree; a **toot**. □ *The guys went off on the honk to end all honks.* **2.** *n.* a white male; a **honk(e)y**. (Black. Not necessarily derogatory.) □ *Who's the honk who keeps driving by?* **3.** *iv.* to vomit. (Onomatopoetic.) □ *I can hear someone in the john honking like mad.* **4.** *tv.* to vomit something. □ *He honked up his whole pizza.*

honked AND **honkers** *mod.* alcohol intoxicated. □ *Wally was too honked to stand up.* □ *Man, is that guy honkers!*

honker 1. *n.* a goose. (Juvenile.) □ *A whole flock of honkers settled on our pond.* **2.** *n.* a strange or eccentric person. □ *Clare is a real honker these days. Is she all right?* **3.** *n.* the nose. □ *Look at the honker on that guy. How can he see around it?*

honkers 1. *n.* a woman's breasts. (Jocular. See also **hooters**. Usually objectionable.) □ *Look at the honkers on that dame!* **2.** Go to **honked**.

honk(e)y AND **honkie** ['hɔŋki] **1.** *n.* a Caucasian. (Black.) □ *The honkies are taking over this neighborhood.* □ *Some honky was around asking for you.* **2.** *mod.* in the manner of a Caucasian; whitelike. (Black.) □ *Where'd you get that honky car?* □ *That's honkey music. I want to hear soul.*

hood 1. *n.* a hoodlum. □ *A couple of hoods hassled us on the street.* **2.** *n.* the neighborhood; the ghetto. □ *Back in the hood, Bob's considered an important guy.*

hood rat *n.* someone who hangs around the [black] neighborhood. □ *Sam's just a wimpy hood rat. He never sees any action.*

hook 1. *tv.* to cheat someone. □ *Watch the clerk in that store. He might try to hook you.* **2.** *tv.* to steal something. □ *Lefty hooked a couple of candy bars just for the hell of it.* **3.** *tv.* to addict someone (to something). (Not necessarily drugs.) □ *The constant use of bicarb hooked him to the stuff.*

hooker *n.* a prostitute. (Usually a female, but of either sex. This has to do with "hooking" men into a situation where they can be exploited sexually or robbed. It has nothing to do with a certain *General Hooker.*) □ *She's a model by day and a hooker by night.* □ *This neighborhood has a few hookers who hang around on the street corners.*

hoops *n.* the game of basketball. □ *You wanna go play some hoops?*

hoot 1. *iv.* to laugh loudly. □ *The audience screamed and hooted with their appreciation.* **2.** *n.* a joke; something laughable. □ *The skit was a hoot, and everyone enjoyed it.* **3.** *iv.* to boo at someone's performance. □ *The audience hooted until the performer fled the stage in disgrace.*

hooted *mod.* alcohol intoxicated. □ *Ted is too hooted to drive.*

hooter 1. *n.* a nose; a big nose. □ *I sort of wish my hooter wasn't so big.* **2.** *n.* a drink of liquor. □ *He tossed back a big hooter of booze and stood there a minute.* **3.** *n.* cocaine. (Drugs.) □ *Albert is known for his high-quality hooter.* **4.** Go to **hooters**.

hooters *n.* a woman's breasts. (Jocular. Usually objectionable.) □ *Look at the hooters on that dame!*

hop 1. AND **hops** *n.* beer. □ *Pretty good hops, Tom. This a new brand?* **2.** *tv.* to get aboard a plane or train. □ *I'll hop a plane and be there in a couple of hours.*

hork 1. *iv.* to vomit. □ *God! I think I'm going to hork!* **2.** *iv.* to spit. □ *Don't you hork on my driveway, you slob!*

horn 1. *n.* the nose. □ *He had the biggest horn I have ever seen on man or beast.* **2.** *n.* the telephone. □ *Get Mrs. Wilson on the horn, please.*

horny *mod.* sexually aroused; in need of sexual release. (Refers to the horns of a goat, not a car horn. The goat is a symbol of lust.) □ *He said he was so horny he could honk. What did he mean?*

horse cock *n.* a large sausage. (Military.) □ *Whack me off a piece of that horse cock, would ya, Clyde?*

horse hockey 1. *n.* horse dung. □ *You don't see horse hockey in the streets anymore.* **2.** *n.* nonsense. □ *I've heard enough of your horse hockey.*

horses *n.* horsepower, as in an engine. □ *Isn't 400 horses a lot for just one car?*

horse's ass *n.* an obnoxious person. (Also a term of address. Usually objectionable.) □ *I don't know why I married that horse's ass, Julian.*

horseshit 1. *n.* the dung of the horse. (Usually objectionable.) □ *After the parade, the street was littered with horseshit.* **2.** *n.* nonsense; bullshit. (Usually objectionable.) □ *I've heard enough of your horseshit!*

hose 1. *n.* the penis. (Usually objectionable.) □ *He held his hands over his hose and ran for the bedroom.* **2.** *tv. & iv.* to copulate [with] a woman. (Usually objectionable.) □ *You don't like her, you just want to hose her!* **3.** *tv.* to cheat or deceive someone; to lie to someone. □ *Don't try to hose me! I'm onto you!*

hoser ['hozɚ] **1.** *n.* a good guy or buddy. □ *Old Fred is a good hoser. He'll help.* **2.** *n.* a cheater or deceiver. □ *You dirty, lying hoser!* **3.** *n.* a moron; a stupid-acting person. (Rude and derogatory.) □ *Come here, you hoser. I'll show you how to do it.*

hot 1. AND **hot under the collar** *mod.* angry. □ *Don't get so hot under the collar. Chill, man.* **2.** *mod.* wanted by the police. (Underworld.) □ *Lefty is hot because of his part in the bank job.* **3.** *mod.* stolen. □ *Rocko won't touch a hot watch or anything else hot.* **4.** *mod.* winning frequently during a session of gambling. □ *I'm hot tonight! Here I go again.* □ *I was hot when I started. I'm broke now.* **5.** *mod.* of great renown; doing quite well for the time being. □ *The dancer was hot and was offered movie roles and all sorts of things.* **6.** *mod.* alcohol intoxicated. □ *Wally was too hot to stand up.* **7.** *mod.* selling well. □ *These things are really hot this season.* □ *Now, here's a hot item.* **8.** *mod.* sexy; sexually arousing. □ *Wow, who was that hot hunk you were with?*

hot item 1. *n.* an item that sells well. □ *This little thing is a hot item this season.* □ *Now here's a hot item that everybody is looking for.* **2.** *n.* a romantically serious couple. □ *Sam and Mary are quite a hot item lately.*

hot number 1. *n.* an exciting piece of music. □ *Now here's a hot number by the Wanderers.* **2.** *n.* an attractive or sexy person, typically a (young) woman. □ *Who's that hot number I saw you with last night?*

hot shit *n.* a male who thinks he is the greatest person alive; a conceited male. (Probably also used for females. Used with or without *a*. Usually objectionable.) □ *The jerk thinks he is real hot shit.*

the **(hot) skinny** *n.* inside information. (See also poop.) □ *What's the skinny on the tower clock? Is it broken?* □ *I've got the hot skinny on Mary and her boyfriend.*

hottie *n.* a sexually attractive person. □ *He's a real hottie! I wonder if he's taken.*

hot under the collar Go to hot.

howl 1. *n.* something funny. □ *What a howl the surprise party turned out to be when the guest of honor didn't show up.* □ *The gag was a real howl.* **2.** *iv.* to laugh very hard. □ *John howled when the joke was told.*

howler *n.* a big but funny mistake; an embarrassing error. □ *Who is responsible for this howler on the Wilson account?*

How('re) they hanging? *interrog.* <an inquiry calling for a report of the state of a male's testicles.> (Usually objectionable.) □ *How they hanging, Fred?*

hughie ['hjui] *iv.* to empty one's stomach; to vomit. (See also cry hughie.) □ *I gotta go hughie.*

humongous [hju'maŋgəs] *mod.* huge. □ *She lives in a humongous house on the hill.* □ *Wally has a humongous nose.*

hump 1. *tv. & iv.* to copulate [with] someone. (Refers to a male arching his back in copulation, as in *fornicate*. Usually objectionable.) □ *The sailor spent his entire leave drinking and humping.* **2.** *n.* an act of copulation. (Usually objectionable.) □ *The sailor said he needed a hump and left the ship for the port.* **3.** *n.* a person who will copulate without much persuasion. (Usually objectionable.) □ *She's just a hump. They're not hard to find these days.*

hump (along) *iv.* to move along in a hurry. □ *I guess I'd better hump along over there.* □ *Come on, move it! Hump to the main office and be fast about it!*

hump it (to somewhere) *tv.* to move rapidly (to somewhere). □ *I have to hump it over to Kate's place right now.*

humpy *mod.* sexually aroused; horny. (See also hump. Usually objectionable.) □ *She gets humpy when she watches those movies.*

hung 1. *mod.* hungover. □ *John is really hung this morning.* **2.** *mod.* annoyed. □ *Fred is hung and looking for somebody to take it out on.* **3.** Go to (well-)hung.

the **hungries** *n.* hunger. □ *Jimmy's crying because he's got the hungries.* □ *I get the hungries about this time every day.*

hungry 1. *mod.* eager to make money. □ *He doesn't sell enough because he's not hungry enough.* **2.** *mod.* ambitious. □ *He gets ahead because he's hungry.*

hunk of ass Go to piece of ass.

hunk of tail Go to piece of ass.

hurl 1. *iv.* to empty one's stomach; to vomit. (Like the *throw* in *throw up.*) □ *I think I gotta go hurl.* **2.** *n.* vomit. □ *There's hurl all over the bathroom floor!*

hurt 1. *mod.* very ugly; damaged and ugly. (Black. Similar to hurting.) □ *Man, are you hurt!* □ *That poor girl is really bad hurt.* **2.** *mod.* drug intoxicated. (Black.) □ *Gert was really hurt and nodding and drooling.* □ *One hit of that dope and he was really hurt.*

hurting *mod.* very ugly; in pain from being ugly. (Similar to hurt.) □ *That dog of yours is something to behold. It's really hurting.*

husky ['həski] *n.* a strong man; a thug. □ *Tell your husky to lay off, Reggie.* □ *A couple of huskies helped me get my car unstuck.*

hustle ['həsəl] **1.** *iv.* to move rapidly; to hurry. □ *Come on, hustle, you guys.* □ *It's late. I've got to hustle.* **2.** *n.* hurried movement; confusion. □ *All the hustle and confusion made it hard to concentrate.* **3.** *n.* a scheme to make money; a special technique for making money. (Underworld. This includes drug dealing, prostitution, and other vice activities.) □ *Each of these punks has a hustle—a specialty in crime.* **4.** *iv.* to use one's special technique for making money. □ *He's out there on the streets hustling all the time.*

hustler ['həslɚ] **1.** *n.* a gambler in a pool hall. □ *Wasn't he the guy who played the hustler in that famous movie?* **2.** *n.* a swindler. □ *The chick is a real hustler. I wouldn't trust her at all.* □ *The hustler conned me out of a month's pay.* **3.** *n.* a prostitute. □ *Gert almost became a hustler to pay for a habit.*

hyped (up) 1. *mod.* excited; stimulated. □ *They were all hyped up before the game.* **2.** *mod.* contrived; heavily promoted; falsely advertised. □ *I just won't pay good money to see these hyped-up movies.*

hyper [ˈhaɪpɚ] **1.** *mod.* excited; overreacting. □ *I'm a little hyper because of the doctor's report.* **2.** *n.* a person who praises or promotes someone or something. □ *She's a hyper, and she doesn't always tell things the way they are.* **3.** *n.* a person who is always overly excited or hyperactive. □ *Pat is such a hyper. Just can't seem to relax.*

iced *mod.* settled once and for all; done easily. (Essentially *frozen*.) □ *I've got it iced. Nothing to it.*

ick ['ɪk] **1.** *n.* any nasty substance. □ *What is this ick on my shoe?* **2.** *exclam.* Nasty! (Usually **Ick!**) □ *Oh, ick! What now?* **3.** *n.* a disliked person. □ *Tell that ick to leave. He's polluting the place.*

icky ['ɪki] *mod.* distasteful; nasty. □ *This was an icky day.*

I.D. 1. *n.* some kind of identification card. □ *Can you show me an I.D.?* **2.** *tv.* to check someone for a valid identification card. □ *They I.D.ed us at the door.*

idiot oil *n.* alcohol. □ *She drinks too much of that idiot oil.*

If that don't fuck all! *exclam.* an exclamation of surprise. (An elaboration of the colloquial *If that don't beat all!* See also **Fuck it (all)!** Taboo. Usually objectionable.) □ *If that don't fuck all! You broke it, and it's my last one!* □ *My uncle left me $40,000! If that don't fuck all!*

ill 1. *mod.* lame; dull; bad. □ *That broad is truly ill and has a face that would stop a clock.* **2.** AND **illing; illin'** *mod.* excellent; cool. □ *We had an ill time at your party. Loved it.*

illing Go to ill.

(I) love it! *exclam.* That is wonderful! (A catchphrase.) □ *It's wonderful, Ted. I love it!*

I'm out of here. AND **I'm outa here.** *sent.* I am leaving this minute. □ *In three minutes I'm outa here.*

in 1. *mod.* current; fashionable. □ *This kind of thing is in now.* **2.** *mod.* private. □ *Is this in information?* □ *If it's in or something, I'm sure they won't spread it around.* **3.** *n.* someone in a special position; someone who is serving in an elective office. □ *Well, now that I am an in, there's going to be some changes.*

in a bad way Go to in bad shape.

in a snit *mod.* in a fit of anger or irritation. □ *Don't get in a snit. It was an accident.*

in a twit *mod.* upset; frantic. □ *She's all in a twit because she lost her keys.*

in bad shape AND **in a bad way 1.** *mod.* injured or debilitated in any manner. □ *Fred had a little accident, and he's in bad shape.* □ *Tom needs exercise. He's in bad shape.* **2.** *mod.* pregnant. □ *Molly's in bad shape again, I hear.* □ *Yup, she's in bad shape all right—about four months in bad shape.*

in deep 1. *mod.* deeply involved (with someone or something). □ *Mary and Sam are in deep with each other.* □ *Carl is in deep with the mob.* **2.** *mod.* deeply in debt. □ *Reggie is in deep with his bookie.* □ *I'm in deep to the department store.*

in drag *phr.* [of a male] appearing in women's clothes. □ *Bob came to the party in drag.*

ink slinger *n.* a professional writer; a newspaper reporter. □ *The ink slingers have been at the candidates again.*

in play 1. *mod.* being played. (Said of a ball in a game.) □ *The ball's in play, so you made the wrong move.* **2.** *mod.* having to do with a company (or its stock) that is a candidate for acquisition by another company. (Financial markets.) □ *The company was in play, but nobody was buying it.* □ *The deal stocks that are in play right now offer excellent buying opportunities.*

intense *mod.* serious; heavy. □ *Oh, wow! Now that's what I call intense!*

in the bag 1. *mod.* achieved; settled. □ *It's in the bag—as good as done.* □ *The election is in the bag unless the voters find out about my past.* **2.** Go to **bagged**.

in the O-zone *mod.* dead; on the verge of death; showing the O-sign. (With the mouth hanging open, like the letter O.) □ *This patient is in the O-zone. Ready to go at any minute.*

in the Q-zone *mod.* dead; on the verge of death; with the mouth showing the Q-sign. □ *Look at that tongue hanging out. This guy's in the Q-zone.*

in there *mod.* sincere; likable. □ *Martha is really in there. Everybody likes her.* □ *I like a guy who's in there—who thinks about other people.*

in the suds *mod.* alcohol intoxicated. □ *Fred is in the suds and can't see straight.*

in the tube 1. *mod.* in the tube of a large wave. (Surfing.) □ *On a day like today, I want to be out there in the tube.* **2.** *mod.* at risk. □ *If you find yourself in the tube in this matter, just give me a ring.*

iron 1. *n.* a gun; a revolver. (Underworld.) □ *Walter never carries iron unless he's going to use it.* **2.** *n.* computer hardware. (See also big iron.) □ *What kind of iron are you people running over there?*

It don't make (me) no nevermind. *phr.* It doesn't matter to me. □ *Go ahead! Do it! It don't make me no nevermind.*

(It's) not my dog. *phr.* It's not my problem. □ *So what! It doesn't matter! Not my dog.*

I've got to fly. AND **I('ve) gotta fly.** *sent.* I have to leave right now. □ *Time's up. I've got to fly.* □ *I've gotta fly. See you later.*

ivories ['aɪvriz] **1.** *n.* the teeth. □ *I gotta go brush my ivories.* **2.** *n.* piano keys. (From the time when piano keys were made from real elephant ivory.) □ *She can really bang those ivories.*

jack 1. *n.* money. □ *I don't have the jack for a deal like that.* □ *How much jack will it take?* **2.** *n.* tobacco for rolling cigarettes. □ *You got some jack I can bum?*

jackal *n.* a low and devious person. □ *What does that jackal want here?*

jack around *iv.* to waste time; to mess around. □ *Stop jacking around and get busy.*

jacked (out) *mod.* angry; annoyed. □ *Boy, was that old guy jacked out at you.* □ *Yup, he was jacked all right.*

jacked up 1. *mod.* excited. □ *Don was really jacked up about the election.* **2.** *mod.* arrested. (Underworld.) □ *What time did Reggie get himself jacked up?* **3.** *mod.* upset; stressed. □ *I was really jacked up by the bad news.*

jack off Go to beat off.

jack-shit 1. *n.* a stupid and worthless person. (Usually refers to a male. Usually objectionable.) □ *What a jack-shit! Not a brain in his head!* **2.** *n.* anything; anything at all. (Always in a negative expression.) □ *This whole thing isn't worth jack-shit!*

jack someone **around** *tv.* to hassle someone; to harass someone. (Compare to **jerk** someone **around**.) □ *The I.R.S. is jacking my brother around.* ⊤ *The boss was jacking around Gert, so she just walked out.*

jack someone or something **up 1.** *tv.* [with *someone*] to motivate someone; to stimulate someone to do something. □ *I'll jack him up and try to get some action out of him.* ⊤ *What does it take to jack up that lazy guy?* **2.** *tv.* [with *something*] to raise the price of something. □ *They kept jacking the price up with various charges, so I walked.* ⊤ *How can they jack up the published price?* **3.** *tv.* [with *something*] to mess something up. □ *Who jacked up*

107

the papers on my desk? **4.** *tv.* [with *someone*] to beat or stab someone. ⊤ *They really jacked up Bobby. He almost died.*

JAFDIP *acronym.* just another fucking day in paradise. (A sarcastic expression for a bad day or a day in an unhappy situation. Usually objectionable.) □ *Everything is going wrong. What do you expect? JAFDIP!*

jag 1. *n.* a Jaguar™ automobile. □ *What I really want is a jag.* **2.** *n.* a drinking bout; a prolonged state of alcohol or drug intoxication. □ *Is he off on another jag, or is this the same one?* **3.** *n.* a prolonged state of emotional excess. □ *She's off on a jag again.*

jag off Go to **beat off.**

jam 1. *n.* a problem; trouble. □ *I hear you're in a bad jam.* **2.** *iv.* [for musicians] to play together, improvising. □ *They jammed until the neighbors complained.* **3.** *tv. & iv.* to force a basketball into the basket; to **slam dunk** a basketball. □ *He tried to jam it but blew it.* **4.** *n.* an act of forcing a basketball into the basket; a **slam dunk.** □ *The jam didn't work, and Fred's team got the ball.*

jammed ['dʒæmd] **1.** *mod.* arrested. (Underworld.) □ *Willie got jammed for speeding.* **2.** *mod.* alcohol intoxicated. □ *I'm a little jammed, but I think I can still drive.* **3.** *mod.* upset; annoyed. □ *He's really jammed because he flunked the test.*

jammed up 1. *mod.* in trouble. □ *He got himself jammed up with the law.* **2.** *mod.* glutted; full of food or drink. □ *I'm jammed up. I can't eat another bite.* □ *After dinner, I am so jammed up that I need a nap.*

jamming *mod.* excellent. □ *This music is really jamming.*

jaw 1. *n.* a chat. □ *I could use a good jaw with my old friend.* **2.** *iv.* to chat. □ *Stop jawing and get to work.* **3.** Go to **jaw(bone).**

jaw(bone) *tv.* to try to persuade someone verbally; to apply verbal pressure to someone. □ *They tried to jawbone me into doing it.* □ *Don't jaw me. I won't do it.*

jazzed (up) 1. *mod.* alert; having a positive state of mind. □ *I am jazzed up and ready to face life.* □ *Those guys were jazzed and ready for the game.* **2.** *mod.* alcohol or drug intoxicated. □ *Dave was a bit jazzed up, but not terribly.* □ *Gert was jazzed out of her mind.* **3.** *mod.* enhanced; with something added; having been made more enticing. □ *The third act was jazzed up with a little skin.* □

It was jazzed enough to have the police chief around asking questions.

jazz someone or something **up** *tv.* to make someone or something more exciting or sexy; to make someone or something appeal more to contemporary and youthful tastes. □ *Let's jazz this up a little bit.* ⊤ *They jazzed up the old girl till she looked like a teenager.* ⊤ *Don't jazz up the first number too much.*

jazzy ['dʒæzi] *mod.* stimulating; appealing. □ *That's a jazzy sweater you got.*

jel ['dʒɛl] *n.* a stupid person with gelatin where brains ought to be. □ *Oh, Wallace, don't act like such a jel!*

jerk *n.* a stupid or worthless person. (For both males and females.) □ *You are such a classic jerk!*

jerker 1. *n.* a drunkard; an alcoholic. (Because of visible shaking.) □ *Some of the jerkers have the D.T.s.* **2.** *n.* a heavy user of cocaine. (Drugs.) □ *The new guy is a jerker. You can see it in his eyes.* □ *The jerkers who need immediate treatment are sent from E.R. up to detox.* **3.** *n.* a male who masturbates habitually. (Usually objectionable.) □ *He's a jerker. He doesn't need women.*

jerk off Go to beat off.

jerk someone **around** *tv.* to hassle someone; to waste someone's time. □ *Stop jerking me around and give me my money back.* ⊤ *They sure like to jerk around people in that music shop.*

jillion ['dʒɪljən] *n.* an enormous, indefinite number. □ *I've got a jillion things to tell you.*

jism AND **chism; gism; gizzum; jizz; jizzum** *n.* semen. (Usually objectionable.) □ *Do you think jism is alive?* □ *This weird doctor took a sample of my gizzum and put it on a microscope slide.*

jive ['dʒaɪv] **1.** *n.* back talk. □ *Cut the jive, man!* □ *Don't you give me any of that jive!* **2.** *n.* lies; deception; nonsense. □ *I've listened to your jive for years. You'll never change.* **3.** *mod.* deceptive; insincere. □ *Don't give me all those jive excuses.*

jive-ass *mod.* foolish. (Black. Caution with ass.) □ *You can tell that jive-ass jerk to forget it.*

jive talk *n.* slang; contemporary fad words. □ *I like to hear jive talk. It's like trying to work a puzzle.* □ *He stands by the window with a pad of paper and takes down the jive talk he hears.*

jive turkey *n.* a stupid person. □ *Get that jive turkey out of here!*

jizz Go to jism.

jizzum Go to jism.

jock 1. *n.* an athlete. (See also **strap**. See also **jockstrap**. Now of either sex.) □ *The jocks are all at practice now.* **2.** *n.* an athletic supporter (garment). □ *Somebody dropped a jock in the hall.*

jockstrap 1. AND **jockstrapper** *n.* an athlete. (From the name of the supporting garment worn by male athletes.) □ *The jockstrappers are all at practice now.* **2.** *iv.* to work as a professional athlete. □ *I jockstrapped for a few years and then lost my interest in it.*

jockstrapper Go to jockstrap.

Joe Six-pack *n.* the average guy who sits around drinking beer by the six-pack. □ *Joe Six-pack likes that kind of television program.*

john 1. *n.* a toilet; a bathroom. □ *Is there another john around here?* **2.** *n.* a man. □ *Some john was around asking for you.* **3.** *n.* a prostitute's customer. □ *She led the john into an alley where Lefty robbed him.* □ *The john looked a little embarrassed.* **4.** *n.* a victim of a crime or deception; a **sucker**. □ *The john went straight to the cops and told the whole thing.*

johnson Go to jones.

joint 1. *n.* a tavern. □ *Lefty has his own joint over on 12th.* □ *I wanted to open a joint, but I don't have the cash.* **2.** *n.* a lowclass establishment. □ *Let's get out of this crummy joint.* □ *This joint bores me.* **3.** *n.* a marijuana cigarette. □ *He always has a joint with him.* **4.** *n.* a jail; a prison. □ *Lefty just got out of the joint.*

joke *tv.* to tease someone; to make fun of someone. □ *Everybody was joking my roommate because of her accent.* □ *Don't joke me, man. I do the best I can.*

jones AND **johnson 1.** *n.* a thing. (Black.) □ *There's a big turf jones down on the corner.* □ *This get-rich-quick jones will land you in the joint, Lefty.* **2.** *n.* a penis. (Black. Caution with topic.) □ *Zip up, man. You want your jones getting out?*

jork *n.* a worthless person; a combination of **jerk** and **dork**. □ *What a jork! How stupid can you get?*

joy juice *n.* liquor; beer. □ *Can I pour you some more of this joy juice?*

the **jug** *n.* jail. □ *A couple of days in the jug would do you fine.*

jug 1. *n.* a jug of liquor; a jar of homemade booze; a can of beer. □ *Where's my jug? I need a swig.* **2.** AND **jug up** *iv.* to drink heavily. □ *Let's jug up and have a good time.* □ *We jugged till about noon and then went to sleep.* **3.** *n.* a glass vial of liquid amphetamine intended for injection. (Drugs.) □ *His mother found a jug and took it to a drugstore to find out what it was.* □ *Any kid can get jugs just by asking around.* **4.** *n.* the jugular vein, used for the injection of narcotics. (Drugs.) □ *He's even got scars on his jugs.* **5.** *n.* a breast. (Usually plural. Usually objectionable.) □ *Look at the jugs on that babe!*

jug up Go to jug.

juice 1. *n.* liquor; wine. □ *Let's go get some juice and get stewed.* **2.** *iv.* to drink heavily. □ *Both of them were really juicing.* **3.** *n.* electricity. □ *The juice has been off since dawn.* □ *Turn on the juice, and let's see if it runs.* **4.** *n.* energy; power; political influence. □ *The boss has the juice with the board to make the necessary changes.* □ *Dave left the president's staff because he just didn't have the juice anymore to be useful.* **5.** *n.* orange juice futures market. (Securities markets.) □ *The juice opened a little high today but fell quickly under profit taking.* □ *It's time to sell juice and buy bellies.* **6.** *n.* anabolic steroids. □ *Fred used too much juice and is growing bitch tits.*

juice house *n.* a liquor store. (Black.) □ *Would you stop by the juice house for some foam?*

juice something **back** *tv.* to drink alcohol. □ *He's been juicing it back since noon.* T *Juice back your drink, and let's go.*

jump 1. *tv.* to attack someone. (General slang.) □ *The gang jumped the old man and robbed him.* **2.** *tv.* to copulate [with] someone. (Usually objectionable.) □ *He was so horny, I just knew he was gonna try to jump me.*

jump start 1. *n.* the act of starting a car by getting power—through jumper cables—from another car. □ *I got a jump start from a friend.* **2.** *tv.* to start a car by getting power from another car. □ *I can't jump start your car. My battery is low.*

jump (street) *n.* the beginning; the start (of something). (Prisons and streets.) □ *I knew from jump that you were going to be trouble.* □ *Way back at jump street, I spotted you as a troublemaker.*

junk 1. *n.* liquor; inferior liquor. □ *Pour this junk down the drain and get me something good.* **2.** *tv.* to dispose of something, such as a piece of equipment. □ *I can't junk it. It's the only one I have.* **3.** *n.* heroin; drugs. □ *Is Sam still on junk? It will kill him.* **4.** *n.* a Caucasian. (Rude and derogatory.) □ *Those cops are junk, and they hate my guts.*

junkie AND **junky** ['dʒəŋki] **1.** *n.* a drug dealer. □ *Junkies should be put into the jug.* **2.** *n.* a drug user; an addict. □ *Junkies have to steal to support their habits.*

Junk it! *command* Throw it away! □ *This is taking up too much space. Junk it!*

just off the boat *mod.* to be freshly immigrated and perhaps gullible and naive. □ *I'm not just off the boat. I know what's going on.*

K ['ke] *n.* a thousand (of anything, such as dollars, bytes, etc.). □ *This car is worth at least 20 K.* □ *I have 640 K memory in my computer.*

Keep in touch. *sent.* Good-bye. (Sometimes a sarcastic way of saying good-bye to someone one doesn't care about.) □ *Nice talking to you. Keep in touch.*

keep one's **cool** *tv.* to remain calm and in control. (Compare to **blow** one's **cool**.) □ *Relax, man! Just keep your cool.*

keep one's **head right** *tv.* to maintain control of oneself. (Black.) □ *Chill, man, chill. You've got to keep your head right.*

Keep your nose out of my business! Go to Get your nose out of my business!

keester AND **keyster; kiester** ['kistɚ] **1.** *n.* a chest; a suitcase. □ *The old lady was hauling the most enormous keester.* **2.** *n.* the buttocks; the anus. □ *He fell flat on his keester.*

keg 1. *iv.* to pay attention. □ *Keep kegging, you guys! This is important.* **2.** *n.* a beer belly. □ *If you didn't drink so much beer, you wouldn't have such a keg.*

kegger 1. *n.* a party where beer is served from a keg. (Teens and collegiate.) □ *Tiffany is having a kegger, and a few of her intimates are invited.* **2.** AND **keggers** *n.* a keg of beer. (Collegiate.) □ *We need another kegger. It's only nine o'clock.* □ *We came here because somebody said there was keggers.*

keg party *n.* a party where liquor, especially beer, is served. □ *The keg party ended early owing to the arrival of uninvited cops.*

kevork *tv.* to kill someone. (Based on the name of *Dr. Jack Kevorkian*, the physician who practices assisted suicide.) □ *This guy looked mean—like he was gonna kevork me.*

kewl *mod.* <an alternate spelling of *cool*>; excellent, neat, and good. □ *Man, this is really kewl, I mean truly phat!*

keyster Go to keester.

kick 1. *n.* a charge or good feeling (from something); pleasure or enjoyment from something. □ *That song really gives me a kick. I love it!* **2.** *n.* a complaint. □ *What's the kick, man?* **3.** *iv.* to complain. □ *Ernie kicks about everything.*

kick around Go to knock around.

kick-ass AND **bust-ass 1.** *mod.* powerful and vigorous. □ *The guy's a real kick-ass bastard!* **2.** *mod.* really fine; excellent; cool. □ *That was a real kick-ass party you had the other night!*

kick-ass on someone *iv.* to give someone a hard time; to try to dominate or overwhelm someone. □ *Don't kick-ass on me! I'm not the one you're after.*

kick back 1. *iv.* to relax (and enjoy something). □ *I like to kick back and listen to a few tunes.* **2.** *n.* money received in return for a favor. (Usually **kickback**.) □ *The kickback the cop got wasn't enough, as it turned out.*

kicker *n.* a clever but stinging remark; a sharp criticism. □ *I waited for the kicker, and finally it came.*

kickin' ['kɪkən] *mod.* wild; super; excellent. □ *I don't know where you get your clothes, but that jacket's kickin'.*

kick in the ass AND **kick in the butt; kick in the pants; kick in the rear** *n.* some kind of action that will motivate someone. (Rarely refers to an actual kick.) □ *What she needs is a kick in the ass!* □ *I thought that the failing grade would be the kind of kick in the butt you needed to get yourself going.*

kick in the butt Go to kick in the ass.

kick in the pants Go to kick in the ass.

kick in the rear Go to kick in the ass.

kick it *tv.* to relax. □ *I need a few minutes to kick it, then I'll get back in the game.*

kick off *iv.* to die. □ *We've been waiting for years for that cat to kick off.* □ *The old girl finally kicked off.*

kicks *n.* cleats or shoes. (Collegiate. See also kick.) □ *Don't you dare wear those kicks in here!*

kick some ass (around) *tv.* to take over and start giving orders. (Caution with **ass**.) □ *Do I have to come over there and kick some ass around?*

kick the shit out of someone Go to beat the shit out of someone.

kicky ['kɪki] *mod.* exciting and energetic. □ *Man, what a kicky idea!*

kiester Go to keester.

killer 1. *n.* a very funny joke. □ *That last one was a killer!* **2.** *n.* something extraordinary. □ *That jacket is a real killer!* □ *That car is a killer. I like it!* **3.** *mod.* extraordinary. □ *What a killer jacket you're wearing!*

kilobucks *n.* a tremendous sum of money. (See also **megabucks**.) □ *How many kilobucks does a set of wheels like that cost?*

kink 1. *n.* a strange person; a kinky person. □ *The guy's a kink. Watch out for him.* **2.** *n.* a sexually deviant person. □ *He was a kink, and I broke up with him.*

kinky 1. *mod.* having to do with someone or something strange or weird. □ *Who is that kinky dame in the net stockings?* **2.** *mod.* having to do with unconventional sexual acts or people who perform them. □ *He showed her a picture of some kind of kinky sex thing.*

kipe *tv.* to steal something. □ *Where did you kipe this thing?* □ *The punk kiped a newspaper just for the heck of it.*

kiper ['kaɪpɚ] *n.* a thief; someone who steals. □ *You dirty little kiper. Give it back!*

kiss-ass 1. *n.* someone who is servile and obsequious. (Rude and derogatory.) □ *Don't be such a sniveling kiss-ass!* **2.** *mod.* servile and obsequious. (Usually objectionable.) □ *He can be so kiss-ass. It makes me sick.*

Kiss my ass! *exclam.* Drop dead!; Go to hell! (Usually objectionable.) □ *Kiss my ass, you creep!*

kiss off 1. ['kɪs ɔf] *n.* the dismissal of someone or something. (Usually **kiss-off**.) □ *The kiss-off was when I lost the Wilson contract.* **2.** ['kɪs ɔf] *n.* death. (Usually **kiss-off**.) □ *When the time comes for the kiss-off, I hope I'm asleep.* **3.** ['kɪs 'ɔf] *iv.* to die. □ *The cat is going to have to kiss off one of these days soon.*

kiss someone's **hind tit** Go to suck someone's hind tit.

kiss the porcelain god *tv.* to empty one's stomach; to vomit. □ *He fled the room to kiss the porcelain god, I guess.*

kiss up to someone *iv.* to flatter someone; to make over someone. □ *I'm not going to kiss up to anybody to get what's rightfully mine.*

kissyface ['kɪsifes] **1.** *n.* kissing. □ *There was a lot of kissyface going on in the backseat.* **2.** *mod.* feeling the need to kiss and be kissed. □ *I feel all kissyface.*

klotz Go to klutz.

klu(d)ge ['klədʒ OR 'kludʒ] **1.** *n.* a patch or a fix in a computer program or circuit. □ *Kluges that are invisible don't bother anybody.* **2.** *tv.* to patch or fix a computer program circuit. □ *I only have time to kludge this problem.*

kludgy ['klədʒi OR 'kludʒi] *mod.* having to do with an inefficient or sloppily written computer program. □ *Who wrote this kludgy mess?* □ *I don't care if it's kludgy. Does it work?*

klutz AND **klotz** ['kləts AND 'klɑts] *n.* a stupid and clumsy person. □ *Don't be a klutz!* □ *Some klotz put mustard in the stew.*

klutzy ['klətsi] *mod.* foolish; stupid. □ *That was really a klutzy thing to do!*

knee-deep navy *n.* the U.S. Coast Guard. (Jocular and derogatory.) □ *Join the knee-deep navy and see the beach!*

knock *tv.* to criticize someone or something. □ *The papers are knocking my favorite candidate again.*

knock around 1. *iv.* to waste time. □ *Stop knocking around and get to work!* **2.** AND **kick around** *iv.* to wander around; to loiter. □ *I think I'll knock around a few months before looking for another job.*

knocked out 1. *mod.* exhausted. □ *We were all knocked out at the end of the day.* **2.** *mod.* overwhelmed. □ *We were just knocked out when we heard your news.* **3.** *mod.* alcohol or drug intoxicated. □ *They were all knocked out by midnight.*

knocked up 1. *mod.* battered; beaten. □ *This book is a little knocked up, so I'll lower the price.* **2.** *mod.* alcohol intoxicated. □ *Bill was knocked up and didn't want to drive.* **3.** *mod.* pregnant. □ *Isn't she knocked up most of the time?*

knock one **back** Go to knock one over.

knock one **over** AND **knock** one **back** *tv.* to take a drink of liquor. □ *He knocked one over right away and demanded another.* ⊤ *He knocked back one and belched grossly.*

knockout 1. *n.* something that is quite stunning. □ *Your new car is a knockout.* **2.** *n.* a good-looking man or woman. □ *Who is that knockout I saw you with last weekend?* **3.** *mod.* very exciting. □ *It was a real knockout evening.*

knock someone **some skin** *tv.* to shake hands with someone. □ *Hey, man, knock me some skin!* □ *Todd knocked Sam some skin, and they left the building together.*

knock someone **up** *tv.* to make a woman pregnant. (Crude.) □ *They say it was Reggie who knocked her up.* ⊤ *He did not knock up Molly. I did.*

knock something **down 1.** *tv.* to drink a portion of liquor. □ *Here, knock this down and let's go.* ⊤ *He knocked down a bottle of beer and called for another.* **2.** *tv.* to earn a certain amount of money. □ *I'm lucky to knock half that down.* ⊤ *She must knock down about 40 thou a year.*

knock the shit out of someone Go to beat the shit out of someone.

know from something *iv.* to know about something. □ *Do you know from timers, I mean how timers work?* □ *I don't know from babies! Don't ask me about feeding them!*

know where one **is coming from** *tv.* to understand someone's motivation; to understand and relate to someone's position. □ *I know where you're coming from. I've been there.*

knuckle-dragger *n.* a strong and stupid man. (Like an ape.) □ *Call off your knuckle-draggers. I'll pay you whatever you want.*

knuckle sandwich *n.* a blow struck in the teeth or mouth. □ *How would you like a knuckle sandwich?*

kong ['kɔŋ] *n.* strong whiskey; illicit whiskey. (Black. From the movie ape King Kong.) □ *How about a big swallow of that kong?*

konk Go to conk.

kook ['kuk] *n.* a strange person. □ *She seems like a kook, but she is just grand, really.*

kookish AND **kooky** ['kukɪʃ] *mod.* strange; eccentric. □ *There's a lot of kookish things going on around here.*

kooky Go to kookish.

L7 ['ɛl 'sɛvən] **1.** *n.* a **square.** □ *That guy is an L7.* **2.** *mod.* dull; square. □ *This guy was real, like, you know, L7.*

labonza [lə'bɑnzə] **1.** *n.* the buttocks. □ *Good grief, what a gross labonza!* □ *She fell flat on her labonza.* **2.** *n.* the pit of the stomach. □ *That kind of beautiful singing really gets you right in the labonza.* □ *She experienced the kind of gut-wrenching anger that starts in your labonza and cuts through right to the top of your head.* **3.** *n.* the belly. □ *I feel the effects of last night's celebration in my wallet and in my labonza.* □ *Look at the labonza on that creep! He's gonna deliver triplets.*

laid-back 1. *mod.* calm and relaxed. □ *Reggie is not what I would call laid-back.* **2.** *mod.* alcohol or drug intoxicated. □ *He's a little laid-back and can't come to the phone.*

laid out 1. *mod.* alcohol or drug intoxicated. □ *Man, you got yourself laid out!* □ *I'm too laid out to go to work today.* **2.** *mod.* well dressed. (Black.) □ *Look at those silks! Man, are you laid out!*

laine Go to **lame.**

lambasted *n.* drunk. □ *He went out and got himself lambasted, then he wrecked his car.*

lame AND **laine; lane 1.** *mod.* inept; inadequate. □ *That guy's so lame, it's pitiful.* □ *This mark is about as laine as they come.* **2.** *n.* a **square** person. (Streets. Underworld.) □ *Let's see if that lame over there has anything we want in his pockets.* □ *He won't drink anything at all. He is such a lame!* **3.** *n.* an inept person. □ *The guy turned out to be a lame, and we had to fire him.* □ *Maybe the lane can work in the front office answering phones or something.*

lamps *n.* the eyes. □ *His lamps are closed. He's asleep or dead.*

lane Go to **lame.**

lard *n.* the police. (Streets. Derogatory. See also **bacon, pig, pork**.) □ *If the lard catches you violating your parole, you're through.*

lard ass 1. *n.* someone with very fat buttocks. □ *Here comes that lard ass again.* **2.** *n.* very large buttocks. □ *I'm gonna have to do something about this lard ass of mine.*

Late. Go to Later.

Later. AND **Late.; Laters.** *interj.* Good-bye. □ *It's time to cruise. Later.* □ *Late. Gotta go.*

Laters. Go to Later.

lats ['læts] *n.* the *latissimus dorsi*; the muscles of the back. (Bodybuilding.) □ *Your lats are coming along fine. Now let's start working on your delts.* □ *Nice lats on that guy.*

launch (one's **lunch)** *tv. & iv.* to empty one's stomach; to vomit. □ *When I saw that mess, I almost launched my lunch.* □ *Watch out! She's going to launch!*

lay a guilt trip on someone Go to lay a (heavy) trip on someone.

lay a (heavy) trip on someone **1.** *tv.* to criticize someone. □ *There's no need to lay a trip on me. I agree with you.* □ *When he finally does get there, I'm going to lay a heavy trip on him like he'll never forget.* **2.** *tv.* to confuse or astonish someone. □ *After he laid a heavy trip on me about how the company is almost broke, I cleaned out my desk and left.* □ *After Mary laid a trip on John about her other self, he sat down and stared at his feet.* **3.** AND **lay a guilt trip on someone** *tv.* to attempt to make someone feel very guilty. □ *Why do you have to lay a guilt trip on me? Why don't you go to a shrink?* □ *Of course, she just had to lay a trip on him about being bossy, self-centered, and aloof.*

lay some sweet lines on someone AND **put some sweet lines on** someone *tv.* to speak kindly to someone; to flatter someone. □ *I just laid some sweet lines on her, and she let me use her car.* □ *If you put some sweet lines on him, maybe he won't ground you.*

leeky store ['liki stor] *n.* a liquor store. (Black. From *liquor*.) □ *Get me some grapes at the leeky store.*

let a fart Go to cut a fart.

let one Go to cut a fart.

lettuce *n.* money. □ *Put your lettuce on the table. Then we'll talk.*

lid *n.* an eyelid. □ *Her lids began to close, and the professor raised his voice to a roar.* □ *Pop your lids open! It's morning!*

lifted *mod.* drunk; high. □ *He was acting a little lifted. He only had 12 beers.*

light *n.* an eye. (Usually plural.) □ *You want I should poke your lights out?* □ *Open your lights and watch for the turnoff sign.*

Like I care. *phr.* You are telling me this news like it matters to me. (Nonchalant and sarcastic.) □ *So, there's problems in South America. Like I care.*

Like it's such a big deal. *phr.* You are making an incredible fuss over some minor issue. □ *So I broke the table. Like it's such a big deal.*

line *n.* a story or argument; a story intended to seduce someone. (See also lines.) □ *Don't feed me that line. Do you think I was born yesterday?*

lines *n.* words; conversation. (Black. See also line.) □ *I like your lines, but I don't have the time.* □ *We tossed some lines back and forth for a while and then split.*

lip 1. *tv. & iv.* to kiss someone intimately. □ *The two of them were in the corner, lipping intently.* **2.** *n.* a lawyer. (Underworld.) □ *So I brought in my lip, and he got me off the rap.* □ *How much do you pay your lip?* **3.** AND **fat lip** *n.* back talk; impudent talk. □ *Don't give me any more of your lip!*

L.I.Q. *n.* a liquor store. (Black. Also an acronym.) □ *Let's stop at the L.I.Q. and get some berries.* □ *I got a headache already. I don't need anything from any L.I.Q. to make it worse.*

liquid laugh *n.* vomit. □ *If you drink much more, you're gonna come out with a liquid laugh.* □ *There's some liquid laugh on your shoe.*

little shit *n.* a stupid and insignificant person. (Rude and derogatory. Usually refers to a male.) □ *What's a little shit like him doing running a big company like this one?*

loady AND **loadie** ['lodi] *n.* a drinker or drug user. (Teens and collegiate.) □ *These loadies are all very difficult to deal with.*

long bread AND **long green** *n.* money. (Black.) □ *Man, that must have cost you some long bread!* □ *Look at the long green you get for doing the job!*

long green Go to long bread.

loo *n.* toilet. (Originally and primarily British.) □ *I gotta use the loo. Be with you in a minute.*

Look (at) what the cat dragged in! *command* Well, look who has just arrived! □ *Look what the cat dragged in! I thought you would never get here.*

loony AND **looney; loonie** ['luni] **1.** *n.* a crazy person. (From lunatic.) □ *I'm beginning to feel like a loonie the longer I stay around here.* **2.** *mod.* crazy. □ *That is a loony idea. Forget it.* **3.** *mod.* alcohol intoxicated. □ *She's acting a little loonie. Let's get her home before she's sick.*

loose cannon *n.* a loudmouth; a braggart. □ *As it turned out, he's not just a loose cannon. He makes sense.* □ *Some loose cannon in the State Department has been feeding the press all sorts of crap as a diversion.*

lorg ['lorg] *n.* a stupid person. □ *Why is Frank such a lorg? Can't he get with it?*

lose it 1. *tv.* to empty one's stomach; to vomit. (Collegiate.) □ *Oh, God! I think I'm going to lose it!* **2.** *tv.* to get angry; to lose one's temper. □ *It was too much for him. Ted lost it.* □ *I sat there calmly, biting my lip to keep from losing it.*

lose one's **doughnuts** Go to blow one's doughnuts.

lose one's **lunch** Go to blow (one's) lunch.

loser ['luzɚ] *n.* an inept person; an undesirable or annoying person. □ *Dave is a real loser.*

love bombs *n.* affirmations of affection. □ *These two were dropping love bombs on each other, even though they hate each other's guts.* □ *What a phony bunch of kooks. They were throwing love bombs all over the place!*

love handles *n.* a roll of fat around the waist. □ *I wish I could get rid of these love handles.* □ *Are you troubled with a spare tire or love handles? Here is a product that has helped thousands and will help you!*

low five *n.* the slapping of hands at waist level as a greeting. (Compare to **high five.**) □ *They turned to each other, throwing a quick low five as they passed.* □ *The two eight-year-olds tried to give each other a low five, but they both hurt their hands.*

lowlife 1. *n.* a low person; a repellent person. □ *Hey, lowlife, keep out of my way.* **2.** *mod.* mean; belligerent. (Black.) □ *We don't need any lowlife characters around here.*

low rent 1. *n.* a low person; someone without grace or spirit. (Also a rude term of address.) □ *Look, low rent, where is what you owe me?* □ *This low rent here thinks he can push Reggie around, huh?* **2.** *mod.* cheap; unfashionable. □ *This place is strictly low rent.* □ *Why don't you go live with some of your low rent friends?*

lube *n.* butter. □ *Pass the lube, will ya, huh?*

lucci *n.* money. (Possibly from *lucre* "money, reward" as in *filthy lucre*.) □ *Can you loan me some of that lucci?*

luck out *iv.* to be fortunate; to strike it lucky. □ *I really lucked out when I ordered the duck. It's excellent.*

lung-butter *n.* vomit. □ *God, you got lung-butter on my shoe!*

lunger *n.* a gob of coughed-up mucus. □ *That's not a fried egg. It's more like a lunger!* □ *He rumbled and coughed up another lunger. This one just dropped onto his shirt.*

lurker *n.* someone who reads the messages in an Internet news group without responding or participating. (Sometimes considered derogatory.) □ *These lurkers read everything but never contribute.*

mace someone's face ['mes . . .] *tv.* to do something drastic to someone, such as spraying mace in the face. (Chemical Mace™ is a brand of tear gas sold in pressurized cans for personal protection.) □ *Do you want me to mace your face? Then shut up!* □ *I look at him, and suddenly I just want to mace his face or something.*

mack *n.* a pimp. (From *mackerel,* a form of which once had the meaning "broker.") □ *This gal's mack was slapping her silly when the police came.*

mack daddy *n.* a man who is popular with the ladies. □ *Sam is a real mack daddy. Sure knows how to treat the ladies.*

mack on someone **1.** *iv.* to make a sexual proposition to someone. □ *You try to mack on anything that wears a skirt!* **2.** *iv.* to kiss and caress someone. □ *Sam is in the back room macking on Mary.*

mac out *iv.* to overeat, especially the type of food served at McDonald's fast food restaurants. (From the Big Mac™ sandwich. See also blimp out, pig out, pork out, scarf out.) □ *I've been in Europe for a month, and I just want to get home and mac out.* □ *I mac out every weekend. It's like going to church.*

maggot 1. *n.* a cigarette. □ *Can I bum a maggot off of you?* **2.** *n.* a low and wretched person; a vile person. □ *You maggot! Take your hands off me!*

magic bullet Go to silver bullet.

mail *n.* money. □ *The bills are due. I need some mail.*

major *mod.* excellent. (Collegiate.) □ *This rally is, like, major!*

Make a lap! *exclam.* to sit down. □ *Hey, make a lap and get out of the way!* □ *Pull up a chair and make a lap!*

make a mountain AND **pitch a tent** *tv.* to have a morning erection that raises the bed covers; to have an erection that makes a bulge in one's clothing; to get an erection. □ *Bobby makes a mountain almost every morning.*

Make my day! *exclam.* Go ahead, do what you are going to do, and I will be very happy to do what I have to do! (A catchphrase said typically by a movie police officer who has a gun pointed at a criminal. The police officer wants the criminal to do something that will justify pulling the trigger, which the police officer will do with pleasure. Used in real life in any context, and especially in sarcasm.) □ *Move a muscle! Go for your gun! Go ahead, make my day!* □ *Make my day! Just try it.*

make waves *tv.* to cause difficulty. □ *Just relax. Don't make waves.* □ *If you make waves too much around here, you won't last long.*

make with the something *iv.* to make something visible; to use something. □ *I want to know. Come on, make with the answers!*

mallet *n.* a police officer. (Black.) □ *Some mallet is going around asking questions about you.*

map 1. *n.* one's face. □ *With a map like that, she could really go somewhere.* **2.** *n.* sheet music. (Jazz musicians. See also **chart**.) □ *I left the map at home. Can I look at yours?*

Mary J. Go to Mary Jane.

Mary Jane 1. AND **Mary J.; Maryjane** *n.* marijuana. (Drugs.) □ *I can't live another day without Mary Jane!* **2.** *n.* a plain-looking girl. □ *She's just a Mary Jane and will never be a glamour girl.*

maw ['mɔ] *tv. & iv.* to kiss and pet; to smooch. (Probably from maul.) □ *Come on, don't maw me. You've been watching too many movies—or too few.* □ *Let's go out somewhere and maw.*

max *n.* the maximum. □ *I want the max. I'm hungry.*

maxed out 1. *mod.* exhausted; tired. □ *I am just maxed out. I haven't been getting enough sleep.* **2.** *mod.* alcohol intoxicated. □ *Sam was maxed out and seemed happy enough to sit under the table and whimper.* □ *I hadn't seen Marlowe so maxed out in years. He was nearly paralyzed.*

mazulla Go to mazuma.

mazuma AND **mazulla** [mə'zumə AND mə'zulə] *n.* money. (From Hebrew *mezu* via Yiddish.) □ *She's got more mazuma than she knows what to do with.*

McD's AND **McDuck's** n. McDonald's, the franchised fast-food restaurant. (Teens and collegiate. The *duck* is a play on the Walt Disney character Donald Duck.) □ *Can you take McD's tonight, or do you want some slow food?*

McDuck's Go to McD's.

meals rejected by the enemy Go to M.R.E.

mean *mod.* having to do with someone or something that is very good. □ *This is the meanest box wine I ever drank.*

mean-green n. money. □ *Can I borrow a little mean-green till payday?*

mega ['mɛgə] *mod.* large. □ *Some mega beast boogied down to the front of the auditorium and started screaming.* □ *You see I have this, like, mega problem, ya know.*

megabucks ['mɛgəbəks] n. a lot of money. (See also kilobucks.) □ *A stereo that size must cost megabucks.*

megadork ['mɛgədork] n. a very stupid person. (See also dork.) □ *Tiffany, you are, like, such a megadork!*

mellow 1. *mod.* relaxed; untroubled. □ *She is the mellowest fox I know.* **2.** *mod.* slightly alcohol or drug intoxicated. □ *I got mellow and stopped drinking right there.*

mellow out 1. *iv.* to calm down; to get less angry. □ *When you mellow out, maybe we can talk.* **2.** *iv.* to become generally more relaxed; to grow less contentious. □ *Gary was nearly 40 before he started to mellow out a little and take life less seriously.* □ *After his illness, he mellowed out and seemed more glad to be alive.*

meltdown n. a total collapse of anything. (From the term used to describe the self-destruction of a nuclear reactor.) □ *There seems to have been a meltdown in the computer center, and all our records were lost.* □ *The meltdown in the financial markets was caused by a combination of things.*

melvin ['mɛlvən] n. a studious or unattractive male. (Teens and collegiate.) □ *Do you think I would go out with that melvin?*

mess 1. n. a hopeless, stupid person. □ *Harry has turned into a mess.* **2.** n. dung. □ *There is a dog mess on the lawn again this morning.*

mess someone's face up *tv.* to beat someone around the face. □ *I had to mess his face up a little, boss, but he's been real coopera-*

tive since then. ⊤ *You want me to mess up your face, or do you want to come along quietly?*

Mickey D's *n.* McDonald's fast-food restaurant. (Teens and collegiate.) □ *Let's hit Mickey D's for chow this noon.*

mickey mouse 1. *n.* nonsense; something trivial. (From the Walt Disney character by the same name.) □ *This is just a lot of mickey mouse.* **2.** *mod.* trivial; time wasting; lousy. □ *I want out of this mickey mouse place.* **3.** *n.* a police officer. (Streets.) □ *Mickey mouse is hanging around asking about you.*

miffed ['mɪft] *mod.* slighted; offended. □ *Don't get so miffed. It was only a joke.*

mink *n.* a woman. (Black.) □ *Take this home to your mink. She'll like it.*

mitt *n.* a hand. □ *Get your mitts off my glass.* □ *The kid's got mitts on him like a gorilla.*

moby ['mobi] **1.** *mod.* enormous; unwieldy. (Like Herman Melville's great white whale, Moby Dick.) □ *This is a very moby old car.* **2.** *n.* a megabyte, a measurement of computer memory size. (A megabyte is whale-sized compared to a kilobyte.) □ *My fixed disks give me a capacity of over 75 mobies.* □ *My new computer has one moby of random access memory.*

mongo *mod.* greatly; hugely. (Probably akin to **humongous**.) □ *When I get some cash, I'm gonna buy me one mongo car with leather seats.*

monkey bite *n.* a kiss that leaves a blotch or mark. (See also hick(e)y.) □ *Who gave you that monkey bite?*

monkey-fart AND **fiddle-fart** *iv.* to waste time; to do something ineffectually or inefficiently. (A blend of *monkey around* and *fart around*.) □ *Stop monkey-farting and get over here and get to work.* □ *He spent the day fiddle-farting with his motorcycle.*

monolithic [mɑnə'lɪθɪk] *mod.* heavily drug intoxicated. (A play on stoned (out).) □ *She's not just stoned, she's monolithic!*

mooley *n.* a clever person who does funny things. □ *What a mooley! Always making us laugh.*

moon 1. *n.* the buttocks. □ *She fell square on her moon and slowly broke into a smile.* **2.** *tv. & iv.* to show (someone) one's nude posterior through a window (usually of an automobile). (Compare to **gaucho**.) □ *When the plane flew over Cuba, this guy named Victor actually mooned a Russian M.I.G. that flew by.*

mope 1. *n.* a tired and ineffectual person. □ *I can't afford to pay mopes around here. Get to work or get out!* **2.** AND **mope around** *iv.* to move around slowly and sadly. □ *He just mopes around all day and won't eat anything.*

mope around Go to **mope**.

motor-mouth Go to **ratchet-mouth**.

mouth-breather *n.* a stupid-acting person. □ *I always end up with a mouth-breather on a blind date.*

mouthwash *n.* liquor; a drink of liquor. □ *You could use a little mouthwash after that long trip, I bet.*

move on someone *iv.* to attempt to pick up someone; to attempt to seduce someone. (Collegiate.) □ *Don't try to move on my date, old chum.*

movies *n.* a case of diarrhea. □ *A case of the movies kept me going all night.*

M.R.E. AND **meals rejected by the enemy** *n.* meals ready to eat, prepackaged food used by the armed forces in combat. □ *Where is my MRE? I'm tired of living.*

M.T. *n.* an empty bottle. □ *Put your M.T.s in the garbage.*

mud duck *n.* an ugly person. □ *Sam is a real mud duck, but the women seem to like him.*

munchkin ['mǝntʃkǝn] *n.* a small or insignificant person. □ *You're not going to let that munchkin push you around, are you?*

munch out *iv.* to eat ravenously. (See also **pig out**.) □ *I had to munch out after the party. I can't imagine why.*

mung 1. AND **MUNG** ['mǝŋ] *n.* something that is mashed until no good; anything nasty or gooey. □ *Get this mung off my plate!* **2.** *tv.* to ruin something. □ *You munged my car!*

mung something **up** *tv.* to mess something up. □ *Don't mung it up this time.* Ⓣ *The team munged up the play, and the coach blasted them but good.*

mungy ['mǝŋi] *mod.* messy. □ *The spaghetti was cold and mungy by the time it was served.*

mush 1. *n.* nonsense. □ *What mush! Come on, talk straight!* **2.** *n.* romance; lovemaking; kissing. □ *When an actor looks at an actress like that, you just know that there's gonna be some mush.* **3.** *n.* one's face. (Crude.) □ *With a mush like that, you ought to be in pictures. Maybe another King Kong remake.*

musical beds *n.* acts of sexual promiscuity; sleeping with many people. (From the name of the game *musical chairs*.) □ *Mary has been playing musical beds for about a year.*

My bad. *phr.* It's my fault and I'm sorry. □ *My bad. It won't happen again.*

M.Y.O.B. *tv.* Mind your own business. □ *This doesn't concern you. M.Y.O.B.*

my tenda *n.* my sweetheart; my lover; my tender [one]. □ *Come here, my tenda. I want some kissing.*

nada ['nɑdɑ] *n.* nothing; none. (Spanish.) □ *The score was nada to nada.*

nads *n.* testicles. (From *gonads*.) □ *He got hit in the nads in the football game.*

narked ['nɑrkt] *mod.* annoyed. (Usually with *at* or *with*.) □ *She is narked with you and your car.*

narky ['nɑrki] *n.* a narcotic drug. □ *They caught him with a lot of narky in his pockets.*

nause someone out *tv.* to nauseate someone. □ *That horrible smell really nauses me out.*

nay *mod.* ugly; unfavorable. (From *nasty*.) □ *What a nay thing to say.*

neat 1. *mod.* great; cool; fine. □ *That was not a very neat thing to do.* **2.** *exclam.* Wow! (Usually **Neat!**) □ *Neat! I'm glad you came.*

the **necessary** *n.* money; an income. □ *I can always use more of the necessary.*

negative 1. *n.* any drawback or bad thing about someone or something. □ *I know another negative you didn't mention.* **2.** *n.* a bad experience. □ *Carl had one negative after another.*

negatory *mod.* no; negative. □ *Q: Are you going to leave now? A: Negatory.*

nerd AND **nurd** ['nɚd] *n.* a dull and bookish person, usually a male. □ *That whole gang of boys is just a bunch of nurds!*

nerd mobile *n.* a full-sized, uninteresting car; a family car. □ *My father always buys some kind of stupid nerd mobile.*

nerd pack *n.* a plastic sheath for holding pens in a pocket, protecting the cloth from ink. (This is the classic symbol of a bookish **nerd**.) □ *A real nerd wears a nerd pack in the pocket of a dirty shirt.*

nerts Go to nurts.

nick 1. *tv.* to arrest someone. □ *The cops nicked Paul outside his house.* **2.** *tv.* to steal something. □ *The thugs nicked a couple of apples from the fruit stand.* **3.** *tv.* to get or take something. □ *Tom nicked a copy of the test for Sam, who also needed one.*

nip 1. *n.* a small, quick drink of liquor. □ *One nip is enough. That is powerful!* **2.** *tv.* to steal something. □ *The punk kid nipped two candy bars from the drugstore.*

nipply *mod.* [of weather] cold. (A play on *nippy* [weather] and what such weather may do to the human nipples.) □ *It's a little nipply out this morning.*

nix ['nɪks] **1.** *interj.* no. (All senses from German *nichts*.) □ *Nix, I won't do it.* **2.** *exclam.* No!; Stop it!; I disagree! (Usually **Nix!**) □ *"Nix," said Paul. "I can't permit that."* **3.** *n.* nothing. □ *What did I get for all my trouble? Nix!* **4.** *tv.* to put a stop to something; to say no to something; to ban something. □ *The boss nixed my plan.*

no great shakes *phr.* someone or something not very good. (There is no affirmative version of this.) □ *Your idea is no great shakes, but we'll try it anyway.*

noid *n.* a paranoid person. □ *Some of those noids write hilarious letters to the editor.*

noodge Go to nudge.

noogie *n.* a painful rubbing of someone's scalp with the knuckles. □ *Bob gave Bill a noogie and Bill punched him in the gut.*

No problem. AND **No prob.** *phr.* All is well.; There is no problem, so don't worry or fret. (Often said after someone else says "I'm sorry.") □ *A: Gee! I'm sorry! B: No prob.*

nose-lunger *n.* a glob of nasal mucus. (*Lunger* is an old slang term for a mass of coughed-up mucus.) □ *He sneezed, and this great nose-lunger flew across the room. Yechchch!*

No shinola! *exclam.* No shit!; You are not kidding are you? (From *know shit from shinola*. Cryptic and jocular.) □ *So you wanna be a radio announcer. No Shinola!* □ *No shinola! I wouldn't lie to you!*

No shit! *exclam.* You are kidding me, aren't you! (Usually objectionable.) □ *You're really gonna do it? No shit!*

no stress *interj.* no problem; no bother. □ *Relax. No stress. It doesn't bother me at all.*

no sweat *interj.* no problem; Don't worry; it is no problem. □ *It's no big deal. No sweat.* □ *No sweat, don't fret about it.*

notch *tv.* to count up something; to add up or score something. □ *Well, it looks like we notched another victory.*

not enough room to swing a cat *phr.* very crowded or cramped; [of a room] small. □ *It's really crowded in here. Not enough room to swing a cat.*

not know one's **ass from a hole in the ground** *tv.* not to be knowledgeable; not to be alert and effective. (Usually objectionable.) □ *That stupid son of a bitch doesn't know his ass from a hole in the ground.* □ *She is so dumb, she doesn't know her ass from a hole in the ground.*

not know shit about something *tv.* not to know anything about something. □ *You've worked here for a month, and you don't know shit about this job!*

not know shit from shinola *tv.* to know what's what; to be knowledgeable in the ways of the world. (See also **No shinola!** Usually objectionable.) □ *That jerk doesn't know shit from shinola! Don't even ask him about it!*

No way! *exclam.* No! □ *Me join the Army? No way!*

nowhere *mod.* bad; no good; dull. □ *This place is really nowhere. Let's go.* □ *I want to get out of this nowhere party.*

nudge AND **noodge** ['nʊdʒ] **1.** *n.* someone who nags. □ *I really can't stand a noodge.* **2.** *iv.* to nag. □ *Don't noodge all the time.* **3.** *tv.* to nag someone. □ *Stop nudging me about that.*

nuggets *n.* the testicles. □ *Man, my nuggets are cold! Let's hurry up and get back in the car.*

nuke 1. *n.* a nuclear weapon. □ *Are there nukes aboard that ship?* **2.** *tv.* to destroy someone or something. (As with a nuclear weapon.) □ *Your cat ran through my garden and totally nuked my flowers!* **3.** *tv.* to cook something with a microwave oven. □ *I'm going to go home and nuke me a nice meal.*

Nuke it! *tv.* Throw it away! □ *You don't need this thing. Nuke it!*

number one 1. *mod.* top rate; best; closest. □ *We heard the number one high school band in the whole state last night.* □ *This is my* *number one buddy, Tom.* **2.** *n.* oneself. □ *I don't know who will pay for the broken window, but old number one isn't!* □ *Everything always comes back to number one. I have to solve everybody's problems.* **3.** *n.* urination; an act of urination. □ *Jimmy made a mess in his pants. But don't worry. It's just number one.*

number two *n.* defecation; an act of defecation. □ *Mommy! I gotta do a number two.*

numbnuts *n.* a jerk; a worthless person. (Usually a male.) □ *Hey, numbnuts! What did you do that for?*

nurd Go to nerd.

nurts AND **nerts** ['nɚts] *n.* nonsense. □ *Don't talk that kind of nurts to me!* □ *Oh, that's just nerts. I don't believe a word of it.*

nut 1. *n.* an odd or strange person; a crazy person. □ *Who is that nut over there in the corner?* **2.** *n.* [someone's] head. □ *The baseball came in fast. "Clonk!" Right on the nut!* **3.** *n.* an enthusiast (about something). □ *Paul is a nut about chocolate cake.*

nuts 1. *mod.* crazy. □ *You're nuts if you think I care.* □ *That whole idea is just nuts!* **2.** *exclam.* No!; I don't believe you!; I don't care! (Usually **Nuts!**) □ *Nuts! You don't know what you are talking about.* □ *Oh, nuts! I forgot my wallet.*

nut up *iv.* to go crazy; to go nuts. □ *I've got to have a vacation soon, or I'm going to nut up.*

occifer Go to ossifer.

off artist Go to rip-off artist.

offed Go to outed.

off the hook 1. *mod.* no longer in jeopardy; no longer obligated. □ *I'll let you off the hook this time, but never again.* **2.** *mod.* crazy. (Referring to the telephone—disconnected.) □ *She's so weird—really off the hook.*

oink ['oɪŋk] *n.* a police officer. (A play on **pig**.) □ *There is an oink following us on a motorcycle.*

O.K. AND **okay 1.** *interj.* accepted. (This may be originally from a jocular *oll kerrect*.) □ *So, he said, like, "okay," and, like, I go "okay." So we both go "Okay." Okay?* **2.** *mod.* acceptable. □ *This cake is okay, but not what I would call first-rate.* **3.** *mod.* acceptably. □ *She ran okay—nothing spectacular.* **4.** *n.* [someone's] acceptance. □ *I won't give the final okay until I see the plans.*

okay Go to O.K.

old skool *mod.* old fashioned; out-of-style; no longer trendy. □ *Man, your haircut is strictly old skool.*

one-eyed pants mouse Go to bald-headed hermit.

on one's **ass** Go to flat on one's ass.

on your six *phr.* behind you. (At one's *six o'clock*.) □ *Look out! On your six!*

O.P.P. *n.* other people's property. □ *You ain't got respect for O.P.P.*

O-sign *n.* the rounded, open mouth of a dead person. (A semijocular usage. Hospitals. See also **Q-sign**.) □ *The guy in room 226 is giving the O-sign.*

ossifer AND **occifer** ['ɑsəfɚ] *n.* a police officer. (Also an ill-advised term of address.) □ *Look here, ossifer, I was just having a little fun.*

out 1. *mod.* alcohol or drug intoxicated. (Probably from **far out**.) □ *Those guys are really out!* **2.** *mod.* out of fashion. (The opposite of in.) □ *That kind of clothing is strictly out.* **3.** *tv.* to make someone's homosexuality public. (Can be reflexive.) □ *He outed himself at the party last Friday.*

outed 1. AND **offed** *mod.* dead; killed. □ *The witness was outed before a subpoena could be issued.* □ *The guy was offed when we found him.* **2.** *mod.* having had one's homosexual identity made public. (Not prenominal.) □ *Yes, he's outed, but he hasn't told his parents.*

out of pocket *mod.* out from under someone's control; not manageable. □ *The guy is wild. Completely out of pocket.*

packing (a gun) *mod.* carrying a gun. ☐ *The crook was packing a gun and carrying a knife in his hand.*

pad *n.* a place to live; one's room or dwelling. ☐ *Why don't you come over to my pad for a while?*

pad out *iv.* to go to bed or to sleep. (See also **pad**.) ☐ *Man, if I don't pad out by midnight, I'm a zombie.* ☐ *Why don't you people go home so I can pad out?*

pain in the ass AND **pain in the butt; pain in the rear (end)** *n.* a very annoying thing or person. (Crude. An elaboration of *pain*. Caution with **ass**. Butt is less offensive. **Rear (end)** is euphemistic.) ☐ *That guy is a real pain in the ass.* ☐ *You are nothing but a pain in the rear.*

pain in the butt Go to pain in the ass.

pain in the neck *n.* a difficult or annoying thing or person. (Compare to **pain in the ass**.) ☐ *This tax form is a pain in the neck.* ☐ *My boss is a pain in the neck.*

pain in the rear (end) Go to pain in the ass.

panic *n.* a very funny or exciting person or thing. ☐ *John's party was a real panic.* ☐ *Paul is a panic. He tells a joke a minute.*

paper 1. *n.* a written document; written evidence supporting something. (Often with *some*.) ☐ *Send me some paper. Let's make this official.* **2.** *n.* a forged check. (See also **paper-pusher**.) ☐ *She was arrested for passing paper.* **3.** *n.* money. ☐ *You don't get the goods till I get the paper.*

paper-pusher 1. *n.* a bureaucrat; a clerk in the military services; any office worker. (See also **pencil-pusher**.) ☐ *If those paper-pushers can't get their work done on time, make them stay late.* ☐ *I don't want to talk to some paper-pusher, I want to talk to the boss.* **2.** *n.* someone who passes bad checks. ☐ *The bank teller spotted* *a well-known paper-pusher and called the cops.* □ *The old lady was charged as a paper-pusher and sent to jail.*

paperweight *n.* a serious student; a hardworking student. □ *What a jerk! Nothing but a paperweight.*

pard *n.* partner. (From *pardner* [partner]. Also a term of address.) □ *Come on, pard, let's go find some action.*

(parental) units *n.* parents. (Teens. Also a term of address.) □ *I don't think my parental units will let me stay out that late.* □ *Hey, units! I need to talk to you about something really important.*

park it (somewhere) *tv.* to sit down somewhere; to sit down and get out of the way. □ *Carl, park it over there in the corner. Stop pacing around. You make me nervous.*

party *iv.* to celebrate; to spend a lot of time at drinking or drugging or other "party" activities. (See also **rally**.) □ *She did nothing but party at school.*

party animal *n.* someone who loves parties. □ *If you weren't such a party animal, you'd have more time for studying.*

pass go *tv.* to complete a difficult or dangerous task successfully. (From "pass go and collect $200" in the game Monopoly™.) □ *Man, I tried to get there on time, but I just couldn't pass go.*

pasting *n.* a beating; a defeat in a game. □ *Our team took quite a pasting last weekend.*

paw 1. *n.* someone's hand. (Jocular.) □ *Get your paws off me!* **2.** *tv.* to feel someone or handle someone sexually. □ *I can't stand men who paw you to pieces.*

payback *n.* retribution. □ *You hit me, I hit you. That's your payback.*

payola [pe'olə] *n.* a bribe. (Originally a bribe paid to a **disk jockey** by record producers to get extra attention for their records.) □ *The announcer was fired for taking payola.*

peanuts *n.* practically no money at all. □ *The cost is just peanuts compared to what you get for the money.*

pec(k)s AND **pects** ['pɛks AND 'pɛkts] *n.* the pectoral muscles. (From weight lifting and bodybuilding.) □ *Look at the pecks on that guy!*

pects Go to pec(k)s.

peep 1. *n.* a noise; an utterance. □ *Don't you make another peep!* **2.** *n.* people. (Often plural, *peeps.*) □ *How many peeps were there?*

peepers *n.* the eyes. □ *Come on, use your peepers. Take a good look.*

pencil-pusher *n.* a bureaucrat; a clerk; an office worker. (See also **paper-pusher**.) □ *City Hall is filled with a bunch of overpaid pencil-pushers.*

penny *n.* a police officer. (A play on **copper**. See the note at **copper**.) □ *The penny over on the corner told the boys to get moving.*

Period! *exclam.* . . . and that's final! (A way of indicating that there will be no more discussion or negotiation.) □ *I don't want to hear any more about it! Period!* □ *My final offer is $30. Period!*

perking *mod.* intoxicated; **stoned (out)**. □ *The guys are really perking. They've had too much to drink.*

petrified *mod.* alcohol intoxicated. (Literally, turned into stone. Another way of saying **stoned (out)**.) □ *He drank beer till he was petrified.*

P.F.M. *n.* pure fucking magic, absolutely astounding. □ *The whole evening was P.F.M.! I had a great time!*

P.G. *mod.* pregnant. □ *Do you think Sally's P.G.?*

phat AND **PHAT 1.** *mod.* good; excellent. (This is essentially a respelling of **fat**, and has the same meaning that **fat** has.) □ *His new car is really phat.* □ *Who is that phat chick you were with?* **2.** *phr.* pretty hips and thighs. (Initialism. A reinterpretation of the spelling.) □ *Now, that's what I like, PHAT.* □ *PHAT is what it's all about.*

phfft ['ffft] **1.** *mod.* done for; dead. (See also **piffed**.) □ *There is my cat, and zoom comes a car. My cat is phfft.* □ *Yup. Deader than a doornail. Phfft!* **2.** *mod.* alcohol intoxicated. □ *You won't wake him up for hours yet. He's phfft.*

phooey AND **fooey 1.** *n.* nonsense. □ *Your story is just a lot of phooey.* □ *I've heard enough fooey. Let's get out of here.* **2.** *exclam.* an expression of disgust, disagreement, or resignation. (Usually **Phooey!** or **Fooey!** Used typically when something smells or tastes bad.) □ *Who died in here? Phooey!* □ *This is the worst food I ever ate. Fooey!*

phreak *n.* <a respelling of *freak*.> □ *You stupid phreak! Why'd you do that?*

phunky Go to funky.

phutz AND **futz** ['fəts] *tv.* to rob, swindle, or cheat someone. □ *Don't futz me! Tell the truth!* □ *The muggers phutzed his wallet and watch.*

pickled *mod.* alcohol intoxicated. (Very common.) □ *It only takes a few drinks to get him pickled.*

piddle (around) *iv.* to waste time; to work aimlessly or inefficiently. □ *Stop piddling around! Get to work!* □ *Can't you get serious and stop piddling?*

piece of ass AND **hunk of ass; hunk of tail; piece of snatch; piece of tail 1.** *n.* someone considered as a partner in copulation. (Usually a female. Usually objectionable.) □ *Man, isn't she a fine looking piece of ass?* **2.** *n.* an act of copulation; copulation with someone. (Usually objectionable.) □ *If Todd doesn't get a hunk of tail once a day, he's real grouchy.*

piece of cake 1. *n.* something easy to do. □ *No problem. When you know what you're doing, it's a piece of cake.* **2.** *exclam.* It's a piece of cake!; It's easy! (Usually **Piece of cake!**) □ *No problem, piece of cake!*

piece of snatch Go to piece of ass.

piece of tail Go to piece of ass.

pie hole Go to word hole.

piff AND **pift** ['pɪf, 'pɪft] *tv.* to kill someone or something. (See also phfft.) □ *He piffed his goldfish by mistake.*

pifted ['pɪftəd] *mod.* dead. □ *What will I do with a pifted cat?*

pifted Go to piffed.

pig 1. *n.* someone who eats too much; a glutton. (All senses are usually derogatory.) □ *Stop being a pig! Save some for other people.* **2.** *n.* an ugly and fat woman. □ *Clare is a pig. Why doesn't she lose a ton or two?* **3.** *n.* a dirty or slovenly person. (Also a rude term of address.) □ *Carl is a pig. I don't think he bathes enough.* **4.** *n.* an officer; a police officer or a military officer. (Derogatory. Used mostly for a police officer. Widely known since the 1960s.) □ *The pigs are coming to bust up the fight.*

pig out *iv.* to overeat; to overindulge in food or drink. (Compare to blimp out, mac out, pork out, scarf out.) □ *I can't help myself when I see ice cream. I have to pig out.*

pile of shit 1. *n.* a mass of lies. (Refers to **bullshit**. Usually objectionable.) □ *He came in and told me this great pile of shit about how his alarm clock was in the shop.* □ *Don't give me that pile of shit! I know the truth!* **2.** *n.* any worthless structure or device. (Usually objectionable.) □ *Take this pile of shit back where you bought it and get your money back.* **3.** *n.* a totally worthless person. (Rude and derogatory.) □ *Don't be such a pile of shit!*

pin 1. *n.* someone's leg. (Usually plural.) □ *My pins are a little wobbly.* **2.** *n.* an important criminal leader. (From *kingpin.*) □ *The mob's getting careless. The cops think they caught the pin this time.*

pinch 1. *n.* a small amount of a powdered substance, such as salt, snuff, a spice, etc. (Not slang.) □ *He put a pinch under his lips and walked up to home plate.* **2.** *tv.* to arrest someone. □ *The police captain pinched her for passing bad checks.* **3.** *n.* the arresting of someone. □ *They made the pinch in front of her house.*

pinstriper *n.* a businessman or businesswoman wearing a pinstriped suit. (Compare to **suit, vest**.) □ *Who's the pinstriper driving the big black car?*

pip *n.* a pimple; a **zit**. □ *Good grief, I've got ear-to-ear pips!*

pipe *n.* an easy course in school. □ *Take this course. It's a pipe.*

piss 1. *iv.* to urinate. (Usually objectionable.) □ *Who pissed on the floor of the john?* **2.** *n.* urine. (Usually objectionable.) □ *You got piss on your pants leg.* **3.** *n.* bad beer; bad liquor; any bad-tasting or poor quality liquid. (Usually objectionable.) □ *How about another can of that piss you serve here?*

pissant AND **piss-ant 1.** *n.* a wretched and worthless person. □ *Look, you silly pissant, beat it!* **2.** *mod.* worthless. □ *I don't want this little pissant piece of pie. Give me a real piece.* □ *Who is this pissant shithead who thinks he can tell me what to do?*

piss around *iv.* to waste time; to be inefficient at something. (Usually objectionable.) □ *I can't piss around here all day! Let's get going!*

piss blood AND **sweat blood 1.** *tv.* to experience great anxiety. (Usually objectionable.) □ *He made me piss blood before he agreed.* **2.** *tv.* to expend an enormous amount of energy. (Usually objectionable.) □ *I pissed blood to come in first in the race.*

piss-cutter AND **piss-whiz** *n.* an extraordinary person; someone who can do the impossible. (Usually objectionable.) □ *Sam is a* *real piss-cutter when it comes to running.* □ *Todd's no piss-whiz as a batter, but he can really pitch!*

pissed 1. *mod.* alcohol intoxicated. (Caution with **pissed**.) □ *He was so pissed he could hardly stand up.* **2.** Go to **pissed (off)**.

pissed (off) *mod.* angry. (Crude. Caution with **piss**. Compare to **piss** someone **off**.) □ *He's come back, and he's sure pissed.*

pissed off about someone or something Go to **pissed (off) (at** someone or something**)**.

pissed (off) (at someone or something**)** AND **pissed off about** someone or something *mod.* very angry with or about someone or something. (Usually objectionable.) □ *She's always pissed off about something.* □ *Man, is that guy pissed off!*

piss elegant *mod.* very pretentious; overly elegant. (Usually objectionable.) □ *Man, this place is piss elegant. Look at them lamp shades!* □ *I ain't never seen such a piss-elegant bathroom!*

pisser 1. *n.* a urinal; a place [room, restroom] to urinate. (Usually objectionable.) □ *Who keeps missing the pisser?* **2.** *n.* a remarkable thing or person. (Usually objectionable.) □ *Man, isn't he a real pisser! Have you ever seen anybody bat like that?* □ *She's no pisser, but she can get the job done.* **3.** *n.* a terribly funny joke. (You laugh so hard you wet your pants. Jocular. Usually objectionable.) □ *He told a real pisser and broke up the entire class.*

piss factory *n.* a bar, tavern, or saloon. (Usually objectionable.) □ *I stopped in at the piss factory for a round or two.*

pisshead 1. *n.* a wretched and disgusting person. (Rude and derogatory.) □ *How can you even think of going out with a pisshead like Sam?* **2.** *n.* a drunkard; a drunken person. (Rude and derogatory.) □ *Some old pisshead in the gutter must have given you that hat.*

pissing *mod.* worthless; minimal. (Usually objectionable.) □ *I'll be there in one pissing minute. Be quiet.*

pissing-match *n.* an argument; a pointless competition. (Usually objectionable.) □ *Let's call a halt to this pissing-match and get to work.*

piss in the wind *iv.* to do something that is futile and counterproductive; to waste one's time doing something. (Usually objectionable.) □ *I'm tired of pissing in the wind. I'm gonna look for a new job.*

piss off AND **P.O.** *iv.* to depart; to go away. (Usually objectionable.) □ *Piss off, you jerk! Get out!* □ *P.O.! Get out!*

Piss on it! *exclam.* To hell with it! (Usually objectionable.) □ *Oh, piss on it! I've had enough!*

piss on someone or something **1.** *iv.* to urinate on someone or something. (Usually objectionable.) □ *That dog pissed on my shoe!* **2.** *iv.* to degrade or denigrate someone or something. (Usually objectionable.) □ *He spent three paragraphs pissing on the play, then he said to go see it.* □ *He pissed on me and then said I tried my best. What does that mean?*

piss-poor 1. *mod.* of very poor quality. (Usually objectionable.) □ *This is piss-poor coffee. Pay the bill and let's go.* **2.** *mod.* without any money; broke. (Usually objectionable.) □ *Tell those piss-poor jerks to go beg somewhere else.*

piss someone **off** *tv.* to make someone angry. (Usually objectionable.) □ *Whatever you do, don't piss him off.*

piss something **away** *tv.* to waste all of something, such as time or money. (Usually objectionable.) □ *He pissed away the best possible chances.*

piss-whiz Go to piss-cutter.

pitch a bitch *tv.* to make a complaint. (Crude.) □ *You really love to pitch a bitch, don't you? What makes you happy?*

pitch a tent Go to make a mountain.

Pitch it! *exclam.* Throw it away. □ *We don't need it. Let's pitch it.*

pits *n.* the armpits. (Usually crude.) □ *Who's got the smelly pits in here?*

the **pits 1.** *n.* anything really bad. □ *This whole day was the pits from beginning to end.* **2.** *n.* the depths of despair. □ *It's always the pits with him.*

pit stop 1. *n.* a pause in a journey (usually by car) to urinate. (From the name of a service stop in automobile racing.) □ *I think we'll pull in at the next rest area. I need a pit stop.* **2.** *n.* an underarm deodorant. (Because it *stops* arm*pit* odor.) □ *Man, do you need some pit stop!*

pizza-face Go to crater-face.

plastered *mod.* alcohol intoxicated. □ *She's so plastered she can't see.*

plastic *mod.* phony; false. □ *She wears too much makeup and looks totally plastic.*

play 1. *n.* a strategy; a plan of action. □ *Here's a play that worked for us last year at this time.* **2.** *n.* an attractive investment; a way to make some money in the financial markets. □ *Not talking it over with your friends first was a bad play.*

playa *n.* a player; a womanizer. □ *Sam is a real playa and already has 8 kids.*

played (out) 1. *mod.* having to do with a portion of marijuana (in a cigarette or a pipe) that has had all of the effective substance smoked out of it. □ *This stuff is played. Get rid of it.* **2.** *mod.* worn-out; exhausted; no longer effective. □ *This scenario is played out. It no longer makes sense.* □ *I'm played. I have no new ideas.*

player *n.* someone who plays around, especially sexually. □ *He's a player, and I'm just a country girl who wanted to go dancing.* □ *I don't want a player. I want a good, solid homemaker type.*

play hide the sausage *tv.* an act of copulation. (Jocular. Usually objectionable.) □ *Then he said he wanted to play hide the sausage.*

play it cool 1. *tv.* to do something while not revealing insecurities or incompetence. (See also **cool**.) □ *Play it cool, man. Look like you belong there.* **2.** *tv.* to hold one's temper. □ *Come on now. Let it pass. Play it cool.*

play the dozens AND **shoot the dozens** *tv.* to trade insulting remarks concerning relatives with another person. (Chiefly black. See also the **(dirty) dozens.**) □ *They're out playing the dozens.* □ *Stop shooting the dozens and go do your homework.*

plootered ['pludɚd] *mod.* alcohol intoxicated. □ *How can anyone get so plootered on a bottle of wine?*

plop 1. *n.* the sound of dropping something soft and bulky, such as a hunk of meat. □ *When I heard the plop, I looked up and saw our dinner on the floor.* **2.** *tv.* to put or place something (somewhere). □ *I don't mind cooking a turkey. You only have to plop it in the oven and forget about it.* **3.** *tv.* to sit oneself down somewhere; to place one's buttocks somewhere. (The *it* in the examples is the buttocks.) □ *Come in, Fred. Just plop it anywhere you see a chair. This place is a mess.* □ *Just plop it down right there, and we'll have our little talk.*

plug 1. *n.* a bite-sized, pressed mass of chewing tobacco. □ *He put a plug in his cheek and walked away.* **2.** *n.* a drink of beer. □ *I just want a plug, not the whole thing.* **3.** *n.* a free advertisement or a commercial boost from someone for a product. □ *How about a free plug during your introduction?*

P.O. Go to **piss off.**

pocket pool *n.* the act of a male playing with his genitals with his hand in his pants pocket. (Usually objectionable.) □ *Stop playing pocket pool and get to work.*

pocket-rocket *n.* the penis. (Usually objectionable.) □ *He held his hands over his pocket-rocket and ran for the bedroom.*

P.O.ed *mod.* pissed off. □ *The teacher was P.O.ed at the whole class.*

poindexter ['pɔɪndɛkstɚ] *n.* a bookish person; a well-mannered good student, usually male. □ *I'm no poindexter. In fact, my grades are pretty low.*

pointy-head *n.* a studious thinker; an intellectual. (Compare to **conehead.**) □ *Why do the pointy-heads spend so much time arguing about nothing?*

poky 1. *n.* jail; a jail cell. □ *Have you ever been in the poky?* **2.** *mod.* slow; lagging and inefficient. □ *Hurry up! Don't be so poky.*

polluted *mod.* alcohol or drug intoxicated. □ *Those guys are really polluted.*

pond scum *n.* a mean and wretched person; a worthless male. (Collegiate. An elaboration of **scum,** less crude than **scumbag.** Also a rude term of address.) □ *Get your hands off me, pond scum!*

poop 1. *n.* information; the detailed knowledge of something. (See also the **(hot) skinny.**) □ *What's the poop on the broken glass in the hall?* **2.** *n.* fecal matter. (Caution with topic.) □ *There's poop on the sidewalk!* **3.** *iv.* to defecate. □ *Your dog pooped on my lawn.*

pooped (out) 1. *mod.* exhausted; worn-out. (Said of a person or an animal.) □ *I'm really pooped out.* □ *The horse looked sort of pooped in the final stretch.* **2.** *mod.* alcohol intoxicated. □ *How much of that stuff does it take to get pooped?* □ *He's been drinking all night and is totally pooped out.*

poop out *iv.* to quit; to wear out and stop. □ *I think I'm going to poop out pretty soon.*

poop sheet *n.* a sheet containing information. □ *Where is the poop sheet on today's meeting?*

pop 1. *tv.* to hit or strike someone. □ *She popped him lightly on the shoulder.* **2.** *mod.* popular. □ *I don't care for pop stuff.* **3.** *n.* popular music. □ *Pop is the only music I like.* **4.** *n.* soda pop; a carbonated soft drink; soda. □ *Can I get some pop? I'm really hot.*

a **pop** *mod.* a time; a try; a piece. □ *I love CDs, but not at $18.95 a pop.*

pop for something *iv.* to pay for a treat (for someone). (See also **spring for** something.) □ *Let's have some ice cream. I'll pop for it.*

pop off 1. *iv.* to make an unnecessary remark; to interrupt with a remark; to sound off. □ *Bob keeps popping off when he should be listening.* **2.** *iv.* to lose one's temper. (Compare to **pop** one's **cork**.) □ *I don't know why she popped off at me. All I did was say hello.* **3.** *iv.* to die. □ *My uncle popped off last week.*

pop one's **cork** *tv.* to release one's anger; to have an angry outburst. □ *She tried to hold it back, but suddenly she popped her cork.*

popped 1. *mod.* arrested. (Similar to *busted.* See also **bust.**) □ *He was popped for hardly anything at all.* **2.** *mod.* alcohol or drug intoxicated. □ *She looks glassy-eyed because she's popped.*

popper 1. AND **popsie** *n.* an ampoule of amyl nitrite, a drug that is inhaled when the ampoule is broken. (Drugs. Often plural.) □ *You got any poppers I can have?* **2.** *n.* a handgun. (Underworld. From the sound of a gunshot.) □ *He carries his popper under his coat.* **3.** *n.* a can of beer (in a pop-top can). □ *You ready for another popper, Tom?*

popsie Go to **popper.**

pork 1. *n.* the police in general; a **pig.** (Underworld.) □ *Keep an eye out for the pork.* **2.** *tv.* & *iv.* to copulate [with] someone. (Usually objectionable.) □ *He's telling everybody that he porked her.*

porked *mod.* copulated with; [of a female] deflowered. (Usually objectionable.) □ *Well, have you been porked?*

pork out *iv.* to overindulge in food and drink. (A play on **pig out.**) □ *Whenever I see French fries, I know I'm going to pork out.*

porky *mod.* fat; obese; piglike. □ *You are beginning to look a little porky.*

pository *mod.* yes; positive. □ *Q: Is this the right one? A: Pository.*

pot 1. *n.* a toilet. □ *Where's the pot around here?* **2.** *n.* cannabis; marijuana. (Originally drugs, now widely known.) □ *The cops found pot growing next to city hall.*

potato *n.* the head. □ *I got a nasty bump on the old potato.*

pound a beer AND **pound** some **beers** *tv.* to drink a beer. □ *Let's go down to the tavern and pound some beers.*

pound one's **ear** *tv.* to sleep. □ *She went home to pound her ear an hour or two before work.*

pounds *n.* dollars; money. (Black.) □ *How many pounds does this thing cost?*

pound some **beers** Go to pound a beer.

pound the books Go to hit the books.

power tool *n.* a student who studies most of the time. (An elaboration of **tool**.) □ *Willard is a power tool if there ever was one. Studies most of the night.* □ *All the power tools always get the best grades.*

prayerbones *n.* the knees. □ *Okay, down on your prayerbones.*

pray to the porcelain god *iv.* to empty one's stomach; to vomit. (Refers to being on one's knees (praying) in front of a porcelain toilet bowl.) □ *Boy, was I sick. I was praying to the porcelain god for two hours.*

prick 1. *n.* the penis. (Usually objectionable.) □ *He held his hands over his prick and ran for the bedroom.* **2.** *n.* a stupid or obnoxious male. (Usually objectionable.) □ *You stupid prick! Get out of here!*

pro 1. *n.* a professional (at anything); someone as good as a professional. □ *When it comes to typing, he's a pro.* **2.** *mod.* professional. □ *I hope to play pro ball next year.* **3.** *n.* a prostitute. □ *Do you think she's a pro or just overly friendly?*

Probablee. *mod.* probably. (As an answer to a question. The last syllable is accented and drawn out.) □ *Q: Will you be there when I get home? A: Probablee.*

prod 1. *n.* a reminder. □ *Call me up and give me a little prod so I won't forget.* **2.** *tv.* to remind someone (about something). □ *Call me up and prod me just before the due date.*

props *n.* evidence of respect; one's proper respect. □ *You gotta give me my props.*

prosty AND **prostie** *n.* a prostitute. □ *The cops haul in about 40 prosties a night from that one neighborhood alone.* □ *This one prosty was high on something and started screaming.*

pseudo ['sudo] **1.** *mod.* false; bogus. □ *She is just too pseudo.* □ *What a pseudo hairdo!* **2.** *n.* a phony person. □ *Randy is such a pseudo! What a fake!*

psyched (out) *mod.* excited; overwhelmed; thrilled. □ *That's great. I'm really psyched!*

psyched (up) *mod.* completely mentally ready (for something). □ *I'm really psyched for this test.*

psycho *n.* a psychopathic person; a crazy person. □ *Get that psycho out of here!*

psych out *iv.* to have a nervous or emotional trauma; to go mad for a brief time. (Compare to **freak (out)**.) □ *Another day like this one and I'll psych out for sure.*

psych someone **out** *tv.* to try to figure out what someone is likely to do. □ *Don't try to psych me out.* ⊤ *The batter tried to psych out the pitcher, but it didn't work.*

psych someone **up** *tv.* to get someone excited or mentally prepared for something. □ *I psyched myself up to sing in front of all those people.* ⊤ *The coach psyched up the team for the game.*

ptomaine-domain AND **ptomaine-palace** ['tomen . . .] *n.* any institutional dining facility; a mess hall; a cafeteria. □ *Time to go over to the ptomaine-palace and eat—if you can call it that.*

ptomaine-palace Go to ptomaine-domain.

puggled 1. *mod.* exhausted; bewildered. □ *I have had a long day, and I'm really puggled.* **2.** *mod.* alcohol intoxicated. □ *When he started pouring his drink down his collar, I knew he was puggled.*

puke 1. *iv.* to vomit. □ *Dinner was gross. I thought I would puke when I smelled it.* **2.** *n.* vomit. □ *Todd put a big hunk of fake plastic puke on the teacher's desk.* **3.** *n.* a totally disgusting and obnoxious person. (Rude and derogatory.) □ *What an ugly puke. Make him leave! Make him handsome!*

the **pukes** *n.* the feeling of nausea; the feeling of impending vomiting. (Especially with *have, get.*) □ *I hate having the pukes.*

pukey AND **pukoid** *mod.* disgusting; repellent. □ *What a pukey day!*

pukoid Go to pukey.

pull *n.* a drink; a drink from a flask. □ *He took another pull and kept on talking.*

pull chocks *tv.* to depart. (*Chocks* are used to block the wheels of a vehicle or a plane.) □ *Let's pull chocks and get out of here.*

pull jive *tv.* to drink liquor. (See also jive. Black.) □ *Let's go pull jive for a while.*

pull oneself **off** Go to beat off.

pull someone's **chain** Go to yank someone's **chain**.

pummelled *mod.* alcohol intoxicated. (Collegiate.) □ *They get pummelled every Friday night.*

pump 1. *tv.* to press someone for an answer or information. □ *Don't pump me! I will tell you nothing!* **2.** *n.* the heart. (See also ticker.) □ *My pump's getting sort of weak.* **3.** *n.* a pumped-up muscle. (Bodybuilding.) □ *Look at the size of that pump.*

pumped (up) *mod.* excited; physically and mentally ready. (Sports.) □ *The team is really pumped up for Friday's game.* □ *She really plays well when she's pumped!*

pump ship 1. *tv.* to urinate. (Crude. From an expression meaning to pump the bilge water from a ship.) □ *He stopped and pumped ship right in the alley.* **2.** *tv.* to empty one's stomach; to vomit. (Crude. Less well-known than sense 1.) □ *After I pumped ship, I felt better.*

pump something **up** *tv.* to flex and tense a muscle until it is expanded to its fullest size, as with thighs and forearms. (Bodybuilding.) □ *He really can pump his pecs up.* ⊤ *She pumped up her thighs and struck a pose.*

punk 1. AND **punk kid** *n.* an inexperienced boy or youth. (Derogatory. Also a term of address.) □ *Ask that punk to come over here.* **2.** *n.* a petty (male) hoodlum; a (male) juvenile delinquent. □ *We know how to deal with punks like you.* **3.** *mod.* poor; dull and inferior. □ *This is pretty punk food.* **4.** *mod.* having to do with punkers or their music. □ *I am tired of your red punk hair. Try it brown for a change.* □ *This music sounds too punk for me.*

punker *n.* a punk rocker; a young person who dresses in the style of punk rockers or has the wild hairstyles. □ *It's not safe to walk on the street with all those weird punkers out there.* □ *The punkers don't even have a sense of rhythm.*

punk kid Go to punk.

punk out 1. *iv.* to chicken out. □ *Come on! Stick with it! Don't punk out!* **2.** *iv.* to become a **punker.** □ *If I punked out, my parents would probably clobber me.*

puppy 1. *n.* a wimpy person; a softie. □ *That silly puppy is still waiting outside your door.* **2.** *n.* a thing; a piece or part of something. □ *Put this little puppy right here.*

push money *n.* extra money paid to a salesperson to aggressively sell certain merchandise. (See also **spiff.**) □ *The manufacturer supplied a little push money that even the store manager didn't know about.* □ *I got about $300 last month in push money for selling some low-grade sweaters.*

push off AND **shove off** *iv.* to leave. (As if one were pushing away from a dock.) □ *Well, it looks like it's time to push off.*

puss ['pʊs] *n.* the face. □ *Look at the puss on that guy! What an ugly face!*

pussy 1. *n.* the female genitals; the vulva. (Usually objectionable.) □ *He said he wanted to get into her pussy.* **2.** *n.* women considered as a receptacle for the penis. (Rude and derogatory.) □ *Man, I gotta get me some pussy.*

put a con on someone *tv.* to attempt to deceive someone; to attempt to swindle someone. (Underworld.) □ *Don't try to put a con on me, Buster! I've been around too long.*

Put a sock in it! Go to Stuff a sock in it!

put-on *n.* a deception; an entertaining deception. □ *Of course, it was a joke. It was a really good put-on.*

putrid *mod.* alcohol intoxicated. (See also **rotten.**) □ *That guy is stinking drunk. Putrid, in fact.*

put some sweet lines on someone Go to lay some sweet lines on someone.

put something **on the street** *tv.* to make something known publicly; to tell everyone one's troubles. □ *Man, can't you keep a secret? Don't put everything on the street.*

put the chill on someone AND **put the freeze on** someone *tv.* to ignore someone. □ *She was pretty snooty till we all put the chill on her.* □ *Let's put the freeze on Ted until he starts acting better.*

put the freeze on someone Go to put the chill on someone.

put the moves on someone *tv.* to attempt to seduce someone. □ *If somebody doesn't try to put the moves on her, she thinks she's a failure.*

put the pedal to the metal *tv.* to press a car's accelerator to the floor. □ *Put the pedal to the metal, and we're out of here.*

put to it *mod.* in trouble or difficulty; hard up (for something such as money). (As if one's back were put to the wall.) □ *Sorry, I can't lend you anything. I'm a bit put to it this month.*

put too much on it *tv.* to make too much fuss over something. □ *Come on, man. Lighten up. Don't put too much on it.*

put your hands together for someone *tv.* to applaud someone. (To put hands together clapping.) □ *Please put your hands together for Ronald and his great musicians!*

putz ['pəts] **1.** *n.* a penis. (Yiddish. Caution with **putz** and topic.) □ *Tell him to cover his putz and run and grab a towel.* **2.** *n.* a stupid person, typically a male; a **schmuck**. (Yiddish. Also a rude term of address.) □ *And this stupid putz just stood there smiling.*

putz around ['pəts . . .] *iv.* to fiddle around; to mess around. □ *Those guys spend most of their time just putzing around.*

pythons *n.* large, muscular biceps. □ *Look at the pythons on that guy! He could lift a piano!*

Q-sign *n.* the rounded, open mouth of a dead person with the tongue hanging out like the tail of a capital Q. (A semi-jocular usage. Hospitals. See also **O-sign**.) □ *The old lady in the corner room is giving the Q-sign.*

quaff a brew ['kwɑf ə 'bru] *tv.* to drink a beer. (See also **brew**.) □ *I went down to the bar to quaff a brew.*

quan Go to quant.

quant 1. AND **quan** *n.* quantitative analysis. (Scientific and collegiate.) □ *I didn't study enough for my quant test.* □ *I flunked quan twice.* **2.** *n.* a technician who works in financial market analysis. □ *The quants have been warning us about the danger for a month.*

quarterback *tv.* to manage, lead, or direct someone or something. □ *Who is going to quarterback this organization after you go?*

queer 1. *n.* a homosexual person. (Usually derogatory. Also a term of address.) □ *Stop acting like a queer, even if you are one.* **2.** *mod.* homosexual; pertaining to homosexual people or things. (Usually male, but also for females. Usually objectionable.) □ *Have you ever been to a queer bar?*

Que pasa? [ke 'pɑsə] *interrog.* Hello, what's going on? (Spanish.) □ *Hey, man! Que pasa?*

quick-and-dirty *mod.* rapidly and carelessly done. □ *I'm selling this car, so all I want is a quick-and-dirty repair job.* □ *They only do quick-and-dirty work at that shop.*

quick buck AND **fast buck** *n.* a quickly or easily earned profit. □ *I'm always on the lookout to make a fast buck.* □ *I need to make a quick buck without much effort.*

quick fix 1. *n.* a quick and probably none too permanent or satisfactory solution to a problem. □ *The quick fix isn't good enough* *in this case.* **2.** *mod.* having to do with a temporary or unsatisfactory solution or repair. (Usually **quick-fix**.) □ *Frank is a master of the quick-fix solution.* □ *This is no time for quick-fix efforts.*

quickie Go to quick one.

quick one AND **quickie 1.** *n.* a quick drink of booze; a single beer consumed rapidly. □ *I could use a quick one about now.* □ *I only have time for a quickie.* **2.** *n.* a quick sex act. (Usually objectionable.) □ *They're in the bedroom having a quick one.*

Quit your bellyaching! *command* Stop complaining! □ *You've been bitching all day! Quit your bellyaching!*

R

rack 1. *n.* a bed. □ *I need some more time in the rack.* **2.** *n.* a pair of [female] breasts. (Usually objectionable.) □ *Look at the rack on that dame! How can she stand upright?*

rack duty Go to rack time.

racked *mod.* struck in the testicles. (Usually objectionable.) □ *The quarterback got racked and didn't play the rest of the quarter.*

racked (up) *mod.* alcohol or drug intoxicated. □ *They drank till they were good and racked.*

racket 1. *n.* noise. □ *Cut out that racket! Shut up!* **2.** *n.* a deception; a scam. □ *He operated a racket that robbed old ladies of their savings.* **3.** *n.* any job. □ *I've been in this racket for 20 years and never made any money.*

rack (out) *iv.* to go to sleep or to bed. □ *What time do you rack out?* □ *If I don't rack by midnight, I'm dead the next day.*

rack something **up 1.** *tv.* to accumulate something; to collect or acquire something. □ *We racked 20 points up in the game last Saturday.* ⊤ *We racked up a lot of money in the stock market.* ⊤ *They all racked up a lot of profits.* **2.** *tv.* to wreck something. □ *Fred racked his new car up.* ⊤ *He racked up his arm in the football game.*

rack time AND **rack duty** *n.* time spent in bed. (Military.) □ *I need more rack time than I'm getting.* □ *I was on rack duty for my entire leave.*

radical *mod.* great; excellent. (California.) □ *It's so, like, radical!* □ *My boyfriend, he's, like, so radical!*

rag 1. *n.* a newspaper. □ *I'm tired of reading this rag day after day. Can't we get a different paper?* □ *What a rag! It's only good for putting in the bottom of bird cages!* **2.** *n.* ugly or badly styled clothing; an ugly garment. □ *I need some new clothes. I can't go around wearing rags like these.* □ *I wouldn't be seen in last sea-*

son's rags. **3.** *n.* any clothing, even the best. (Always plural.) □ *Man, I got some new rags that will knock your eyes out!* **4.** *n.* a sanitary napkin; a tampon. (For use in the menstrual cycle. Usually objectionable.) □ *God, I've got to change this rag!*

rag out *iv.* to dress up. □ *I like to rag out and go to parties.*

railroad tracks *n.* dental braces. □ *I can't smile because of these railroad tracks.* □ *My railroad tracks cost nearly $1,200.*

rainbow *n.* a bowlegged person, typically a male. (Also a rude term of address.) □ *Hey, rainbow! Are you a cowboy?*

rain on someone or something Go to rain on someone's parade.

rain on someone's **parade** AND **rain on** someone or something *iv.* to spoil something for someone; to ruin someone or something. □ *I hate to rain on your parade, but your plans are all wrong.*

rake something **in** *tv.* to take in a lot of something, usually money. □ *Our candidate will rake votes in by the thousand.* Ⓣ *They were raking in money by the bushel.*

rally ['ræli] **1.** *n.* a party or get-together of some kind. □ *The rally was a flop. Everyone left early.* **2.** *iv.* to hold a party of some kind; to party. (Collegiate.) □ *Let's rally tonight about midnight.*

ralph AND **rolf** ['rælf AND 'rɔlf] *iv.* to empty one's stomach; to vomit. (Teens and collegiate.) □ *She went home and ralphed for an hour.* □ *I think I'm going to rolf.*

ralph something **up** *tv.* to vomit (something). □ *The doctor gave him some stuff that made him ralph it up.* Ⓣ *He ralphed up his dinner.*

rambo ['ræmbo] *tv.* to (figuratively) annihilate someone or something. (Collegiate. From the powerful film character Rambo.) □ *The students ramboed the cafeteria, and the cops were called.*

rammy ['ræmi] *mod.* sexually excited or aroused. (Refers to the ram, a symbol of arousal.) □ *Your rammy boyfriend is on the telephone.*

ramrod *tv.* to lead something; to act as the driving force behind something. □ *Who is going to ramrod this project?*

ranch 1. *n.* semen. (Similar in appearance and consistency to ranch [salad] dressing. Usually objectionable.) □ *God! There's ranch on the bathroom floor!* **2.** *iv.* to ejaculate. (Usually objectionable.) □ *Just looking at her makes me want to ranch.*

rank *tv.* to harass someone; to annoy someone. □ *The dean was ranking the boys for pulling the prank.* □ *When he finished with the boys, he started ranking their parents.*

rank someone **out** *tv.* to annoy or chastise someone. (Compare to rank.) □ *He really ranks me out. What a pest!* T *I ranked out the whole gang, but good!*

rap 1. *iv.* to talk or chat about something. □ *The kids sat down and rapped for an hour or so.* **2.** *n.* a conversation; a chat. □ *Let's have a rap sometime.* **3.** *n.* sweet talk; seductive talk; line. □ *Don't lay that rap on me! You're not my type.* **4.** *n.* a criminal charge; the blame for something. (Underworld.) □ *The cops tried to make the rap stick, but they didn't have enough evidence.*

rap session *n.* an informal conversation session. □ *The rap session was interrupted by a fire drill.*

(rap) sheet *n.* a criminal record listing all recorded criminal charges. (See also rap.) □ *This guy has a rap sheet a mile long.* □ *The sergeant asked if there was a sheet on the prisoner.*

raspberry ['ræzbɛri] *n.* a rude noise made by vibrating the lips with air blown between them. □ *The entire audience gave the performer the raspberry.*

rasty ['ræsti] *mod.* having to do with a harsh-looking young woman. (Collegiate.) □ *That dark lipstick makes you look a little rasty.*

rat 1. *n.* a wretched-acting person. (Also a term of address.) □ *Stop acting like a dirty rat!* **2.** Go to rat (on someone).

rat around *iv.* to waste time loafing around; to loiter. (Collegiate.) □ *If kids don't have jobs, they just rat around.*

rat-bastard *n.* a really wretched or despised person. (Rude and derogatory.) □ *You dirty rat-bastard! I could kill you!*

ratchet-mouth AND **motor-mouth** *n.* someone who talks incessantly. (Also a term of address.) □ *Tell that ratchet-mouth to shut up!* □ *Hey, motor-mouth, quiet!*

rat fink *n.* an informer. (Also a term of address. See also rat.) □ *That guy is nothing but a rat fink. A dirty squealer!*

rathole 1. *n.* a run-down place. □ *I refuse to live in this rathole any longer.* **2.** *n.* a bottomless pit; an endless cause for the expenditure of money. (Typically with *throw . . . down.*) □ *The trans-*

portation system is beyond help. Giving it more subsidies is just throwing money down a rathole.

rat (on someone) *iv.* to inform (on someone). □ *Bill said he was going to rat on that punk.*

rat out *iv.* to quit; to quit (on someone or something). □ *He tried to rat out at the last minute.*

rattled 1. *mod.* confused; bewildered. □ *Try not to get her rattled.* **2.** *mod.* tipsy; alcohol intoxicated. □ *After an hour of drinking, Bill was more than a little rattled.*

rattling *mod.* excellent. (Collegiate. Compare to rocking.) □ *Her party was really rattling.* □ *What a rattling place to live!*

raw 1. *mod.* harsh and cold, especially weather. □ *The weather was cold and raw.* **2.** *mod.* inexperienced; brand new. □ *The raw recruit did as well as could be expected.* □ *She'll get better. She's just a little raw.* **3.** *mod.* vulgar; crude. □ *I've had enough of your raw humor.*

rays *n.* sunshine. (Collegiate. See also catch some rays.) □ *I'm going to go out and get some rays today.*

razz ['ræz] *tv.* to tease someone. □ *Please stop razzing me.*

real gone *mod.* really cool; mellow and pleasant. □ *Man, this music is real gone.*

ream someone **out** *tv.* to scold someone severely. □ *The teacher really reamed him out.* T *The coach reamed out the whole team.*

rear (end) *n.* the tail end; the buttocks. (Euphemistic.) □ *She fell right on her rear.* □ *The dog bit her in the rear end.*

rear-ender AND **back-ender** *n.* an automobile wreck where one car runs into the back of another. (Compare to fender-bender.) □ *It wasn't a bad accident, just a rear-ender.*

red hot 1. *mod.* important; in great demand. □ *This is a red hot item. Everybody wants one.* **2.** *n.* a hot dog (sausage). □ *"Get your red hots right here!" shouted the vendor.*

red tide *n.* a menstrual period. (Punning on the name of a tidal phenomenon where the water appears reddish owing to the presence of certain kinds of microscopic creatures.) □ *Sorry, she's down with the red tide and really prefers to stay home.*

regs *n.* regulations. □ *Follow the regs or pay the penalty.*

rent(al)s *n.* one's parents. (Teens. See also **(parental) units**. Also a term of address.) □ *I'll have to ask my rents.* □ *Hey, rentals, let's go out for dinner.*

rep ['rɛp] **1.** *n.* a representative, usually a sales representative. □ *Please ask your rep to stop by my office.* **2.** *n.* someone's reputation. □ *I've got my own rep to think about.* **3.** *n.* repertory theater. □ *Rep is the best place to get experience, but not to make connections.*

repo ['ripo] **1.** *n.* a repossessed car. □ *I'd rather have a plain used car than a repo.* **2.** *tv.* to repossess a car. □ *Some guy came around and tried to repo my car.*

ret ['rɛt] *n.* a tobacco cigarette. (Collegiate. A front clipping.) □ *You got a ret I can bum?*

retread ['ritrɛd] *n.* a burned-out person; a made-over person. □ *Chuck is just a retread. He's through.*

revved (up) *mod.* excited, perhaps by drugs. □ *Bill is revved from too much dope.*

ride shotgun *tv.* to ride in the front seat of a car, next to the driver. (A term from the days of stagecoaches and their armed guards.) □ *I have to take the beer over to the party. Why don't you come along and ride shotgun?* □ *Who's going to ride shotgun with Bill?*

rif ['rɪf] **1.** *tv.* to dismiss an employee. (From the initials *R.I.F.*, reduction in force.) □ *They're going to rif John tomorrow.* **2.** *n.* a firing; a dismissal. □ *Who got the rif today?*

riff ['rɪf] **1.** *n.* a short, repeated line of music played by a particular performer. □ *Jim just sat there and forgot his riff.* □ *Listen to this riff, Tom.* **2.** *n.* a digression while speaking. □ *Excuse the little riff, but I had to mention it.*

riffed ['rɪft] **1.** *mod.* alcohol or drug intoxicated. □ *That guy is really riffed!* **2.** AND **rift** *mod.* fired; released from employment. (From *R.I.F.*, reduction in force.) □ *Most of the sales force was riffed last week.*

rift Go to **riffed**.

righteous ['raɪtʃəs] *mod.* good; of good quality. (Originally black.) □ *She is a righteous mama.* □ *This stuff is really righteous!*

right guy *n.* a good guy; a straight guy. □ *Tom is a right guy. No trouble with him.*

rinky-dink ['rɪŋki'dɪŋk] *mod.* cheap; inferior; broken down. □ *What a rinky-dink job! I quit!*

riot ['raɪət] *n.* someone or something entertaining or funny. □ *Tom was a riot last night.*

rip 1. *n.* a drinking bout. □ *Fred had another rip last night. He's rotten now.* **2.** *n.* the loot from a rip-off. □ *I want my share of the rip, now!* **3.** *n.* a theft; a rip-off. □ *The crooks pulled a rip on Fourth Street last night.*

rip-off 1. *n.* a theft; a deception; an exploitation. (See also rip.) □ *What a rip-off! I want my money back.* **2.** *mod.* having to do with theft and deception. □ *I consider myself to be rip-off champion of North America.*

rip-off artist AND **off artist** *n.* a con artist. □ *Beware of the rip-off artist who runs that shop.*

rip on someone *iv.* to give someone a hard time; to annoy someone. □ *Fred was ripping on me, and I heard about it.*

ripped *mod.* muscular. □ *I worked and worked to get ripped, but I'm just not made that way.*

rip someone or something **off 1.** *tv.* [with *someone*] to assault, kill, beat, rob, rape, or cheat someone. (Note the *for* in the example.) □ *They ripped me off, but they didn't hurt me.* Ⓣ *Man, they ripped off the old lady for three hundred dollars.* **2.** *tv.* [with *something*] to steal something. □ *They ripped them all off.* Ⓣ *The crooks ripped off the hubcaps of each car on the block.*

rivets ['rɪvəts] *n.* dollars; money. □ *You got enough rivets on you for a snack?*

roach-coach *n.* a truck or van from which snacks and sandwiches are sold. □ *Let's go get a sandwich at the roach-coach.*

road apple *n.* a lump of horse excrement. (Compare to alley apple.) □ *Don't step on the road apples.*

road hog *n.* someone who takes too much space on a road or highway; someone who tries to run other people off the road. □ *Get over! Road hog!* □ *Some road hog nearly ran me off the road.*

roadie AND **roady** ['rodi] **1.** AND **roadster** ['rodstɚ] *n.* a young person who helps rock groups set up for performances. □ *I was a* *roadster for a while, but I didn't like it.* **2.** AND **roadster** *iv.* to help rock groups set up. □ *Let's go downtown and roadie tonight. The Red Drips are in town.* □ *I hate to roady. It's, like, work!* **3.** *mod.* eager to travel; eager to get on the road. □ *We'd better get going. Your father looks a little roadie.*

roadster Go to roadie.

roast 1. *tv.* to put on an entertaining program where the guest of honor is teased and insulted. □ *They roasted Dave when he retired.* **2.** *n.* an entertaining program where the guest of honor is insulted all in fun. □ *It was a wonderful roast. The guest of honor was pleased with the quality of the insults.* □ *It was a little too polite for a real roast.*

rock 1. AND **rock candy** *n.* crack, a crystallized form of cocaine. (See also **rocks**.) □ *Some call it rock, and some call it crack.* **2.** *n.* a crystallized form of heroin used for smoking. □ *Carl is hooked on rock—the kind that you smoke.* **3.** *n.* a diamond or other gemstone. □ *Look at the size of that rock in her ring.*

rock candy Go to rock.

rocking *mod.* excellent. (Collegiate.) □ *Man, what a rocking party!*

rocks 1. *n.* ice cubes. □ *Can I have a few rocks in my drink, please?* **2.** *n.* Xerox, Inc. (Securities markets, New York Stock Exchange.) □ *When she says, "Buy me a thousand rocks at the market," that means she wants one thousand shares of Xerox at whatever the market price is at the moment.* **3.** *n.* money; a dollar. (Underworld.) □ *How many rocks do you want for that?* **4.** *n.* the testicles. (See also **stones**. Usually objectionable.) □ *I was afraid I'd get kicked in the rocks, so I stayed back.*

rolf Go to ralph.

roni *n.* pepperoni, as used in pizza. □ *I want roni and shrooms on my pizza.*

rotorhead *n.* a helicopter pilot or member of a helicopter crew. (Military. Also a term of address.) □ *Radio those rotorheads and tell them to get back to the base, now!* □ *Hey, rotorhead, where's your eggbeater?*

rotsee ['rɑtsi] *n.* R.O.T.C., the Reserve Officers Training Corps. □ *I joined rotsee to help pay my way through school.*

rotten 1. *mod.* smelly; disgusting. (Not slang.) □ *What is that rotten smell?* **2.** *mod.* alcohol intoxicated. (See also **putrid**.) □ *When he gets rotten, he's sort of dangerous.* **3.** *mod.* poor or bad. (From sense 1.) □ *This is the most rotten mess I've ever been in.*

rough time *n.* a hard time; a bad time. □ *I didn't mean to give you such a rough time. I'm sorry.*

round tripper *n.* a home run in baseball. □ *He hit a round tripper in the fourth inning.*

roundup *n.* a collection or summary of news items, such as a weather roundup, news roundup, etc. □ *Tune in at noon for a roundup of the day's news.*

rubber 1. *n.* automobile tires; the rubber of automobile tires left on the street from spinning tires. □ *The rubber on my car is practically ruined.* **2.** *n.* a condom. □ *Bill has carried a rubber in his wallet since he was 12. The same one!* □ *He always carries a rubber "just in case."*

rubber sock *n.* a timid person; a passive and compliant person. □ *Come on! Stand up for your rights. Don't be such a rubber sock!*

rubbish *n.* nonsense. (Also an exclamation.) □ *I'm tired of listening to your rubbish.*

rug *n.* a wig or toupee. (See also **divot**.) □ *Is that guy wearing a rug, or does his scalp really slide from side to side?* □ *I wear just a little rug to cover up a shiny spot.*

rug rat AND **ankle biter** *n.* a child. (Also a term of address.) □ *You got any rug rats at your house?*

rule *iv.* to dominate; to be the best. (Slang only in certain contexts. Typical in graffiti.) □ *Pizza rules around here.*

ruley *mod.* ideal; excellent. (Said of something that **rules**.) □ *Her idea is ruley! She knows what we ought to do!*

run 1. *n.* a session or period of time spent doing something; a period of time when something happens. □ *The market had a good run today.* □ *We all have enjoyed a good run of luck.* **2.** *tv.* to transport contraband, alcohol, or drugs. □ *The farmers were caught running guns.* **3.** *n.* an act of transporting contraband. □ *Four soldiers were killed during a run.* □ *In their final run the cocaine smugglers made over four million dollars.*

run down some lines

run down some lines 1. *iv.* to converse (with someone). □ *I was running down some lines with Fred when the bell rang.* **2.** *iv.* to try to seduce someone; to go through a talk leading to seduction. (See also run one's rhymes.) □ *I was just standing there running down some lines with Mary when those guys broke in.*

run it down *tv.* to tell the whole story; to tell the truth. □ *Come on! What happened? Run it down for me!*

run off *iv.* to have diarrhea. □ *Jimmy has been running off since midnight.*

run off at the mouth *iv.* to talk too much; to have diarrhea of the mouth. □ *I wish you would stop running off at the mouth.*

run one's rhymes *tv.* to say what you have to say; to give one's speech or make one's plea. (Collegiate.) □ *Go run your rhymes with somebody else!*

run out of gas *iv.* to lose momentum or interest. □ *His program is running out of gas.*

the runs *n.* diarrhea. □ *I can't believe those cute little hamburgers could give anybody the runs.*

rush 1. *n.* a quick print of a day's shooting of a film. (Film making. Usually plural.) □ *Take these rushes right over to Mr. Hitchcock's office.* **2.** *n.* a period of time when fraternities and sororities are permitted to pursue new members. (Collegiate.) □ *I've got to be at school in time for rush.* **3.** *tv.* [for a fraternity or sorority member] to try to persuade someone to join. □ *The frat tried to rush me, but I'm too busy.* **4.** *tv.* to court or date someone, usually a woman. □ *Tom's trying to rush Betty, but she's not interested.*

ruth ['ruθ] **1.** *n.* a women's restroom. (Compare to john.) □ *Point me toward the ruth!* **2.** *iv.* to empty one's stomach; to vomit. (See also cry ruth.) □ *I gotta go ruth!*

sack 1. *n.* a bed. □ *I was so tired I could hardly find my sack.* **2.** *tv.* to dismiss someone from employment; to fire someone. □ *The boss sacked the whole office staff last week.* **3.** *tv.* to tackle someone in football. □ *I tried to sack him, but he was too fast.* **4.** *n.* the completion of a tackle in football. □ *Andy made the sack on the 10-yard line.*

the sack *n.* a dismissal from employment. □ *The boss gave them all the sack.*

sack out *iv.* to go to bed or go to sleep. □ *It's time for me to sack out.*

saltine *n.* a white person. (A play on a kind of salted white cracker (biscuit). A *cracker* is a derogatory term for a white person.) □ *What are those saltines doing in this neighborhood?*

savage *mod.* excellent. (Collegiate.) □ *This is really a savage piece of music.*

scag Go to skag.

scam ['skæm] **1.** *n.* a swindle; a hustle. (See also What's the scam?) □ *I lost a fortune in that railroad scam.* **2.** *tv.* to swindle someone; to deceive someone. □ *They were scammed by a sweet-talking southern lady who took all their money.* □ *She scammed them for every cent they had.* **3.** *iv.* to seek out and pick up young women, said of males. (Collegiate.) □ *Bob was out scamming last night and ran into Clare.* **4.** *iv.* to copulate. (Caution with topic.) □ *I think those people over there are scamming.* **5.** *iv.* to fool around and waste time. □ *Quit scamming and get busy.*

scammer ['skæmɚ] **1.** *n.* a swindler; a hustler. □ *Carl is a scammer if I ever saw one.* **2.** *n.* a lecher; a fast worker with the opposite sex. □ *Bob thinks he's a great scammer, but he's just a wimp.*

scank Go to skank.

scarf 1. *tv.* to eat something. □ *Andy scarfed the whole pie.* **2.** *iv.* to eat. □ *I'll be with you as soon as I scarf.* **3.** *n.* food. □ *I want some good scarf. This stuff stinks.*

scarf out *iv.* to overeat. (See also blimp out, mac out, pig out, pork out.) □ *I scarf out every weekend.*

scarf something **down** *tv.* to eat something, perhaps in a hurry; to swallow something, perhaps in a hurry. □ *Are you going to scarf this whole thing down?* ⊤ *Here, scarf down this sandwich.*

schiz(z) out ['skɪz . . .] *iv.* to freak out; to lose mental control. □ *I schizzed out during the test. Got an F.*

s(c)hlep ['ʃlɛp] **1.** *tv.* to drag or carry someone or something. (From German *schleppen* via Yiddish.) □ *Am I supposed to schlep this whole thing all the way back to the store?* □ *I am tired of shlepping kids from one thing to another.* **2.** *n.* a journey; a distance to travel or carry something. □ *It takes about 20 minutes to make the schlep from here to there.* □ *That's a 10-mile schlep, and I won't go by myself.* **3.** *n.* a stupid person; a bothersome person. (Literally, a drag.) □ *What a schlep! The guy's a real pain.*

s(c)hlepper ['ʃlɛpɚ] *n.* an annoying person who always wants a bargain or a favor. (See also s(c)hlep.) □ *Why am I surrounded by people who want something from me? Is this a schlepper colony or what?* □ *Tell the shleppers that they'll get their money after I close the sale on my wife and kids.*

schmoose Go to s(c)hmooze.

s(c)hmooze AND **schmoose** ['ʃmuz] **1.** *iv.* to chat or gossip. (From Hebrew *schmuos* via Yiddish.) □ *You were schmoozing when you should have been listening.* **2.** *n.* a session of chatting or conversing. □ *Come over, and let's have a schmooze before you go.*

schmoozer *n.* someone who chats or converses well. □ *Two old schmoozers sat muttering to one another all afternoon by the duck pond.*

schmuck ['ʃmək] **1.** *n.* a jerk; a repellent male. (Also a rude term of address. Yiddish.) □ *Ask that schmuck how long he will be on the phone.* **2.** *n.* a penis. (Yiddish. Caution with topic.) □ *If I hear that joke about a camel's schmuck one more time, I'm going to scream.* □ *There are probably better names than schmuck for what you are talking about.*

school someone *tv.* to teach someone something, usually as a demonstration of power. (As in *I'll teach you a thing or two.* which suggests violence.) □ *Am I gonna have to school you in how to act?*

Sco. ['sko] *command* Let's go. □ *It's late. Sco.*

scoff ['skɔf] **1.** *tv. & iv.* to eat (something). (Compare to scarf.) □ *She scoffed three hamburgers and a large order of fries.* **2.** *n.* food. □ *This scoff is gross!*

scope on someone Go to scope someone.

scope someone AND **scope on** someone *tv. & iv.* to visually evaluate a member of the opposite sex. □ *He scoped every girl who came in the door.*

scope someone **out** *tv.* to look someone over. Ⓣ *Dave was scoping out all the girls.* □ *Nobody was scoping Dave out, though.*

score 1. *iv.* to succeed. □ *I knew if I kept trying I could score.* **2.** *tv. & iv.* to obtain something; to obtain drugs or sex. (Very close to sense 1.) □ *Albert spent an hour trying to score some pot.* **3.** *n.* the result of a scoring: drugs, loot, winnings, etc. □ *Where's the score? How much did you get?* □ *The crooks dropped the score as they made their getaway.* **4.** *iv.* [for a male] to copulate with a female; [for a female] to copulate with a male. (Usually objectionable.) □ *Fred can't think about anything but scoring with Martha.* □ *He will spend his vacation trying to score.* **5.** *n.* the client of a male or female prostitute. □ *She conked the score over the head and robbed him.* **6.** *n.* a summary; a conclusion; the sum total. □ *The score is that you are in trouble with the Internal Revenue Service.* □ *Okay, waiter, what's the score?*

scraggy ['skrægi] *mod.* bony. □ *I lost weight till I was scraggy as a hungry bear.*

scratch 1. *n.* money. □ *I just don't have the scratch.* □ *How much scratch does it take to buy a car like this one?* **2.** *tv.* to eliminate something from a list; to cancel something. □ *Scratch Fred. He can't make the party.* □ *We decided to scratch the idea of a new car. The old one will have to do.* **3.** *mod.* impromptu; temporary. □ *We started a scratch game of basketball, but most of the girls had to leave at dinnertime.* □ *This is just a scratch tape. After you use it for your computer program, someone else will write something over it.*

screw 1. *tv. & iv.* to copulate [with] someone. (Usually objectionable.) □ *The sailor wanted to screw somebody bad.* **2.** *tv. & iv.* to cheat or deceive someone. □ *The salesclerk screwed me on this watch.* **3.** *n.* an act of copulation. (Usually objectionable.) □ *The sailor said he needed a good screw.* **4.** *n.* a person with whom one can copulate. (Usually objectionable.) □ *His teeth are crooked and his hands are callused, but he's a good screw.*

screw around *iv.* to mess around; to waste time. □ *Stop screwing around and get to work!*

screwed 1. *mod.* copulated with. (Usually objectionable.) □ *I got myself good and screwed, and I haven't felt better in months.* **2.** *mod.* cheated. □ *Wow, you got screwed on that watch.*

screw someone over *tv.* to give someone a very bad time; to scold someone severely. □ *Those guys really screwed you over. What started it?* ⊤ *Let's get those kids in here and screw over every one of them. This stuff can't continue.*

screw up 1. *iv.* to mess up. □ *I hope I don't screw up this time.* **2.** *n.* a mess; a blunder; utter confusion. (Usually **screw-up.**) □ *One more screw up like that and you're fired.*

scrog ['skrɔg] *tv. & iv.* to have sex; to copulate (with someone). (Caution with topic.) □ *You know what? I think those people over in the corner are scrogging!*

scrub *tv.* to cancel something. □ *We had to scrub the whole plan because of the weather.*

scruff(y) ['skrəf(i)] *mod.* sloppy; unkempt. □ *Her boyfriend is a little scruffy, but he's got money!* □ *Why don't you clean up this scruff car? It's—like—grody!*

scrump ['skrəmp] *tv. & iv.* to copulate (with someone). (Caution with topic.) □ *The movie showed a scene of some woman scrumping her lover.*

scrunge ['skrəndʒ] *n.* nastiness; gunk. □ *What is this scrunge on my shoe?*

scrungy ['skrəndʒi] **1.** *mod.* filthy. □ *This place is too scrungy for me. I'm outa here.* □ *What a scrungy guy. Put him somewhere to soak for a day or two.* **2.** *mod.* inferior; bad. □ *You have a very scrungy outlook on life.*

scum 1. *n.* a totally worthless and disgusting person. (Rude and derogatory.) □ *You scum! Get out of here!* **2.** *n.* lowlife in general; disgusting and worthless people. (Rude and derogatory.) □ *Fourth Street is where all the scum in town hangs out.* **3.** *n.* semen; seminal fluid. (Usually objectionable.) □ *You'd better clean up the scum from the backseat before you take the car home.*

scumbag 1. *n.* a condom; a used condom. (Usually objectionable.) □ *I saw a used scumbag in the school parking lot.* **2.** *n.* a totally disgusting person. (Rude and derogatory.) □ *Oh, he's a scumbag. I wouldn't be seen dead with him!*

scurvy ['skɚvi] *mod.* repulsive; **gross.** (Collegiate.) □ *Who is that scurvy guy who just came in?*

scuz(z) ['skəz] **1.** *n.* filth. □ *What is this scuzz all over the floor?* **2.** *n.* a nasty person; an undesirable person; a scraggly person. □ *And this scuzz comes up to me and asks me to dance, and I'm like, "What?"* □ *I told the scuz, like, I was feeling sick, so I couldn't dance with anybody.*

scuzzbag *n.* a despicable person. (Also a rude term of address.) □ *Who is that scuzzbag who just came in?*

scuzzo *n.* a repellent person. □ *There's the scuzzo who thinks I like him.*

scuzz someone out *tv.* to nauseate someone. □ *He had this unreal face that almost scuzzed me out!* ⊤ *It's not nice to scuzz out people like that, especially when you hardly know them.*

scuzzy ['skəzi] *mod.* repellent; unkempt. □ *His clothes are always so scuzzy. He probably keeps them in a pile in his room.* □ *Whose scuzzy car is that in the driveway?*

sell a wolf ticket AND **sell wolf tickets** *tv.* to boast, bluff, or lie. (Originally black.) □ *Freddie is out selling wolf tickets again.*

sell buicks *tv.* to vomit. □ *I hear somebody in the john selling buicks.*

sell wolf tickets Go to **sell a wolf ticket.**

serious *mod.* good; profound; excellent. (See also **heavy.**) □ *He plays some serious guitar.* □ *Man, these tunes are, like, serious.*

set 1. *n.* a period of time that a band plays without a break; a 30-minute jam session. □ *I'll talk to you after this set.* □ *We do two sets and then take a 20-minute break.* **2.** *n.* a party. □ *Your set was a totally major bash!*

seven-seven-three-aitch AND **773H** *n.* hell. (This is the printed word *HELL* rotated 180 degrees. Jocular.) □ *What the 773H is going on around here?*

sexy 1. *mod.* having great sex appeal. □ *What a sexy chick!* **2.** *mod.* neat; exciting. □ *That's a sexy set of wheels.*

shades *n.* dark glasses. (See also **sunshades.**) □ *Where are my shades? The sun is too bright.*

shag ass (out of some place**)** Go to **bag ass (out of** some place**).**

shag (off) *iv.* to depart. □ *I gotta shag. It's late.* □ *Go on! Shag off!*

shank 1. *n.* a knife. □ *The mugger pulled a shank on the victim.* **2.** *iv.* to dance. □ *They were busy shankin' and didn't hear the gunshots.*

shank it *tv.* to use one's legs to get somewhere; to walk. □ *My car needs fixing so I had to shank it to work today.*

sharp 1. *mod.* clever; intelligent. □ *She's a real sharp chick! Got lots of savvy.* **2.** *mod.* good-looking; well-dressed. □ *That's a sharp set of wheels you got there.*

sheen ['ʃin] *n.* a car. (From *machine.*) □ *You have one fine sheen there.*

shekels ['ʃɛkəlz] *n.* dollars; money. □ *You got a few shekels you can spare?*

shellac [ʃə'læk] *tv.* to beat someone; to outscore someone. □ *We're gonna shellac those bums Friday night.*

shellacked 1. *mod.* beaten; outscored. □ *The team got shellacked in last week's game.* **2.** *mod.* alcohol intoxicated; overcome by booze. □ *Ernie was so shellacked he couldn't see.*

shellacking *n.* a beating. □ *We gave them a shellacking they'll never forget.*

shit 1. *n.* dung. (Usually objectionable.) □ *Gee! I stepped in some shit!* **2.** *iv.* to defecate. (Usually objectionable.) □ *This dog needs to shit. Take it for a walk.* **3.** *n.* any trash or unwanted material; junk; clutter. (Usually objectionable.) □ *Clean up this shit and don't let this place get so messy.* **4.** *n.* a wretched person; a despised person. (Rude and derogatory.) □ *You stupid shit! Look what you did!* **5.** *n.* one's personal belongings. (See also **get** one's **shit together.** Usually objectionable.) □ *I gotta get my shit from the kitchen and get outa here.* □ *Is this your shit? Move it!* **6.** *n.* lies; nonsense. (From **bullshit.** Usually objectionable.) □ *All I ever* *hear out of you is shit.* **7.** *tv.* to deceive someone; to lie to someone. □ *Stop shittin' me, you bastard!* □ *You wouldn't shit me, would you?* **8.** *n.* drugs, especially heroin or marijuana. (Usually objectionable.) □ *You are going to have to get off this shit or you're gonna die.* **9.** *exclam.* a general expression of disgust. (Usually Shit! Usually objectionable.) □ *Oh, shit! What a mess!* □ *Shit! That's terrible.*

shit-ass 1. *n.* a disgusting and wretched person. (Rude and derogatory.) □ *The guy's a shit-ass. What're you gonna do?* **2.** *mod.* pertaining to someone or something disgusting and wretched. (Usually objectionable.) □ *He's nothing but a shit-ass bastard!*

shit-bag 1. *n.* an unpleasant or inept person. (Rude and derogatory.) □ *I don't want that shit-bag working for me anymore!* **2.** *n.* a collection of unpleasant problems or annoyances. (Usually objectionable.) □ *You can just take your whole shit-bag and bother somebody else with it.* □ *This place has been a regular shit-bag of grief this morning.*

shitcan 1. *n.* a toilet; an outhouse. (Usually objectionable.) □ *I gotta spend some time on the shitcan.* **2.** *n.* a trash can. (Military. Usually objectionable.) □ *Just throw all this stuff in the shitcan.* **3.** *tv.* to throw something in the garbage can. (Usually objectionable.) □ *Shitcan this thing, will you?*

shit-faced *mod.* drunk. (Usually objectionable. See also faced.) □ *He was so shit-faced, he couldn't walk.*

shithead *n.* a stupid and obnoxious person, usually a male. (Rude and derogatory.) □ *You stupid shithead! Get out of my life!*

shit-house AND **crap-house** *n.* an outdoor toilet; an outhouse. (Usually objectionable.) □ *There is a hornets' nest in the crap-house.*

shit-list AND **crap-list** *n.* a list of people who are as worthless as dung; a list of problem people. (The phrase with crap is milder. Usually objectionable.) □ *From now on you are on my shit-list!* □ *Trouble with Tom is that everybody he knows is on his crap-list.*

shitload of something *n.* a whole lot of something. (Usually objectionable.) □ *I ended up with a whole shitload of bills and no job.*

shit on a shingle AND **S.O.S.** *n.* creamed chipped beef on toast. (Military. Usually objectionable.) □ *Oh, no, it's shit on a shingle again tonight.*

shit on someone **1.** *iv.* to defecate on someone. (Usually objectionable.) □ *That damn cat shit on me!* **2.** *tv.* to treat someone very badly. (Usually objectionable.) □ *The prof shit on the whole class by assigning a paper due Monday morning.* □ *The Internal Revenue Service really shit on me this year.*

Shit or get off the pot! *iv.* Do something or go away!; Do something or give someone else a chance!; Hurry up! (Usually objectionable.) □ *Hurry up with it, Fred! Shit or get off the pot!*

the **shits** *n.* diarrhea. (Usually objectionable.) □ *I can't eat that stuff. It always gives me the shits.*

shitsky ['ʃɪtski] **1.** *n.* dung. (Caution with shit.) □ *Some rude dog has left a little pile of grade-A shitsky on the sidewalk.* **2.** *n.* a despicable person. (Provocative. Caution with shit.) □ *The stupid shitsky is back on skag again.*

shitstick 1. *n.* a wretched and undesirable person. (Rude and derogatory.) □ *Why are you such a shitstick all the time?* **2.** *n.* a rod of dung. (Usually objectionable.) □ *Who left the shitsticks floating in the john?*

shitty 1. *mod.* covered or soiled with dung. (Usually objectionable.) □ *Get that shitty shovel out of the garage and clean it.* **2.** *mod.* lousy; rotten. (Usually objectionable.) □ *This has been a real shitty trip for me.*

shlep Go to s(c)hlep.

shlepper Go to s(c)hlepper.

shmen ['ʃmɛn] *n.* freshmen. □ *The shmen are having a party all to themselves this Friday.*

shoot 1. *tv. & iv.* AND **shoot up** to inject drugs, especially heroin. (Drugs.) □ *He actually had to leave the meeting to shoot.* **2.** *n.* an injection of heroin. (Drugs. Usually **shoot-up**.) □ *"Just one more shoot. That's all. Then, never again!" moaned Ernie, rather unconvincingly.* **3.** *tv.* to add liquor to a nonalcoholic drink. □ *I'm gonna shoot the punch with rum.* **4.** *iv.* to begin to tell [something]. □ *We're ready. Go ahead. Shoot!*

shoot one's **breakfast** Go to shoot one's cookies.

shoot one's **cookies** AND **shoot** one's **breakfast; shoot** one's **supper** *tv.* to empty one's stomach; to vomit. □ *I think I'm gonna shoot my cookies.*

shoot one's **supper** Go to shoot one's cookies.

shoot the bull AND **shoot the crap; shoot the shit** *tv.* to chat and gossip. (Caution with crap, shit.) □ *Let's get together sometime and shoot the bull.* □ *You spend too much time shooting the crap.*

shoot the crap Go to shoot the bull.

shoot the dozens Go to play the dozens.

shoot the shit Go to shoot the bull.

shoot up Go to shoot.

the **shorts** AND a **case of the shorts** *n.* a time when one is short of money; a time when one lacks money. □ *Here I am with a case of the shorts again.*

shot 1. *n.* a try at something. □ *Go ahead. Give it another shot.* **2.** *mod.* exhausted; ruined. □ *Here's your pen back. It's shot anyway.* **3.** *n.* a rocket launching. □ *The shot was canceled because of the weather.*

shot down 1. *mod.* demolished; destroyed. □ *Her idea was shot down after all her work.* **2.** *mod.* rejected by a young woman. □ *Fred's shot down, thanks to his best girl. He'll get over it.*

shot to the curb *mod.* without money or a place to live; living in the gutter; down and out. □ *I'm totally out of bills, man. Shot to the curb.*

shove off Go to push off.

shredded *mod.* alcohol intoxicated. (Collegiate.) □ *We are all too shredded to drive home. What shall we do?*

shuck ['ʃək] **1.** *n.* an insincere person. □ *The guy's a shuck. Don't believe a thing he says!* **2.** *tv. & iv.* to kid someone; to tease someone. □ *Stop shucking me!* **3.** *tv.* to swindle someone; to deceive someone. □ *The con man shucked a number of people in the town before moving on.* **4.** *n.* a hoax. □ *How could you fall for that old shuck?*

shutters *n.* the eyelids. □ *She blinked those yummy shutters over those bedroom eyes, and my knees turned to mush.*

shwench ['ʃʍɛntʃ] *n.* a female freshman. (Collegiate.) □ *There's a shwench in my English class who knows more than the prof.*

sicks *n.* nausea; vomiting. □ *Oh, man, I got the sicks.*

sick (up) *iv.* to empty one's stomach; to vomit. □ *I think I'm going to sick up. Isn't there supposed to be a barf bag in one of these seat pockets?* □ *He's got to sick, and there's no air sickness bag. Help!*

sicky *n.* someone who seems mentally deranged. □ *Some sicky drew these obscene pictures on the wall.*

side *n.* a side of a record. □ *Now here's a side you may remember.*

sieg-heil someone ['sɪg'haɪl] *tv.* to show homage to someone; to salute and obey someone. (From German. Use caution with this reminder of Nazi Germany.) □ *The guy expects all his underlings to sieg-heil him and worship the ground he walks on.* □ *I won't sieg-heil her. She'll have to earn my respect.*

signify 1. *iv.* to cause trouble for fun; to stir things up. (Black.) □ *Why's that dude signifying over there?* **2.** *iv.* to try to look more important than one really is; to brag. (Black.) □ *See that dude signify like somebody important?*

silk *n.* a Caucasian. (Black.) □ *He told his mama that if she doesn't treat him better, he's gonna bring some silk home for dinner and let her see what the neighbors think.*

silks *n.* clothing. □ *Look at the silks on that dude!*

silky *mod.* smooth; unctuous. □ *Beware of anybody that silky.*

silver bullet AND **magic bullet** *n.* a specific, fail-safe solution to a problem. (From the notion that a silver bullet is required to kill a werewolf.) □ *I'm not suggesting that the committee has provided us with a silver bullet, only that its advice was timely and useful.* □ *Okay, I've got the magic bullet you need for your problem. Your favorable vote on the pork storage units for my district would be greatly appreciated, of course.*

sin-bin *n.* a van fitted with bedding as a place for necking and love-making. □ *Wally said he was saving his money to buy a sin-bin so he could have more fun on dates.* □ *Some rusty old sin-bin was parked in front of the house when I got there.*

sink *tv.* to swallow some food or drink. □ *Here, sink a bite of this stuff.*

skag AND **scag** ['skæg] **1.** *n.* a rotten thing or person. □ *Don't be such a skag. Who do you think you are?* **2.** *n.* a very ugly woman. (Collegiate.) □ *She looks like a scag without makeup.*

skank AND **scank** ['skæŋk] **1.** *n.* an ugly (young) woman. (Collegiate.) □ *What a skank she is! Give her a comb or something.* **2.** *iv.* to appear ugly. □ *My face is skanking like mad. Must be the zits.*

skanky ['skæŋki] *mod.* ugly; repellent, usually said of a woman. (Collegiate.) □ *She is so skanky! That grody hairdo doesn't help either.*

skanless *mod.* scandalous □ *Who did that? That skanless! Just skanless.*

skat ['skæt] *n.* beer. □ *You got any pretzels to go with the skat?*

skate 1. *n.* a drinking bout. □ *He's off on another three-day skate.* **2.** *n.* a drunkard; a person on a drinking spree. □ *A couple of skates celebrating the new year ran into my car.* **3.** *n.* something really easy. □ *The test was a skate!* □ *Don't sweat the game. It'll be a skate.* **4.** *iv.* to get drunk. □ *Let's go out and skate, okay?*

skeet *n.* a blob of nasal mucus. (Collegiate.) □ *God, Fred, there's a gross skeet hanging outa your nose!*

skeet-shooting *n.* blowing the nose with the thumb. □ *Stop skeet-shooting and use a snot-rag.*

skeevy ['skivi] *mod.* sleazy and disgusting. □ *This is a skeevy joint. Let's get out.*

skid-lid *n.* a motorcycle helmet. □ *The law has no business telling me I gotta wear a skid-lid.*

skin 1. *n.* a dollar bill. □ *This ticket cost me a couple of skins—and it's not worth it.* **2.** AND **skinhead** *n.* someone with a shaved or bald head. □ *Who's the skin with the earrings?* **3.** *tv.* to cheat or overcharge someone. □ *The guy who sold me this car really skinned me.*

skin a goat *tv.* to empty one's stomach; to vomit. □ *Was my cooking so bad that everybody had to skin a goat?*

skinhead Go to skin.

Skin me! *exclam.* Give me some skin!; Shake my hand! (Originally black.) □ *Hey, old buddy. Don't walk on! Skin me!*

skins *n.* drums. (Musicians. The same as **hides**.) □ *Andy can really make the skins talk.*

skosh ['skoʃ] *n.* a bit more. □ *I need a skosh more room.* □ *Move down a skosh so I can sit down.*

skrag ['skræg] *tv.* to murder someone. (Underworld.) □ *These thugs tried to skrag me, I swear.*

skrilla AND **skrill** *n.* money. □ *I'm totally outa skrilla, man. Shot to the curb.*

skulled *mod.* alcohol or drug intoxicated. □ *He's too skulled to drive.*

skurf ['skɚf] *iv.* to skateboard. (From the words *skate* and *surf*.) □ *He skurfed from city hall to the post office.*

sky *iv.* to travel (to somewhere) in an airplane. □ *Let's sky to New York and then go on to London.*

slackmaster *n.* someone who slacks off a lot; someone who doesn't work hard enough or at all. □ *He never does his share. Nothing but a slackmaster!*

slam 1. *tv.* to criticize someone or something. □ *Please don't slam my car. It's the best I can do.* **2.** *n.* a criticism. □ *Harry took another slam at the sales record the sales force had produced for the meeting.* □ *I don't want to hear another nasty and hateful slam at my sister. Is that clear?*

slam-dancing *n.* a style of punk dancing where the dancers jump about, bumping into each other, trying to knock each other down. □ *Haven't you about had enough of that juvenile slam-dancing?*

slam dunk 1. *tv. & iv.* to force a basketball into the basket from above. (See also *jam*.) □ *Wilbur slam dunked another one, raising the score from 108 to 110.* **2.** *n.* an act of making a basket as in sense 1. □ *Another slam dunk and Wilbur ties the score again!*

slammer 1. *n.* a jail. □ *I got out of the slammer on Monday and was back in by Wednesday.* **2.** *n.* a **slam dunk.** □ *He really has that slammer perfected!*

slam some **beers** *tv.* to drink beer; to drink a number of beers. □ *Fred and Larry went out to slam some beers.*

sleaze AND **sleez** ['sliz] **1.** *n.* a low and despicable person. □ *God, what a sleaze! How can anybody be so skanky?* □ *You'd expect to find a sleaze like that in a sleazoid joint like this.* **2.** *n.* something worthless; junk. □ *I won't sell sleez like that! I won't even have it in my store.* □ *Look at this sleaze—and look at the price! Outra-*

geous! **3.** *iv.* to act low; to be sexually promiscuous. □ *She earned quite a reputation sleazing around with just anybody.*

sleazebag *n.* a repellent person or place. □ *I won't go into a sleazebag like that.* □ *Who is the sleazebag leaning against the wall?*

sleazeball *n.* a repellent person. □ *He's okay if you're into sleazeballs.*

sleaze-bucket *n.* a repellent person, thing, or place. □ *God, what a sleaze-bucket! Let me out of here!*

sleazo(id) 1. ['slizo AND 'slizoid] *mod.* low; disreputable; sleazy. □ *Let's get out of this sleazo joint.* □ *Who wants a sleazoid car with no backseat?* **2.** *n.* a sleazy person. □ *Who is this sleazoid?* □ *Who was that sleazo I saw you with last night?*

sleepwalk *n.* a movement toward something without effort. (A movement that could be done in one's sleep. See also **cakewalk**, a **walk**.) □ *Getting the degree was a sleepwalk. Getting a job was hell.*

sleez Go to sleaze.

slime 1. *n.* a worthless person; a low and wretched person. □ *What a slime that guy is!* **2.** *n.* degrading matters; corrupt people or situations. □ *I don't want to be involved in slime like that.* □ *The press uncovered even more slime at city hall.*

slime bag AND **slime bucket; slimeball** *n.* a despicable person, usually a male. (See also **slime**.) □ *Gee, a slime bag like that in the same room with me! Yuck!* □ *Who's the slime bucket in the 1962 Bonneville?*

slimeball Go to slime bag.

slime bucket Go to slime bag.

Slip me five! Go to Give me (some) skin!

slip someone **five** Go to give someone five.

slop(s) *n.* bad beer; inferior liquor. □ *Why do we have to drink slops like this? Can't Tom afford to give his guests something decent?* □ *Tom's slop is better than water—dishwater anyway.*

slosh 1. *n.* beer; liquor. □ *How about a glass of slosh?* **2.** *tv. & iv.* to drink liquor, including beer; to drink to excess. □ *Are you going to slosh gin all night?*

sludgeball ['slədʒbɑl] *n.* a despicable and repellent person. □ *Mike is such a sludgeball! Why do you keep seeing him?*

smacker 1. *n.* the face. □ *She ought to give that ugly smacker back to the horse before it runs into something.* **2.** *n.* a dollar. (Underworld.) □ *You got a couple of smackers for the tollbooth?* **3.** *n.* a kiss. □ *He planted a smacker square on her lips. She kicked him in the shins for his trouble.* □ *Marlowe was greeted at the door by a lovely, cuddly chick in a nightie—eyes closed and lips parted for a better-than-average smacker. He really wished—just for a moment—that he hadn't rung the wrong doorbell.*

smarmy ['smɑrmi] *mod.* insincere and obsequious. □ *The guy is so smarmy, I can't stand him.*

smarts *n.* intelligence. □ *I got the smarts to do the job. All I need is someone to trust me.*

smash *n.* wine. (Black. Because it is made from smashed grapes.) □ *I got a bottle of smash in my car.*

smashed *mod.* alcohol or drug intoxicated. □ *He was so smashed he couldn't stand up.* □ *Molly can drink a lot without ever getting smashed.*

smash hit *n.* a play, movie, musical, etc., that is a big success. □ *Her first book was a smash hit. The second was a disaster.* □ *A smash hit doesn't always make people rich.*

smear *tv.* to defeat someone; to outscore someone. □ *They said they would smear us, but we smeared them.*

smeller *n.* [someone's] nose. □ *I think my smeller's gone bad because of my cold.*

smile AND **smiler; smiley** *n.* a drink of liquor; liquor. □ *Come over and join me for a smiley.* □ *Here, have a smiler on me.*

smiler Go to smile.

smiley Go to smile.

smoke 1. *n.* a tobacco cigarette; a pipe; a cigar. □ *I think I'll have a smoke now.* □ *You got a smoke I can owe you?* **2.** *n.* the act of smoking anything smokable, including drugs. □ *I need a smoke—of anything.* **3.** *n.* exaggeration; deception. (See also blow smoke.) □ *That's not a report. That's just smoke.*

smoke eater *n.* a firefighter. □ *A couple of off-duty smoke eaters wandered around the store doing a little shopping.* □ *The smoke eaters took a long time getting there.*

smokin' ['smokən] *mod.* really hot; overpowering. □ *Those threads on that dude are really smokin'.* □ *If you wanna hear some smokin' vinyl, just stay tuned.*

smoking gun *n.* the indisputable sign of guilt. □ *Mr. South was left holding the smoking gun.*

smurf ['smɚf] **1.** *n.* someone who cleans ill-gotten money by buying cashier's checks at banks and shifting funds from place to place. (Underworld. From the name of a type of cartoon character.) □ *I think the guy at the first window is a smurf. He's in here twice a week with $9,500 in cash each time.* □ *Did you get a good look at this alleged smurf?* **2.** *tv. & iv.* to shift illicit money from place to place to conceal its origin. (Underworld.) □ *I smurf for a living. It doesn't pay much, but you meet some very interesting people.* □ *I smurfed a fortune for a famous drug kingpin and got 14 years up the river—with some very interesting people.*

smurfbrain ['smɚfbren] *n.* a simple-minded person. (A smurf is an innocent little cartoon character.) □ *You can be such a smurfbrain!*

smurfed ['smɚft] *mod.* having to do with a bank that has been used to launder money. (See also **smurf**.) □ *The teller came slowly into the office. "I think we were smurfed," she said.* □ *See that this cash is smurfed by Friday.*

snag 1. *n.* a difficulty. □ *There's a little snag in our plan.* □ *We ran into a little snag, I'm sorry to say.* **2.** *n.* an ugly (young) woman. □ *She's not a snag! She's lovely.* **3.** AND **SNAG** *n.* a Sensitive New-Age Guy. □ *Tim is a wimp, a SNAG, a twit!* **4.** *tv.* to procure, grab, or steal something. □ *Somebody snagged the jacket I just bought.*

snake 1. *iv.* to scheme; to plot and plan. (Prisons.) □ *He spent a lot of time snaking about that job.* **2.** *tv.* to steal something. □ *Where did you snake that bike?*

snap 1. *n.* a snapshot. □ *I got some good snaps of the fish you caught.* **2.** *iv.* to go crazy. □ *Suddenly Walter snapped and began beating her savagely.* □ *His mind snapped, and he's never been right since.* **3.** Go to **be a snap.**

snap one's **cookies** *tv.* to vomit; to regurgitate. (See also **blow** one's **cookies**.) □ *I think I'm gonna snap my cookies!*

snitzy ['snɪtsi] *mod.* classy; ritzy. □ *This is a pretty snitzy place—tablecloths and everything.*

snookered ['snʊkɚd] *mod.* cheated; deceived. □ *I got snookered at the service station.*

snoozamorooed ['snuzəmə'rud] *mod.* alcohol intoxicated. □ *The groom went and got himself snoozamorooed before the wedding.*

snotted *mod.* very drunk. □ *She gets totally snotted almost every night.*

snow 1. *n.* deceitful talk; deception. □ *All I heard for an hour was snow. Now, what's the truth?* **2.** *tv.* to attempt to deceive someone. □ *You can try to snow me if you want, but I'm onto your tricks.* **3.** *n.* a powdered or crystalline narcotic: morphine, heroin, or cocaine. (Now almost always cocaine.) □ *The price of snow has come down a lot as South America exports more of it.*

snow job *n.* a systematic deception. □ *You can generally tell when a student is trying to do a snow job.*

snuff it *tv.* to die. □ *The cat opened its eyes, leapt straight up in the air, and snuffed it.*

S.O.B. *n.* a son of a bitch; a despised person, usually a male. (Crude. Also a rude and provocative term of address. Never an acronym.) □ *Tell that S.O.B. to mind his own business.*

sofa spud ['sofə 'spəd] *n.* someone who spends a great deal of time sitting and watching television. (A play on **couch potato**.) □ *Sofa spuds have been getting a lot of attention in the newspapers.*

software rot *n.* an imaginary disease that causes computer programs to go bad over a long period of time. (Computers.) □ *What you have here is not a bug, but just plain old software rot.*

soldier 1. *n.* a liquor bottle; an empty liquor bottle. (Compare to **dead soldier**.) □ *There was a broken soldier on the floor and a cap on the table.* **2.** *n.* a whole tobacco cigarette. □ *The old man almost fell over trying to pick up the soldier from the sidewalk.* □ *"Look, Jed. A soldier. My lucky day!" said the old soak to his buddy.*

solid 1. *mod.* good; great; **cool**. □ *Man, this music is solid!* **2.** *mod.* consecutive; consecutively. □ *Larry ate for four solid days.*

someone's ass is grass *phr.* someone has had it; It is the end for someone. □ *You do that again, and your ass is grass!*

some pumpkins AND **some punkins** *n.* someone or something great or special. □ *That chick is some punkins!*

some punkins Go to some pumpkins.

sorry-ass(ed) 1. *mod.* sad and depressed. (Usually objectionable.) □ *Man, old Charlie was about the most sorry-ass dude you ever saw.* **2.** *mod.* worthless; poor quality. (Usually objectionable.) □ *This is really a sorry-ass movie. I want my money back.* □ *How much longer do I have to drive this sorry-ass excuse for an automobile?*

S.O.S. Go to shit on a shingle.

(So) sue me! *phr.* So, if you are so bothered or offended, take me into court and sue me! (A way of saying "There is nothing you can do about it.") □ *You don't like the way I talk? So, sue me!*

soul kiss 1. *n.* a kiss where the kissers' tongues interact; a French kiss. □ *Yes, a soul kiss sounds silly—till you try it with somebody you really like.* **2.** *iv.* [for two people] to kiss with interacting tongues. □ *They were soul kissing and making noises.*

sounds *n.* music; records. □ *I got some new sounds. Ya wanna come over and listen?*

Soup's on! *iv.* Dinner is ready. □ *Time to eat! Soup's on!*

sozzle ['sazəl] *iv.* to drink to excess. □ *I wish you'd stop coming home every night and sozzling to oblivion.*

spaced (out) AND **spacy** *mod.* silly; giddy. □ *I have such spaced-out parents!* □ *I love my spacy old dad.*

space-out *n.* a giddy person. □ *Terry is becoming such a space-out!*

space (out) *iv.* to become giddy; to become disoriented. □ *She is spacing again. She doesn't even know where she is.* □ *I spaced out after the long climb.*

space someone out *tv.* to cause someone to become giddy. □ *The whole business just spaced me out.* ⊤ *The spectacle spaced out the entire audience.*

spacy Go to spaced (out).

spam 1. *n.* something disliked, typically, but not necessarily, food. (From the brand name of a canned meat product.) □ *I can't eat this spam. It could be spoiled.* **2.** *n.* one or a series of uninvited e-mail messages advertising money-making schemes, pornography, or sales of any kind. □ *If I don't recognize the sender, I assume the message is spam and I delete it.* **3.** *tv.* to clutter or fill someone's e-mail account with spam (sense 2). □ *Some jerk is spamming me with an advertisement for dirty pictures.*

spanked *mod.* drunk. □ *Those gals are spanked. Who served them all that booze?*

spastic *mod.* overly responsive; out of control. □ *Tell the spastic jerk to shut up.*

spaz ['spæz] **1.** *n.* a fit or an attack; a strong reaction to a bad or funny situation. □ *My father had a spaz when he heard.* □ *Take it easy! Don't have a spaz.* **2.** *n.* a total jerk; someone who over-reacts to something. (Not used for a congenitally spastic condition.) □ *Some spaz is in the other room screaming about a stolen car.*

spaz around *iv.* to waste time; to mess around. □ *You kids are always spazzing around. Why don't you get a job?*

spaz out 1. *iv.* to overreact to something; to become overly excited about something. □ *I knew you would spaz out! It's not that bad!* **2.** *n.* an emotional display. (Usually **spaz-out**.) □ *There's no need for a spaz-out!*

specs ['spɛks] *n.* eyeglasses; spectacles. □ *I broke my specs.*

speeder *n.* a speeding ticket. □ *The cop that gave Mary a speeder Wednesday gave her another one Friday.* □ *Actually, that's three speeders in one week, counting the one she got Monday.*

spiff *n.* extra money paid to a salesperson to sell certain merchandise aggressively. (See also **push money**.) □ *The manufacturer supplied a little spiff that even the store manager didn't know about.* □ *I got about $300 last month in spiff for selling some low-grade shoes.*

spiffed out *mod.* nicely dressed up; decked out. □ *I like to get all spiffed out every now and then.*

spiffed up *mod.* dressed up, brushed up, and polished up nicely. □ *See if you can get yourself a little spiffed up before we get to the front door. We wouldn't want the Wilmington-Thorpes to think you only have one suit.* □ *The house doesn't have to be too spiffed up for the Franklins. They are used to clutter.*

spiffy ['spɪfi] *mod.* excellent. □ *This is a real spiffy place you've got here, Sam.*

spike *tv.* to puncture an idea. □ *I explained the plan, but the boss spiked it immediately.*

spiked 1. *mod.* having to do with a drink with alcohol added; having to do with a punch with an alcoholic content. □ *Is the punch spiked? I want some without alcohol.* **2.** *mod.* having to do with hair that stands up straight. □ *His spiked hair wouldn't look so bad if it wasn't orange.*

spill one's **guts on** someone Go to spill one's guts (to someone).

spill one's **guts (to** someone) AND **spill** one's **guts on** someone *tv.* to tell all; to confess; to pour one's heart out to someone. □ *I had to spill my guts to someone about the broken window.*

spinach *n.* money. (Because it is green.) □ *Look at this! One hundred dollars in good old American spinach!*

split *iv.* to leave. □ *I've got to split. See you later.*

sponged *mod.* thirsty. □ *I gotta get a drink, man. I'm sponged!*

sponge off someone *n.* to live off someone; to abuse someone by taking food and shelter from them without compensation. □ *Go get a job! Stop sponging off me!*

spook 1. *tv.* to frighten or startle someone or something. □ *Don't spook the cattle. They'll stampede.* **2.** *n.* a spy; a C.I.A. (U.S. Central Intelligence Agency) agent. □ *I just learned that my uncle had been a spook for years.*

spook factory *n.* the C.I.A. (U.S. Central Intelligence Agency) in Washington, D.C., where spies are said to be trained. □ *Tom got a job in the spook factory.*

spot 1. *n.* a small drink of liquor. □ *I'll just have a spot, please.* **2.** *n.* a nightclub; a night spot. □ *It was a nice little spot, with a combo and a canary.* □ *We went to a spot with a jukebox for entertainment.*

spot someone (something) **1.** *tv.* to give an advantage to someone. □ *I'll spot you 20 points.* **2.** *tv.* to lend someone something. □ *Can you spot me a few bucks?* □ *I can spot you a whole hundred!*

spring for something AND **bounce for** something *iv.* to treat (someone) by buying something. (See also **pop for** something.) □ *I'm bouncing for pizza. Any takers?* □ *Ralph sprang for drinks, and we all had a great time.*

spud ['spəd] **1.** *n.* a potato. □ *Mashed spuds are the best of all.* **2.** *n.* vodka, presumed to be made from potatoes. □ *How about a glass of spud?*

spunk ['spəŋk] *n.* courage. □ *Show some spunk. Get in there and stand up for your rights.*

square 1. *mod.* old-fashioned; law-abiding; stodgy. □ *Man, you are really square.* **2.** *n.* a person who behaves properly. □ *You are a square if I ever saw one.* **3.** AND **square joint** *n.* a tobacco cigarette, compared to a marijuana cigarette. □ *You got a square joint on you?* □ *No, thanks. I've heard that them squares will give you cancer.* **4.** *tv.* to settle or to make something right. □ *Let's talk about squaring this matter.*

square joint Go to square.

squat 1. *iv.* to sit (down). □ *Squat over here by the fire.* **2.** *n.* nothing. (See also diddly-squat.) □ *I worked all day on this, and she didn't pay me squat.*

squeal *iv.* to inform (someone about something). □ *Who squealed to the cops?* □ *Molly is the one who squealed.*

squeeze 1. *n.* liquor. (Black. See also grape(s).) □ *Let's stop on the way and get some squeeze.* **2.** *tv.* to put pressure on someone. □ *The mob began to squeeze Carl for money.* **3.** *n.* a tight situation; a situation where pressure is felt. □ *I'm in sort of a squeeze. Can you wait a month?* **4.** *n.* one's lover. (Black.) □ *I'll see if my squeeze wants to go.*

squib ['skwɪb] *n.* a notice; a small advertisement. □ *There was a squib in the paper about your project.*

squid ['skwɪd] *n.* an earnest student. (Collegiate.) □ *I'm no squid. I went out on a date last month.*

squiff ['skwɪf] *n.* a drunkard. □ *It's no fun living with a squiff.*

squiff out *iv.* to collapse from drink. □ *She kept from squiffing out because she didn't trust her date.*

squirrel 1. *n.* a strange or eccentric person. □ *Martin can be such a squirrel.* **2.** *n.* a car engine's horsepower. □ *What kind of squirrels you got under the hood?*

the **squirts** *n.* a case of diarrhea. □ *He's got the squirts and can't go out.*

squooshy ['skwuʃi AND 'skwuʃi] *mod.* soft, wet, and gooey. □ *I like to walk barefooted in squooshy mud.*

stache Go to stash.

stanza ['stænzə] *n.* an inning in baseball or some other division of a ball game. □ *He's doing better than he was in the last stanza.* □ *Jerry Clay is pitching again in this stanza.*

starched AND **starchy** *mod.* alcohol intoxicated. (Compare to stiff.) □ *No, he wasn't quite stiff, but he was starched.*

starchy Go to starched.

stash 1. AND **stache** *n.* a mustache. □ *Jerry has this enormous stash that he keeps waxed and trimmed.* **2.** *tv.* to hide something (somewhere). □ *Stash this under the chair until I can think of a place to put it.* **3.** *n.* a concealed supply of drugs, especially marijuana; drugs and drug paraphernalia stored in a secret place. (Drugs.) □ *Albert's stash was never located by the fuzz.*

stat ['stæt] **1.** *n.* a thermostat. □ *Who turned down the stat?* **2.** AND **STAT** *mod.* a medical notation meaning "immediately." (From Latin *statim* "immediately.") □ *The order is marked stat, so do it now.*

stay loose Go to hang loose.

steam 1. *tv.* to anger someone. □ *She steamed him by being two hours late.* **2.** *iv.* to be angry. □ *They steamed for a while and then did as they were told.*

steamed (up) *mod.* angry. □ *Now, now, don't get so steamed up!*

steam someone's beam *tv.* to make someone angry. □ *Being stood up really steams my beam!*

stems *n.* legs. □ *Look at the stems on that dame!*

step off the curb *iv.* to die. □ *Ralph almost stepped off the curb during his operation.*

Step on it! *iv.* Hurry up! (As if one were pressing down on the gas pedal. Not limited to vehicles, though.) □ *We're late. Come on! Step on it!*

stern *n.* the posterior. □ *The little airplane crashed right into the stern of an enormous lady who didn't even notice.* □ *Haul your stern over here and sit down.*

stick like shit to a shovel Go to cling like shit to a shovel.

stiff 1. AND **stiffed** *mod.* alcohol intoxicated; dead drunk. □ *Kelly was too stiff to find his keys.* **2.** *n.* a drunkard. □ *Some stiff staggered by—belching clouds of some beery smell.* **3.** *n.* a corpse. (Underworld.) □ *They pulled another stiff out of the river last* *night. Looks like another mob killing.* □ *They took me into a room full of stiffs to identify Walter's body.* **4.** *tv.* to fail to tip someone who expects it. □ *Ya know, you can tell right away when a guy's gonna stiff you—ya just know.* □ *I guess I get stiffed two or three times a day.*

sting 1. *tv.* to cheat or swindle someone; to overcharge someone. □ *They are likely to sting you in any of those pawnshops.* **2.** *n.* a well-planned scheme to entrap criminals. □ *The sting came off without a hitch.* **3.** *tv.* to entrap and arrest someone. □ *The feebies stung the whole gang at once.*

stinger *n.* the drawback; the catch; the hitch. □ *Sounds good, but what's the stinger?*

stink 1. *iv.* to be repellent. □ *This whole setup stinks.* **2.** *n.* a commotion. □ *The stink you made about money has done no good at all. You're fired.* □ *One more stink like that and out you go.*

stinker 1. *n.* an unpleasant or wicked person. □ *Jerry is a real stinker. Look what he did!* **2.** *n.* a serious problem. □ *This whole business is a real stinker.*

stink on ice *iv.* to be really rotten. (So rotten as to reek even when frozen.) □ *The whole idea stank on ice.*

stinkpot 1. *n.* a baby with a dirty diaper. (Also a term of address.) □ *Jimmy's a stinkpot. Better change him.* **2.** *n.* anything smelly. □ *Why don't you drive this stinkpot into a service station and get it tuned?*

stoked (on someone or something**)** *mod.* excited by someone or something. (Compare to **stokin'**.) □ *We are totally stoked on Mary. She is the greatest.*

stoked out *mod.* exhausted. □ *Alex is totally stoked out.*

stokin' *mod.* excellent; wild. □ *That car is really stokin'.*

stone *mod.* completely; totally. □ *This lecture is stone dull.* □ *I am stone mad at you.*

stoned (out) *mod.* alcohol or drug intoxicated. □ *I have never seen anybody so stoned who could still talk.*

stone fox *n.* an attractive woman; a very sexy woman. □ *She is a stone fox if I ever saw one.*

stone groove *n.* something really cool; a fine party or concert. □ *This affair is not what I would call a stone groove. Stone beige, maybe.* □ *Ted's do was a stone groove.*

stones 1. *n.* the testicles. (Also a standard English euphemism. See also **rocks**.) □ *You scared me so much, I almost lost my stones.* **2.** *n.* courage; bravado. □ *Hey, man, you got no stones!*

stonkered ['stɔŋkɚd] **1.** *mod.* killed. □ *The car crashed into him and he was stonkered for sure.* **2.** *mod.* alcohol intoxicated. □ *My buddy here is stonkered and needs a ride, and can I have one, too?*

storked *mod.* pregnant. □ *I hear that Molly is storked again.*

straight 1. *mod.* honest; unembellished. □ *This is the straight truth.* □ *Have I ever been anything but straight with you?* **2.** *n.* a tobacco cigarette; a tobacco cigarette butt. (As opposed to a marijuana cigarette.) □ *No, I want a straight. That pot makes me sneeze.* **3.** *mod.* having to do with undiluted liquor. □ *I'll take mine straight.* □ *Make mine straight with a little ice.* **4.** *mod.* relieved and satisfied by a dose of drugs. (Drugs.) □ *It only takes a few bucks and a little time to get straight.* **5.** *mod.* off drugs; no longer addicted to drugs. □ *I'm straight now, and I'm gonna stay that way.* **6.** *n.* a square person (who does not use drugs, etc.). □ *The guy's a straight. He's gonna turn us over to the cops!* **7.** *n.* a non-homosexual; a heterosexual. (Often from the homosexual point of view.) □ *Walter invited a few straights to the affair, just to keep things calm.* **8.** *mod.* not homosexual; not having a homosexual orientation. □ *He wandered into a straight bar by mistake.* **9.** *mod.* excellent. □ *This news is truly straight and I am happy to hear it.* □ *You are a straight G.*

straight (dope) *n.* the true information. □ *He gave us the straight dope.* □ *I want the straight. I can take it.*

straight low *n.* the absolute truth; the true lowdown on something. □ *Nobody ain't gonna tell no warden the straight low; you can be sure of that.*

straight up 1. *mod.* upright. □ *She is one of the most straight-up brokers in town.* **2.** *mod.* without ice; neat. □ *I'll have a bourbon, straight up, please.*

strap *n.* an athlete, not necessarily male. (From *jockstrap*.) □ *A whole gang of straps came in the bar and ordered milk.*

strapped 1. *mod.* broke; short of money. □ *They're really strapped for money at the present time.* **2.** *mod.* wearing a gun holster. □ *Be careful. He's strapped. I see it under his jacket.*

the **street 1.** *n.* the real, free world, as opposed to prison. □ *It's good to be back on the street.* **2.** *n.* Wall Street in New York City. □ *The street doesn't seem to believe the policy makers in Washington.*

streeter *n.* an urban street person. □ *These streeters have to be bright and clever just to survive.*

street smart *mod.* wise in the ways of urban life; wise in the ways of tough neighborhoods. □ *Freddy was street smart at age eight.*

street smarts *n.* the knowledge and ability to survive on the urban street. □ *If you don't have street smarts, you won't last long out there.*

street sweeper *n.* a machine gun. □ *In my neighborhood, the sound of street sweepers is about as common as the sound of horns honking.*

stress 1. *iv.* to suffer annoyance; to experience stress. □ *Clare finds that she is stressing more and more about little things.* **2.** *tv.* to annoy or bother someone. □ *Don't stress Wally! He's had a hard day.*

stressed *mod.* upset; annoyed. □ *Come on, man, don't get stressed! It's only a gag.*

stretch 1. *n.* a period of time. (Folksy.) □ *Let's talk here for a stretch and then go up and see if dinner's ready.* □ *I sat there for a stretch and then got up and kept going.* **2.** *n.* a prison term. □ *I was away for a stretch of about seven years.* **3.** *iv.* to hang (as with a death sentence). □ *You will stretch for this, Lefty!* **4.** *tv.* to cut or dilute a drug. □ *Let's stretch this stuff, sell it, and then get out of town.* **5.** *n.* a nickname for a tall person, usually male. (Usually **Stretch.**) □ *Well, Stretch, think you'll go out for basketball this season?*

stroke *tv. & iv.* to flatter someone; to soothe and comfort someone. □ *She strokes everybody to keep them on her side during the bad times.*

stud ['stəd] *n.* a human male viewed as very successful with women. (From the term for a male horse used for breeding purposes.) □ *Fred thinks he is a real stud.*

studhammer *n.* a male who is successful sexually with women. □ *The guy thinks he is a studhammer, but he is just a jerk.*

stud-muffin *n.* a really good-looking guy; a stud. □ *Who's the stud-muffin with Sally?*

Stuff a sock in it! AND **Put a sock in it!** *exclam.* Shut up! (That is, stuff a sock in your mouth.) □ *Stuff a sock in it! You are a pain.*

stumper *n.* a shoe. (Black. Usually plural. See also **stumps**.) □ *Make those stumpers shine!*

stumps *n.* a person's legs. □ *My stumps are sore from all that walking.*

stupid-ass Go to dumb-ass.

style *iv.* to show off; to strut around. (Black.) □ *Why don't you style over here and meet my man?*

suave ['swɑv] *n.* personal polish and smoothness. □ *You need some suave to carry off this sham.*

suck 1. AND **suck** something **up** *tv.* to drink beer or liquor. □ *Let's go out and suck a few up.* **2.** *iv.* [for someone or something] to be bad or undesirable. □ *I think that the whole business sucks.*

sucker 1. *n.* a dupe; an easy mark. □ *The sucker says he doesn't need a bridge, thank you.* **2.** *tv.* to trick or victimize someone. □ *That crook suckered me. I should have known better.* **3.** *n.* an annoying person. (Also a rude term of address.) □ *Look, sucker, get out of my way!* **4.** *n.* a gadget; a thing. □ *Where is that sucker that looks like a screw?*

suck face *tv.* to kiss. (Compare to **swap spits**.) □ *The kid said he was going out to suck face. It sounds awful.*

suck (some) brew AND **suck (some) suds** *tv.* to drink beer. (See also **quaff a brew**.) □ *Wanna go suck some brew?* □ *I'm tired of sucking suds. Got any whiskey?*

suck someone's **hind tit** AND **kiss** someone's **hind tit** *tv.* to be obsequious to someone. (Usually objectionable.) □ *What does he want me to do, suck his hind tit or something?*

suck (some) suds Go to suck (some) brew.

suck something **up** Go to suck.

sucky *mod.* poor; undesirable. □ *This is the suckiest movie I ever saw.* □ *This food is sucky. It is really vile!*

suds 1. *n.* beer. □ *How about some suds, Bill?* **2.** *iv.* to drink beer. □ *They were sudsing when they should have been studying.*

sugar daddy *n.* an older man who takes care of a younger person, especially a young man or woman. □ *Mr. Wilson is sort of a sugar daddy to the whole team.*

suit *n.* a businessman or businesswoman; someone who is in charge. □ *This suit comes up and asks to go to the airport.*

sunshades *n.* sunglasses. (See also shades.) □ *Where are my sunshades? Did you borrow them again?*

superfly *mod.* excellent; wonderful. □ *I don't care about this superfly friend of yours. If he doesn't have a job, I don't want you seeing him anymore. Ya hear?*

superjock 1. *n.* an excellent athlete. □ *Mike is a real superjock. He plays four sports.* **2.** *n.* a very well-built man regardless of athletic ability. □ *My boyfriend is a superjock, and does he look good!*

super-strap *n.* an earnest and hardworking student. (As compared to a jock, strap, superjock.) □ *He's just a super-strap and he doesn't do anything but study.*

surf the net *tv.* to browse through the offerings of the Internet. □ *He surfs the net for three hours each evening.*

Suzy Homemaker *n.* a personification of the quintessential female American housewife. □ *Well, aren't you just Miss Suzy Homemaker! You're even wearing an apron!*

swacked ['swækt] *mod.* alcohol intoxicated. □ *Molly is too swacked to drive home. Can somebody give her a lift?*

swallow 1. *n.* a puff of cigarette smoke. □ *He took just one swallow and started coughing.* **2.** *tv.* to believe or accept something. □ *Nobody's gonna swallow that nonsense.*

swap spits *tv.* to kiss with someone. □ *A couple of kids were in the car swapping spits.*

sweat 1. *tv. & iv.* to fret (about something) while waiting for an outcome. □ *This whole promotion business really has me sweating.* **2.** *n.* trouble; bother. □ *I can handle it. It won't cause me any sweat.*

sweat blood Go to piss blood.

swift 1. *mod.* smart and clever. □ *Dave is doing well in school. He's swift, and he likes his classes.* **2.** *mod.* sexually fast or easy, usually said of a woman. □ *Molly is swift they say, but I find her to be a perfect lady.*

swing 1. *iv.* [for someone] to be up to date and modern. □ *Tom really swings. Look at those blue suede shoes!* **2.** *iv.* [for a party or other event] to be fun or exciting. □ *I've never been to a gathering that swings like this one.* **3.** *iv.* to be involved in sexual fads, group sex, or the swapping of sexual partners. □ *Carol says that Tom, Ted, and Alice swing. How does she know?*

swipe 1. *tv.* to drink liquor rapidly and to excess; to bolt a drink of liquor. □ *Fred sat at the bar and swiped two gins and ate an egg.* **2.** *n.* inferior or homemade liquor. □ *This swipe is gross. I'd rather drink water.* **3.** *tv.* to steal something. □ *Carl swiped a pack of cigarettes from the counter.* **4.** *n.* a blow or an act of striking someone or something. □ *The cat gave the mouse a swipe with its paw.*

swish ['swɪʃ] **1.** AND **swishy** *mod.* overly fancy; effeminate; displaying effeminacy. □ *The lobby of the theater was a little swish, but not offensive.* **2.** *n.* elaborate decoration; effeminacy. □ *What this place needs is more swish. Hang some baubles here and there.* **3.** *n.* a gay male. (Rude and derogatory.) □ *This place is full of swishes. Let's leave.*

switch *n.* a switchblade knife. □ *They found a switch in his pocket when they searched him.*

swoozled AND **swozzled** ['swuzəld AND 'swɑzəld] *mod.* alcohol intoxicated. □ *How can anybody be so swozzled on three beers?*

swozzled Go to swoozled.

tabbed *mod.* well dressed. (Black.) □ *That dude is well tabbed.* □ *She's really tabbed in some nice threads.*

tag 1. *n.* a name. □ *I know the face, but I forgot the tag.* **2.** *n.* a car license plate or sticker. □ *The car had Kansas tags and was towing a trailer.*

tagger *n.* a gang member who puts gang signs and themes on things with spray paint. □ *Sam is our tagger. Man, he's an artist.*

take a crap Go to take a shit.

take a dirt nap *tv.* to die and be buried. □ *Isn't Tom a little young to take a dirt nap?*

take a dump Go to take a shit.

take a hike AND **take a walk** *tv.* to leave; to beat it. □ *Okay, I've had it with you. Take a hike! Beat it!* □ *I had enough of the boss and the whole place, so I cleaned out my desk and took a walk.*

take a shit AND **take a crap; take a dump; take a squat** *tv.* to defecate. □ *Hurry up in there! I gotta take a shit.*

take a squat Go to take a shit.

take a walk Go to take a hike.

take five *tv.* to take a five-minute break. □ *Okay, gang, take five. Be back here in five minutes, or else.*

taken AND **had; took 1.** *mod.* cheated; deceived. (Correct grammar is usually avoided in the slang senses of these words.) □ *You were really took, all right.* **2.** *mod.* drug intoxicated; unconscious from drugs. □ *The guy in the corner booth was taken and crying in his beer.* □ *His eyes were bloodshot, his hands were shaking—he was had.* **3.** *mod.* dead. □ *I'm sorry, your cat is taken—pifted.* □ *Your cat's took, lady, tough luck.*

take names *tv.* to make a list of wrongdoers. (Often figuratively, as with a schoolteacher whose major weapon is to take names and send them to the principal.) □ *Gary is coming by to talk about the little riot last night, and I think he's taking names.*

take someone or something **out 1.** *tv.* [with *someone*] to block someone, as in a football game. □ *I was supposed to take out the left end, but I was trapped under the center.* Ⓣ *Okay, Andy, you take out the center this time.* **2.** *tv.* [with *something*] to bomb or destroy something. □ *The enemy took out one of the tanks, but not the one carrying the medicine.* Ⓣ *The last flight took out two enemy bunkers and a radar installation.* **3.** *tv.* [with *someone*] to date someone. □ *I hope he'll take me out soon.*

take the spear (in one's **chest)** *tv.* to accept full blame for something; to accept the full brunt of the punishment for something. □ *The admiral got the short straw and had to take the spear in his chest.* □ *I sure didn't want to take the spear.*

taking care of business *tv.* doing what one is meant to do; coping with life as it is. (Black.) □ *Walter is taking care of business. Back in a minute.*

talking head *n.* a television news reader or announcer whose head and neck appear on the screen. □ *I've had it with talking heads. I can read the paper and learn as much in 20 minutes.* □ *Some of those talking heads make millions a year.*

talk on the big white phone *iv.* to vomit into a toilet. □ *She was talking on the big white phone all night.*

tall 1. *mod.* high on drugs; intoxicated with marijuana. (Drugs.) □ *When Jerry gets a little tall, he gets overwhelmed with a sense of guilt.* **2.** *mod.* high quality. □ *This is one tall pizza, man.*

tall in the saddle *mod.* proud. (Often with *sit.*) □ *I'll still be tall in the saddle when you are experiencing the results of your folly.* □ *Despite her difficulties, she still sat tall in the saddle.*

tank 1. AND **tank up** *iv.* to drink too much beer; to drink to excess. □ *The two brothers were tanking up and didn't hear me come in.* **2.** *tv. & iv.* to lose a game deliberately. □ *The coach got wind of a plan to tank Friday's game.* **3.** *iv.* for something to fail. □ *The entire stock market tanked on Friday.*

tanked 1. AND **tanked up** *mod.* alcohol intoxicated. □ *She was too tanked to drive.* **2.** *mod.* defeated; outscored. □ *The team was tanked again—20 to 17.*

tanked up Go to tanked.

tank up Go to tank.

tap dance like mad *iv.* to be busy continuously; to have to move fast to distract someone. □ *When things get tough, Congress tap dances like mad.* □ *Any public official knows how to tap dance like mad and still seem honest.*

taped ['tept] *mod.* finalized; settled. (As if one were taping a package.) □ *Until this thing is taped, we can't do anything.*

tap out *iv.* to lose one's money in gambling or in the financial markets. □ *I'm gonna tap out in about three more rolls—just watch.*

tapped (out) **1.** *mod.* broke. □ *The consumer is just about tapped. Don't expect much buying in that sector.* □ *I'm tapped out. Nothing left for you or anybody else this month.* **2.** *mod.* exhausted. □ *I need a nap. I'm tapped out.* □ *I've had it. I'm tapped.* **3.** *mod.* ruined. □ *We are tapped. That really did it to us.* □ *The project is completely tapped out.*

tawny ['tɔni] *mod.* excellent. □ *Who is throwing this tawny party anyway?* □ *This pizza is, like, tawny!*

tchotchke AND **chotchke** ['tʃætʃki] *n.* a trinket or ornament. (From Yiddish.) □ *Her whole house is filled with tchotchkes and old photographs.*

technicolor yawn *n.* vomit. □ *This garbage will bring on a few technicolor yawns if we serve it.*

tee someone **off** *tv.* to make someone angry. □ *That really teed me off!* ⊤ *Well, you sure managed to tee off everybody!*

T.G.I.F. 1. *interj.* Thank God it's Friday. □ *Everybody was muttering T.G.I.F. by Friday afternoon.* **2.** *n.* a party held on Friday in honor of the end of the workweek. □ *Everyone is invited to the T.G.I.F. tonight.*

That's so suck! *phr.* That's so awful. □ *Eat sweet potatoes? That's so suck!*

third wheel *n.* an extra person; a person who gets in the way. (Such a person is as useful as a third wheel on a bicycle.) □ *Well, let's face it. We don't need you. You are a third wheel.*

thou ['θɑʊ] *n.* one thousand. □ *I managed to get a couple of thou from the bank, but I need a little more than that.* □ *It only costs four thou. I could borrow it from my uncle.*

threads *n.* clothing. □ *When'd you get new threads, man?* □ *Good-looking threads on Wally, huh?*

throat *n.* an earnest student; a very hardworking student. (Collegiate. From *cutthroat*.) □ *Merton is not a throat! He's not that smart.* □ *All the throats got A's, of course.*

the **throne** *n.* a toilet; a toilet seat. □ *And there was the cat—right on the throne, just staring at me.*

throw a map *tv.* to empty one's stomach; to vomit. □ *I felt like I was going to throw a map.*

throw one's **cookies** Go to **toss** one's **cookies**.

throw one's **voice** *tv.* to empty one's stomach; to vomit. □ *Wally's in the john throwing his voice.* □ *Another drink of that stuff and Don'll be throwing his voice all night.*

throw salt on someone's **game** *tv.* to mess up someone's plans. □ *I don't mean to throw salt on your game, but I don't think you can pull it off.*

throw something **back** *tv.* to eat or drink something. ⊤ *Did you throw back that whole pizza?* ⊤ *Jed threw back a quick drink and went on with his complaining.*

throw up one's **toenails** *tv.* to wretch; to vomit a lot. □ *It sounded like he was throwing up his toenails.* ⊤ *Who's in the john throwing up her toenails?*

thunderbox *n.* a portable stereo radio, often played very loudly in public. □ *Someday I'm going to smash one of these thunderboxes!*

thunder-thighs *n.* big or fat thighs. (Cruel. Also a rude term of address.) □ *Here comes old thunder-thighs.*

tick *n.* a minute; a second. □ *I'll be with you in a tick.* □ *This won't take a tick. Sit tight.*

ticked (off) *mod.* angry. □ *Wow, was she ticked off!* □ *Kelly was totally ticked.*

ticker 1. *n.* a heart. □ *I've got a good, strong ticker.* **2.** *n.* a watch. □ *My ticker stopped. The battery must be dead.* □ *If your watch runs on a battery, can you really call it a ticker?*

ticket 1. *n.* the exact thing; the needed thing. □ *This degree will be your ticket to a bright and shining future.* **2.** *n.* a license. □ *I finally got a ticket to drive a big truck.*

TIIC *n.* the idiots in charge. □ *I can't give you the answer until I consult with TIIC.*

Time (out)! *exclam.* Stop talking for a minute! (A way of interrupting someone.) □ *Time! I have something to say.*

time to cruise *n.* Time to leave. □ *Time to cruise. We're gone.*

tingle 1. *n.* a party. □ *This tingle is really da bomb.* **2.** *iv.* to party. □ *Hey, man, let's tingle.*

tinsel-teeth *n.* a nickname for someone who wears dental braces. (Also a term of address.) □ *Tinsel-teeth is having a hard time talking.*

tints *n.* sunglasses. □ *Somebody sat on my tints!* □ *I have to get some prescription tints.*

titless wonder 1. *n.* an oafish or awkward person. (Usually objectionable.) □ *That stupid jerk is the classic titless wonder. What a twit!* **2.** *n.* an unsatisfactory thing or situation. □ *I've got to take this titless wonder into the shop for an oil change.*

tits *n.* breasts, usually a woman's. (Usually objectionable.) □ *She's nothing but tits and teeth! Not a brain in her head!*

toast 1. *n.* a drunkard. □ *The old toast stumbled in front of a car.* **2.** *mod.* excellent. (Black.) □ *This stuff is toast!* □ *Your silks are real toast.* **3.** *mod.* done for; in trouble. □ *If you don't get here in 20 minutes, you're toast.*

toe jam *n.* a nasty, smelly substance that collects between the toes of unwashed feet. □ *Wash your feet, you turkey! I don't want you getting all your toe jam all over the room!*

toe tag *tv.* to kill someone. (Bodies in the morgue are identified by tags on their big toes.) □ *Man, you treat me that way one more time and I'm gonna toe tag you!*

tokus AND **tukkis; tuchus** ['tokəs AND 'tʊkəs] *n.* the buttocks. (Yiddish.) □ *She fell right on her tokus!* □ *Look at the tukkis on that fat guy.*

took Go to taken.

tool 1. *n.* an earnest student. (Compare to **power tool**.) □ *Of course he's a tool. See the plastic liner in his pocket?* **2.** *n.* a dupe; someone who can be victimized easily. □ *They were looking for some tool to drive the getaway car.* **3.** *iv.* to speed along (in a car).

(Compare to **tool around**.) □ *We were tooling along at about 75 when the cop spotted us.*

tool around *iv.* to drive or cruise around. (Compare to **tool**.) □ *We tooled around for a while and then rented a horror flick.*

toot 1. *n.* a binge or a drinking spree. □ *Harry's on a toot again.* □ *He's not on one again. It's the same old toot.* **2.** *tv. & iv.* to drink copiously. □ *She could toot booze from dusk to dawn.* **3.** *n.* an emotional state of some kind; an obsessive act or display. □ *She's on a toot about how nobody loves her anymore.*

torqued ['torkt] **1.** *mod.* angry; bent. □ *Now, now! Don't get torqued!* **2.** *mod.* drunk. □ *Mary gets torqued on just a few drinks.*

toss 1. *iv.* to empty one's stomach; to vomit. □ *I was afraid I was going to toss.* **2.** *tv.* to throw something away. □ *Toss it. It's no good.* **3.** *tv.* to search someone. (Underworld.) □ *The cops tossed him and found nothing.*

Toss it! *tv.* Throw it away! □ *You don't need that hat. Toss it!*

toss off Go to **beat off**.

toss one's **cookies** AND **throw** one's **cookies**; **toss** one's **lunch**; **toss** one's **tacos** *tv.* to empty one's stomach; to vomit. □ *If you feel like tossing your cookies, please leave quietly.*

toss one's **lunch** Go to **toss** one's **cookies**.

toss one's **tacos** Go to **toss** one's **cookies**.

toss something **off 1.** *tv.* to do something quickly without much time or effort. □ *It was no big deal. I tossed it off in 30 minutes.* Ⓣ *We can toss off the entire order in—let's say—three hours.* **2.** *tv.* to drink something quickly. □ *He tossed it off and ordered another.* Ⓣ *She tossed off a scotch in one big swig.* **3.** *tv.* to ignore criticism; to ignore defeat or a setback. □ *She just tossed it off like nothing had happened.* Ⓣ *How could she just toss off the whole problem?*

totalled 1. *mod.* wrecked; damaged beyond repair. (From *totally wrecked.*) □ *The car was totalled. There was nothing that could be saved.* **2.** *mod.* alcohol intoxicated. □ *Tom was too totalled to talk.*

totally *mod.* absolutely; completely. (Standard. Achieves slang status through overuse.) □ *How totally gross!* □ *This place is totally dull.*

tough shit AND **T.S.** *n.* tough luck; too bad. (Usually objectionable.) □ *If you really think I did wrong, then tough shit! I don't care.*

tough something **out** *tv.* to carry on with something despite difficulties or setbacks. □ *I think I can tough it out for another month.*

trailer trash *n.* the poorest of people who live in rundown house trailers. (Used with singular or plural force. Rude and derogatory.) □ *She's just trailer trash. Probably doesn't even own shoes.*

trammeled ['træməld] *mod.* alcohol intoxicated. (Collegiate.) □ *Jim came home trammeled and was sick on the carpet.*

tranny ['træni] *n.* an automobile transmission. □ *It looks like you get a new tranny, and I get 900 bucks.*

trans ['trænts] *n.* an automobile. (From *transportation*.) □ *I don't have any trans—I can't get myself anywhere.*

trash 1. *tv.* to throw something away. □ *Trash this stuff. Nobody will ever use it.* **2.** *n.* a low, worthless person; worthless people. □ *The guy is trash! Stay away from him.* **3.** *tv.* to vandalize something. □ *Somebody trashed the statue with spray paint.* □ *Who trashed my room?*

trashed *mod.* alcohol or drug intoxicated. (Collegiate.) □ *They were trashed beyond help.*

Trash it! *tv.* Throw it away! □ *We don't have space for this old chair. Trash it!*

tribe *n.* a group of friends or relatives. □ *When are you and your tribe going to come for a visit?*

trip 1. *n.* a prison sentence; a trip to prison. (Underworld.) □ *Yeah, me and Lefty both was on a little trip for a few years.* **2.** *n.* intoxication from a drug. (Drugs.) □ *The trip was great, but once was enough.* **3.** *n.* an annoying person or thing. □ *Class was a trip today.* **4.** *iv.* to leave. (Black.) □ *I gotta trip, man.*

TRIs *n.* the triceps. □ *I'm working on building up my TRIs. Been doing lots of pushups.*

troll 1. *n.* an ugly person; a grouchy person. □ *Gee, that dame is a real troll. What's her problem?* **2.** *n.* an Internet user who sends inflammatory or provocative messages designed to elicit negative responses. (As a fisherman trolls for an unsuspecting fish.) □ *Don't answer those silly messages. Some troll is just looking for* *an argument.* **3.** *n.* a message sent by a **troll** (sense 2). □ *Every time I get a troll, I just delete it.*

trollkin *n.* a youthful or inexperienced **troll** (sense 2). □ *Some trollkin sent me a message trying to make me angry.*

trounce ['traʊnts] *tv.* to beat someone; to outscore someone. (Sports.) □ *Western trounced Eastern for the 47th year in a row.*

Tru dat. *n.* That's true.; I agree. □ *Tru dat. I know just what you mean.*

Trust me! *exclam.* Believe me!; Honestly! □ *It's true! Trust me!*

T.S. Go to **tough shit.**

Tsup? *interrog.* What's up?; What is happening?; What have you been doing? □ *Hi! Tsup?* □ TONY: *Tsup?* TIFFANY: *Like, nothing.*

tube 1. *n.* a can of beer. (See also **crack a tube.**) □ *Toss me a tube, will ya?* **2.** *n.* the inner curve of a tall wave. (Surfing. See also **tubular.**) □ *I'm waiting for the best tube.* **3.** *iv.* to fail; to go down the tube(s). □ *The whole plan tubed at the last minute.* **4.** *n.* a television set. □ *What's on the tube tonight?* **5.** *n.* a cigarette. □ *There's a pack of tubes in my jacket.*

tubed *mod.* alcohol intoxicated. □ *They were both tubed and giggling.*

tube it *tv.* to fail a test. (See also **tube.**) □ *I tubed it, and I'll probably get a D in the course.*

tube steak *n.* a frankfurter or a wiener. □ *Are we having tube steak again for dinner?*

tub of guts Go to **tub of lard.**

tub of lard AND **tub of guts** *n.* a fat person. (Cruel. Also a rude term of address.) □ *Who's that tub of guts who just came in?*

tubular *mod.* excellent. (Surfing and later general youth slang. Having to do with a **tube** [wave] that is good to surf in.) □ *That pizza was totally tubular!*

tuchus Go to **tokus.**

tude ['tud] *n.* a bad attitude. □ *Hey, you really got a tude, dude.* □ *Are you pulling a tude with me?*

tukkis Go to **tokus.**

tunes *n.* a record; a record album or compact disc. □ *I got some new tunes. Wanna come over and listen?*

turd 1. *n.* a formed mass of fecal material; a fecal bolus. (Usually objectionable.) □ *Don't step on that dog turd.* **2.** *n.* a wretched or worthless person. (Rude and derogatory.) □ *You stupid turd!* □ *Don't be such a goddamn turd!*

turd face *n.* a wretched and obnoxious person. (Rude and derogatory.) □ *You stupid turd face! Why did you do that?*

turkey 1. *n.* a failure; a sham. □ *The turkey at the town theater closed on its first night.* **2.** *n.* a stupid person. □ *Who's the turkey who put the scallops in the scalloped potatoes?*

turn belly-up AND **go belly-up 1.** *iv.* to fail. □ *I sort of felt that the whole thing would go belly-up, and I was right.* **2.** *iv.* to die. (As a fish does when it dies. See also **belly-up**.) □ *Every fish in Greg's tank went belly-up last night.*

turnoff *n.* something that repels someone. □ *The movie was a turnoff. I couldn't stand it.*

turn one's **toes up** *tv.* to die. □ *I'm too young to turn my toes up.* Ⓣ *The cat turned up its toes right after church. Ah, the power of prayer.*

turn turtle *iv.* to turn over, as with a ship. (When a ship is upside down in the water, its hull looks like the shell of a huge turtle.) □ *The car struck a pole and turned turtle.*

tweased ['twizd] *mod.* alcohol intoxicated. □ *Jim came in a little tweased last night.*

tweeked ['twikt] *mod.* alcohol intoxicated. (Collegiate.) □ *They're not really bombed—just tweeked a little.*

twenty-four, seven AND **24-7** *mod.* all the time, twenty-four hours a day, seven days a week. □ *He's always at home, 24-7!*

twerp Go to twirp.

twirp AND **twerp** ['twɚp] *n.* an annoying runt of a person. (Also a term of address.) □ *Some little twerp threatened to kick me in the shin.*

twit *n.* an irritating and stupid person. (Also a term of address. See also **in a twit**.) □ *Get out of here, you twit!*

twofer ['tufɚ] *n.* an item that is selling two for the price of one. □ *Here's a good deal—a twofer—only $7.98.*

two-time *tv.* to deceive one's lover. □ *Sam wouldn't two-time Martha. He just wouldn't!*

two-time loser *n.* a confirmed loser. □ *Poor Carl is a two-time loser.*

two-topper *n.* a restaurant table that will seat two people. (Restaurant jargon.) □ *There are two-toppers on each side of the kitchen door.*

two umlauts ['tu 'umlɑuts] *n.* a Löwenbräu™ beer. □ *I'll take a two umlauts.*

U

uke Go to (y)uke.

umpteen ['əmptin] *mod.* many; innumerable. □ *There are umpteen ways to do this right. Can you manage to do one of them?*

umpteenth Go to umpty-umpth.

umpty-umpth AND **umpteenth** ['əmpti'əmpθ AND 'əmp'tintθ] *mod.* thousandth, billionth, zillionth, etc. (Represents some very large but indefinite number.) □ *This is the umpteenth meeting of the joint conference committee, but still there is no budget.*

uncut 1. *mod.* unedited; not shortened by editing. □ *I saw the whole uncut movie.* **2.** *mod.* not circumcised. □ *My brother and I are both uncut.*

unit ['junət] **1.** *n.* a gadget. □ *Now, take one of the red units—put the copper strip in the slot—place the whole thing in this larger unit—and you're done.* □ *Hand me that unit on the thingy there.* **2.** *n.* the penis. (Usually objectionable.) □ *Why are you always scratching your unit?*

up 1. *mod.* happy; cheery; not depressed. □ *This is not an up party. Let's cruise.* **2.** *tv.* to increase something. □ *The bank upped its rates again.*

upchuck ['əptʃək] **1.** *tv. & iv.* to vomit (something). □ *Wally upchucked his whole dinner.* **2.** *n.* vomit. □ *Is that upchuck on your shoe?* □ *There is still some upchuck on the bathroom floor.*

up for grabs 1. *mod.* available for anyone; not yet claimed. □ *It's up for grabs. Everything is still very chancy.* □ *I don't know who will get it. It's up for grabs.* **2.** *mod.* in total chaos. □ *This is a madhouse. The whole place is up for grabs.*

up for something *mod.* agreeable to something. □ *I'm up for a pizza. Anybody want to chip in?* □ *Who's up for a swim?*

up front 1. *mod.* at the beginning; in advance. □ *The more you pay up front, the less you'll have to finance.* **2.** *mod.* open; honest; forthcoming. (Usually **up-front**) □ *She is a very up-front gal—trust her.*

up shit creek (without a paddle) AND **up the creek (without a paddle); up a creek** *mod.* in an awkward position with no easy way out. (Usually objectionable with **shit**.) □ *I'm sort of up the creek and don't know what to do.*

up the creek (without a paddle) Go to up shit creek (without a paddle).

uptight *mod.* anxious. □ *Don't get uptight before the test.*

Up yours! *exclam.* Go to hell!; Drop dead! (Usually objectionable.) □ *I won't do it! Up yours!*

urp Go to earp.

U.V.s ['ju'viz] *n.* ultraviolet rays from the sun; sunshine. □ *I wanna get some U.V.s before we go home.*

vanilla 1. *mod.* plain; dull. □ *The entire production was sort of vanilla, but it was okay.* **2.** *n.* a Caucasian. □ *Some vanilla's on the phone—selling something, I guess.*

V-ball *n.* volleyball. (Compare to **B-ball**.) □ *You wanna play some V-ball?*

veg (out) ['vɛdʒ 'aʊt] *iv.* to cease working and take it easy; to vegetate. □ *Someday, I just want to veg out and enjoy life.*

vest 1. *n.* an important businessman or businesswoman. (See also **suit**.) □ *Some vest jumped out the window this afternoon.* **2.** *n.* a bulletproof vest. □ *The cop wasn't wearing a vest, and the shot killed him.*

vette ['vɛt] *n.* a Corvette™ automobile. □ *I'd rather have a vette than a caddy.* □ *Vettes aren't as popular as they once were.*

vibes *n.* vibrations; atmosphere; feelings. (Usually with *good* or *bad*.) □ *I just don't get good vibes about this deal.*

vic ['vɪk] **1.** *n.* a victim. (Streets. See also **vivor**.) □ *We're all vics, but we all keep going.* □ *Harry is a con artist, not a vic.* **2.** *n.* a convict. □ *We try to give the vics a chance at employment where they won't be treated badly.*

vicious ['vɪʃəs] *mod.* great; excellent. □ *Man, this burger is really vicious.*

Vickie *n.* a (Ford) Crown Victoria™ police car; the police in a Crown Victoria car. □ *Two cops in a Vickie followed the suspect's car.*

vid *n.* a video [tape]. □ *I rented some vids for tonight so we can stay in and drink beer.*

vines *n.* clothing. (Black.) □ *I like those smokin' vines you're in.*

vinyl ['vaɪnəl] *n.* phonograph records. □ *I got some new vinyl. Come over and listen.*

vivor ['vɑɪvɚ] *n.* a survivor; a street person who manages to survive. (Streets. Compare to **vic**.) □ *Harry's a vivor, and I like him.*

viz ['vɑɪz] *n.* Levis™; blue jeans. □ *How do you like my new viz?*

vomity ['vɑmɪdi] *mod.* nasty. (Crude.) □ *What is this vomity stuff on my plate?*

V.S.A. *mod.* vital signs absent, dead. (Hospital jargon.) □ *The intern made a note in the chart: V.S.A., 10:18 A.M.*

wacked (out) Go to **whacked (out).**

wack off Go to **beat off.**

wad ['wɑd] *n.* a bundle of money; a bankroll. (Originally underworld.) □ *I lost my wad on a rotten horse in the seventh race.* □ *You'd better not flash a wad like that around here. You won't have it long.*

wailing AND **whaling** *mod.* excellent. (Teens.) □ *Man, that's wailing!* □ *What a whaling guitar!*

wail on someone *iv.* to beat someone. □ *Who are those two guys wailing on Sam?*

a **walk** *n.* something easy. (See also **cakewalk, sleepwalk.**) □ *That game was a walk!*

walk 1. *iv.* to walk out on someone. □ *Much more of this and I'm going to walk.* **2.** *iv.* to walk away from something unharmed. □ *It couldn't have been much of an accident. Both drivers walked.* □ *It was a horrible meeting, but when it was over I just walked.*

walk heavy *iv.* to be important. (Black.) □ *Harry's been walking heavy since he graduated.*

the **walking wounded 1.** *n.* soldiers who are injured but still able to walk. (Standard English.) □ *There were enough walking wounded to start another division.* □ *Many of the walking wounded helped with the more seriously injured cases.* **2.** *n.* a person who is injured—mentally or physically—and still able to go about daily life. □ *The outpatient clinic was filled with the walking wounded.* **3.** *n.* stupid people in general. □ *Most of network programming seems to be aimed at the walking wounded of our society.*

walk on sunshine *n.* to be really happy. □ *I'm in love and I'm walking on sunshine.*

walkover *n.* an easy victory; an easy task. (From sports.) □ *The game was a walkover. No problem.* □ *Learning the computer's operating system was no walkover for me.*

walk tall *iv.* to be brave and self-assured. □ *I know I can walk tall because I'm innocent.*

waltz *n.* an easy task. □ *The job was a waltz. We did it in a day.*

wank off Go to beat off.

wannabe AND **wanabe** ['wɑnə bi OR 'wɔnə bi] *n.* someone who wants to be something or someone. □ *All these teenyboppers are wannabes, and that's why we can sell this stuff to them at any price.*

washboard abs *n.* heavily marked abdominal muscles, divided into six equal sections. □ *If I work out hard enough I can build those washboard abs.*

Wassup? Go to Wusup?

waste *tv.* to kill someone. (Underworld.) □ *Reggie had orders to waste Carl.*

wasted 1. *mod.* dead; killed. □ *Carl didn't want to end up wasted.* **2.** *mod.* alcohol or drug intoxicated. □ *I've never seen a bartender get wasted before.*

way 1. *mod.* extremely; totally. □ *Oh, this is way gross!* **2.** *interj.* "There is too," as an answer to **No way!** □ *A: I won't do it. No way! B: Way! Yes, you will.* □ *She says "no way," and I say "way." Nobody ever wins!*

the **way it plays** *phr.* the way it is; the way things are. □ *The world is a rough place, and that's the way it plays.*

wedgie Go to wedgy.

wedgy AND **wedgie** *n.* a situation where one's underpants are drawn up tightly between the buttocks. □ *Wally skipped up behind Greg and gave him a wedgy.*

weed 1. *n.* tobacco; a cigarette or cigar. □ *This weed is gonna be the death of me.* **2.** *n.* marijuana; a marijuana cigarette. □ *This is good weed, man.*

weeds *n.* clothing. □ *Good-looking weeds you're wearing.* □ *These weeds came right out of the catalog. Would you believe?*

weenie AND **wienie 1.** *n.* a stupid and inept male. □ *Tell that stupid weenie to get himself over here and get back to work.* **2.** *n.* the penis. (Usually objectionable.) □ *He held his hands over his weenie and ran for the bedroom.*

weird out *iv.* to become emotionally disturbed or unnerved; to flip (out). □ *The day was just gross. I thought I would weird out at noon.*

(well-)hung *mod.* having large [male] genitals. (Widely known and very old. Usually objectionable.) □ *If Tom was as hung as he thinks he is, he wouldn't even say anything at all.*

(Well,) pardon me for living! AND **Excuse me for breathing!; Excuse me for living!** *tv.* I am SOOO sorry! (A very sarcastic response to a rebuke, seeming to regret the apparent offense of even living.) □ *A: You are blocking my view. Please move. B: Well, pardon me for living!*

wet rag Go to wet sock.

wet sock AND **wet rag** *n.* a wimpy person; a useless jerk. (See also rubber sock.) □ *Don't be such a wet sock! Stand up for your rights!* □ *Well, in a tight situation, Merton is sort of a wet rag.*

whacked (out) AND **wacked (out) 1.** *mod.* alcohol or drug intoxicated. □ *Dave was so whacked out he couldn't stand up.* **2.** *mod.* crazy; silly. □ *Bill is totally whacked and can't find his car.*

whack off Go to beat off.

whack someone or something **(out)** AND **wack** someone or something **(out) 1.** *tv.* [with *someone*] to kill somebody. (Underworld.) □ *Willie made another try at whacking Albert out last evening.* T *He really wants to whack out Mr. Big.* **2.** *tv.* [with *something*] to rob a place; to swindle a business establishment. (Underworld.) □ *Did your guys wack the church collection box?*

whack someone or something **up** AND **whack** someone or something **up** *iv.* to damage someone or something. □ *Bob got mad at Greg and whacked him up.*

whaling Go to wailing.

whank off Go to beat off.

whatever *mod.* I don't care; it doesn't matter which choice; whatever you want. □ *Q: I have chocolate, vanilla, strawberry, kiwi, and lime. Which do you want? A: Oh, whatever.*

What (in) the fucking hell! *exclam.* an angry and surprised elaboration of What? (Taboo. Usually objectionable.) □ *What the fucking hell! Who are you and how'd you get in here?*

What's going down? *interrog.* What's happening? □ *Hey, man, what's going down?*

What's happ(ening)? *interrog.* Hello, what's new? (See also Tsup?) □ *What's happ? How's it goin'?*

What's shakin' (bacon)? *interrog.* How are you?; What is new? □ *Hi, Jim. What's shakin'?*

What's the deal? Go to What's the scam?

What's the scam? AND **What's the deal?** *interrog.* What is going on around here? (See also scam.) □ *I gave you a twenty, and you give me five back? What's the deal? Where's my other five?*

What's up? *interrog.* What is going on?; What is happening? (See also Tsup?) □ *Haven't seen you in a month of Sundays. What's up?*

What's up doc? *interrog.* What is happening here? □ *What's up doc? How're things going?*

What's your damage? *interrog.* What's your problem? (Like a damage report.) □ *You look beat, man. What's your damage?*

wheel *tv. & iv.* to drive a car. (Black.) □ *Let's wheel my heap over to Marty's place.*

wheels *n.* transportation by automobile. □ *I'll need a ride. I don't have any wheels.*

whenchy AND **wenchy** ['wɛntʃi OR 'mɛntʃi] *mod.* bitchy; snotty. (Collegiate.) □ *Then she began to get whenchy, so I left.*

when (the) shit hit the fan *tv.* when the trouble broke out; when things became difficult. (Usually objectionable.) □ *We had one hell of an afternoon around here. Where were you when the shit hit the fan?*

whip off Go to beat off.

whip one's **wire** Go to beat the dummy.

whipped 1. *mod.* exhausted; beat. □ *Wow, you look whipped.* **2.** *mod.* alcohol intoxicated. □ *She was too whipped to find money to pay her bill.* **3.** *mod.* great. □ *The band was whipped and the food was unbelievable.*

whip the dummy Go to beat the dummy.

whitebread *mod.* plain; dull. □ *If I wanted a whitebread vacation, I'd have gone to the beach.*

white-knuckle 1. *mod.* having to do with an event that creates a lot of tension, especially an airplane flight. □ *We came in during the storm on a white-knuckle flight from Chicago.* **2.** *mod.* of a person who is made tense by something such as flying or sailing. □ *I'm afraid I'm a white-knuckle sailor, and you'd all be much happier if I stay on dry land.* □ *My cousin is a white-knuckle flyer and would rather take the train.*

whiz 1. *n.* a talented or skilled person. □ *I'm no math whiz, but I can find your errors.* **2.** *iv.* to urinate. (Caution with topic.) □ *I gotta stop here and whiz.* □ *You can't whiz in the park!*

the **whole ball of wax** *n.* everything; the whole thing. □ *Your comments threatened the whole ball of wax, that's what.*

the **whole enchilada** [. . . ɛntʃə'lɑdə] *n.* the whole thing; everything. (From Spanish.) □ *Nobody, but nobody, ever gets the whole enchilada.* □ *Carl wants the whole enchilada.*

wicked *mod.* Excellent!; impressive. □ *Now this is what I call a wicked guitar.*

wicky *mod.* wicked; excellent. □ *Whose wicky red convertible is parked in front of the house?*

wienie Go to weenie.

wimp out (of something**)** *iv.* to chicken out (of something); to get out of something, leaving others to carry the burden. □ *Come on! Don't wimp out now that there's all this work to be done.*

wimpy *mod.* weak; inept; square. □ *You are just a wimpy nerd!*

wing *iv.* to travel by airplane. □ *We winged to Budapest to attend a conference.* □ *They winged from there to London overnight.*

wing it *tv.* to improvise; to do something extemporaneously. □ *Don't worry. Just go out there and wing it.*

winks *n.* some sleep. □ *I gotta have some winks. I'm pooped.*

wired 1. *mod.* nervous; extremely alert. □ *The guy is pretty wired because of the election.* **2.** AND **wired up** *mod.* alcohol or drug intoxicated. □ *Ken was so wired up he couldn't remember his name.*

wired into someone or something *mod.* concerned with someone or something; really involved with someone or something. □ *Mary is really wired into classical music.*

wired up Go to wired.

within spitting distance *mod.* close by. □ *The house you're looking for is within spitting distance, but it's hard to find.*

wombat ['wɑmbæt] *n.* a strange person; a **geek**. (Collegiate.) □ *Why does everybody think Merton is such a wombat?* □ *Who's the wombat in the 1957 Chevy?*

wonk ['wɔŋk] *n.* an earnest student. (Collegiate.) □ *Who's the wonk who keeps getting the straight A's?* □ *Yes, you could call Merton a wonk. In fact, he's the classic wonk.*

wonky ['wɔŋki] *mod.* studious. (Collegiate.) □ *Merton is certainly the wonky type.*

woody 1. *n.* a wooden surfboard; a surfboard. □ *Get your woody, and let's get moving.* **2.** *n.* an erection of the penis. □ *He always gets a woody when he doesn't need it and never when he does.*

word hole AND **cake hole; pie hole** *n.* the mouth. □ *Put this food in your word hole, chew it up, and swallow it.*

work one's **ass off** AND **work** one's **butt off** *tv.* to work very hard. (Use caution with **ass**.) □ *It was really busy at the shop. I worked my ass off all day.* □ *I'm tired of working my butt off for low pay.*

work one's **butt off** Go to work one's **ass off**.

worship the porcelain god *tv.* to empty one's stomach; to vomit. (Collegiate.) □ *Somebody was in the john worshiping the porcelain god till all hours.* □ *I think I have to go worship the porcelain god. See ya.*

wrinkle-rod *n.* the crankshaft of an engine. □ *A wrinkle-rod'll set you back about $199, plus installation charges, of course.*

wrongo ['rɔŋo] **1.** *mod.* wrong. □ *Wrongo, wrongo! You lose the game!* **2.** *n.* an undesirable thing or person; a member of the underworld. □ *The guy's a total wrongo. He's got to be guilty.*

wuss(y) ['wʊs(i)] *n.* a wimpy or weak person. □ *Don't be such a wuss. Stand up for your rights.* □ *Wussies like you will never get ahead.*

Wusup? AND **Wassup?** *interrog.* What's up? □ *Wusup! What's going on around here?*

yank 1. *tv.* to harass someone. (See also **yank** someone **around**.) □ *Stop yanking me!* **2.** *n.* a Yankee; a U.S. soldier. (Sometimes capitalized.) □ *I don't care if you call me a yank. That's what I am.*

yank one's **strap** Go to beat the dummy.

yank someone **around** *tv.* to harass someone; to give someone a hard time. (Compare to **jerk** someone **around**.) □ *Listen, I don't mean to yank you around all the time, but we have to have the drawings by Monday.* □ *Please stop yanking me around.*

yank someone's **chain** AND **pull** someone's **chain** *tv.* to harass someone; to give someone a hard time. (As if one were a dog wearing a choker collar, on a leash.) □ *Stop yanking my chain!* □ *Do you really think you can just yank my chain whenever you want?*

yeaster *n.* a beer-drinker. □ *A couple of yeasters in the back of the tavern were singing a dirty song.* □ *Who's the yeaster with the bloodshot eyes?*

yola *n.* cocaine. □ *Albert spends too much time snorting yola.*

york ['jork] **1.** *iv.* to empty one's stomach; to vomit. □ *He ate the stuff, then went straight out and yorked.* **2.** *n.* vomit. □ *Hey, Jimmy! Come out in the snow and see the frozen york!*

You got that? *interrog.* Do you understand? □ *You are not to go into that room! You got that?*

yu(c)k ['jək] **1.** *n.* someone or something disgusting. (Also a term of address.) □ *I don't want any of that yuck on my plate!* **2.** *exclam.* Horrible! (Usually **Yuck!**) □ *Oh, yuck! Get that horrible thing out of here!* **3.** *n.* a joke. □ *Come on! Chill out! It was just a yuck.*

yu(c)ky AND **yukky** ['jəki] *mod.* nasty. □ *What is this yucky pink stuff on my plate?*

(y)uke ['juk] **1.** *iv.* to empty one's stomach; to vomit. (Collegiate. Compare to puke.) □ *I think somebody yuked in the backseat, Tom.* **2.** *n.* vomit. (Collegiate.) □ *That is uke on the floor, isn't it?*

yukky Go to yu(c)ky.

Z

za [ˈzɑ] *n.* pizza. (Collegiate.) □ *I'm gonna spring for some za.*

zap 1. *tv.* to shock someone. □ *That fake snake zapped me for a minute.* **2.** *tv.* to impress someone. □ *My big idea really zapped the boss. I may get a raise.* **3.** *exclam.* Wow! (Usually **Zap!**) □ *Zap! I did it again!*

zapped 1. *mod.* tired; exhausted. □ *I'm way zapped. Good night.* **2.** *mod.* alcohol or drug intoxicated. □ *We all got zapped and then went home.*

zarf [ˈzɑrf] *n.* an ugly and repellent male. □ *Ooo, who is that zarf who just came in?*

zero *n.* an insignificant person; a nobody. □ *I want to be more in life than just another zero.*

zip 1. *n.* nothing. □ *I got zip from the booking agency all week.* **2.** *n.* a score or grade of zero. □ *Well, you got zip on the last test. Sorry about that.* **3.** *n.* vigor; spunk. □ *This whole thing lacks the zip it needs to survive.*

zit [ˈzɪt] *n.* a pimple. □ *Don't squeeze your zits on my mirror!*

zonk [ˈzɔŋk] **1.** *tv.* to overpower someone or something. □ *We zonked the dog with a kick.* □ *It took two cops to zonk the creep.* **2.** *tv.* to tire someone out. □ *The pills zonked me, but they made my cold better.*

zonked (out) AND **zounked (out)** [ˈzɔŋkt . . . AND ˈzɑʊŋkt . . .] **1.** *mod.* alcohol or drug intoxicated. □ *She's too zonked to drive.* □ *Jed was almost zounked out to unconsciousness.* **2.** *mod.* exhausted; asleep. □ *She was totally zonked out by the time I got home.* □ *I'm zounked. Good night.*

zonk out *iv.* to collapse from exhaustion; to go into a stupor from drugs or exhaustion. □ *I went home after the trip and just zonked out.*

zot(z) ['zɑt(s)] *n.* zero; nothing. □ *I went out to get the mail, but there was zot.* □ *All I got for a raise was little more than zotz.*

zounked (out) Go to zonked (out).

Hidden-Word Index

Use this index to locate a phrasal entry by one of the major words inside the phrase. If you can't find a phrase by looking up the first word in the phrase, pick out some other major word and look it up here. Then look up the simplest form of that word in this index to find the phrase as it is used in the dictionary. Third, look up the phrase in the main body of the dictionary.

Some words are omitted because they occur so frequently that their lists would cover many pages. The entries based on the first words of phrasal entries are omitted. Most of the grammar words, such as prepositions, pronouns, and articles, are not indexed.

abs washboard abs
action chill someone's action
air come up for air
aitch seven-seven-three-aitch
all be all over something
all Fuck it (all)!
all have it all together
all If that don't fuck all!
along hump (along)
already Enough, already!
altar bow to the porcelain altar
anchor boat anchor
animal party animal
apeshit go ape(shit) (over someone or something)
applause anal applause
apple alley apple
apple road apple
artillery heavy artillery
artist bullshit artist
artist con artist
artist off artist
artist rip-off artist

ass someone's ass is grass
ass bag ass (out of some place)
ass barrel ass (out of some place)
ass be ass out
ass bust (one's) ass (to do something)
ass bust-ass
ass candy-ass
ass candy-ass(ed)
ass chew someone's ass out
ass cut ass (out of some place)
ass drag ass (out of some place)
ass drag ass around
ass dumb-ass
ass fat-ass(ed)
ass flat on one's ass
ass flat-ass
ass Get off my ass!
ass Get your ass in gear!
ass gripe one's ass
ass hairy-ass(ed)
ass half-ass(ed)
ass haul ass (out of some place)
ass have a wild hair up one's ass

cobra crotch-cobra

cock horse cock

coin hard coin

collar hot under the collar

coming know where one is coming
    from

commerce chamber of commerce

con put a con on someone

cookies blow one's cookies

cookies drop one's cookies

cookies shoot one's cookies

cookies snap one's cookies

cookies throw one's cookies

cookies toss one's cookies

cool blow one's cool

cool keep one's cool

cool play it cool

cork blow one's cork

cork pop one's cork

counter bean-counter

counter comma-counter

cow cash cow

cracking Get cracking!

crap Cut the crap!

crap shoot the crap

crap take a crap

creek up shit creek (without a
    paddle)

creek up the creek (without a
    paddle)

cruise time to cruise

curb shot to the curb

curb step off the curb

cutter piss-cutter

D's Mickey D's

daddy mack daddy

daddy sugar daddy

dagger bull-dagger

damage What's your damage?

dance tap dance like mad

dancer grave-dancer

dancing slam-dancing

dangle dingle(-dangle)

dat Tru dat.

day Make my day!

deal Here's the deal.

deal Like it's such a big deal.

deal What's the deal?

deep in deep

deep knee-deep navy

deuces double-deuces

dime get off the dime

dink rinky-dink

dirt take a dirt nap

dirty quick-and-dirty

dish dish the dirt

disk disk jockey

distance within spitting distance

doc What's up doc?

doctor dome-doctor

dog (It's) not my dog.

dog bird-dog

domain ptomaine-domain

dong ding-dong

doors blow someone's doors off

dope straight (dope)

doughnuts blow one's doughnuts

doughnuts lose one's doughnuts

down bring-down

down burn someone down

down chow something down

down chow down

down come down

down cool down

down flake down

down garbage something down

down get down

down go down

down go down in flames

down go down the chute

down go down the tube(s)

down knock something down

down run down some lines

down run it down

down scarf something down

down shot down

down What's going down?

dozens the (dirty) dozens

spud sofa spud
squat (doodly-)squat
squat cop a squat
squat diddly-squat
squat take a squat
squeezer duck-squeezer
start jump start
station fuzz station
stay stay loose
steak tube steak
stick boom sticks
stick carry the stick
stink big stink
stop pit stop
store leeky store
strap yank one's strap
street jump (street)
street put something on the street
stress no stress
stuck bleed like a stuck pig
stuff fluff-stuff
stuff green stuff
such Like it's such a big deal.
suck That's so suck!
suds bust (some) suds
suds in the suds
suit all over someone like a cheap suit
Sunday dark Sunday
sunshine walk on sunshine
supper shoot one's supper
sweat no sweat
sweeper street sweeper
sweet lay some sweet lines on someone
sweet put some sweet lines on someone
swing not enough room to swing a cat
tacos toss one's tacos
tag toe tag
tail fuzzy (tail)
tail Get off my tail!
tail hunk of tail
tail piece of tail

talk jive talk
tall walk tall
tank avenue tank
teeth tinsel-teeth
ten hang ten
tenda my tenda
tent pitch a tent
thighs thunder-thighs
three seven-seven-three-aitch
ticket get one's ticket punched
ticket sell a wolf ticket
ticket sell wolf tickets
ticks a few ticks
tide red tide
time bean time
time face time
time rack time
time rough time
time two-time
time two-time loser
tit bitch tits
tit go tits up
tit kiss someone's hind tit
tit suck someone's hind tit
toenails throw up one's toenails
toes turn one's toes up
together get one's shit together
together have it all together
together put your hands together for someone
toke harsh toke
tool power tool
top blow one's top
topper four-topper
topper two-topper
touch Keep in touch.
tough hang tough (on something)
tracks railroad tracks
train gravy train
trap fox trap
trash trailer trash
tree Go climb a tree!
trip bum trip
trip down trip